Behavioral Sciences and the Mass Media

Publications of Russell Sage Foundation

Russell Sage Foundation was established in 1907 by Mrs. Russell Sage for the improvement of social and living conditions in the United States. In carrying out its purpose the Foundation conducts research under the direction of members of the staff or in close collaboration with other institutions, and supports programs designed to improve the utilization of social science knowledge. As an integral part of its operations, the Foundation from time to time publishes books or pamphlets resulting from these activities. Publication under the imprint of the Foundation does not necessarily imply agreement by the Foundation, its Trustees, or its staff with the interpretations or conclusions of the authors.

Behavioral Sciences and the Mass Media

Contributors   Ben H. Bagdikian
Leo Bogart
Edgar F. Borgatta
Marvin Bressler
John Mack Carter
Wayne A. Danielson
W. Phillips Davison
Emmett Dedmon
Eli Ginzberg
Ernest Havemann
Herbert H. Hyman
Robert L. Jones
Alfred J. Kahn
Joseph T. Klapper
Melvin L. Kohn
Daniel Lerner
Ronald Lippitt
John W. Riley
Earl Ubell
Richard C. Wald
Stanton Wheeler
Robin M. Williams

Editor   Frederick T. C. Yu

A Report of an Arden House
Conference jointly
sponsored by Russell Sage Foundation and the
Graduate School of Journalism, Columbia University

Publisher   Russell Sage Foundation, New York, 1968

© 1968 by Russell Sage Foundation
Printed in United States of America by
Connecticut Printers, Inc., Hartford, Connecticut
Designed by Bennett Robinson

Library of Congress Catalog Card Number: 68–25421

Editor's Foreword

About the Conference

In the spring of 1966, the Russell Sage Foundation and the Graduate School of Journalism of Columbia University invited sixty prominent scholars and journalists to a Conference on Behavioral Sciences and the Mass Media. The three-day conference, which was held on April 1–3 at Arden House, Harriman, New York, aimed at exploring ways to achieve closer cooperation and interplay between the two fields and thus to increase and improve public understanding of behavioral sciences. This book is the outcome of that conference.

It is no new knowledge that public understanding of behavioral sciences is at best superficial. This is easily understandable. One obvious reason is the newness of this field of study. Another is the layman's understandable impatience with the theoretical abstraction and methodological precision that are the benchmarks of the behavioral sciences. Still another is the increasingly high degree of specialization and professionalization of the field, and this has resulted in the piling up of technical terms and jargons that at once intimidate, irritate, and infuriate the educated as well as the unwashed.

But the need for improved public understanding of behavioral sciences has become increasingly great. While the nation's general level of information on the work in this young and expanding field of study still remains low, the American public is sufficiently educated to know that behavioral scientists play an increasingly important role in various areas of public affairs: education, social work, public health, business, national defense and others. It is too early and too much to expect the American public to make much sense out of what it has read or heard about this body of knowledge. But it is a reasonably safe guess that the American people have probably enough exposure to behavioral sciences to be at least curious about the effects of the research in this field on themselves. They may have only the foggiest idea about the squabbles over the uses, misuses, and abuses of behavioral sciences, but they probably know enough to want to know a bit more about the accomplishments, limitations, and consequences of this burgeoning area of knowledge.

The public needs information, far more than it now possesses. But it is not getting it.

The problem is not one of popularizing behavioral sciences. Too many such attempts have already been made, and often represent vulgarization of the worst sort. Responsible behavioral scientists and public communicators should never be tricked into doing this under the guise of keeping the public informed. The problem, to put it simply, is one of making available to the public a continuous flow of full, honest, and understandable information on a wide gamut of subjects, questions, methods, experiments, and findings in this rapidly growing field of study.

But how is this to be done?

It is all very easy to suggest that behavioral scientists and journalists should cooperate. The harsh fact is that until recent years the two groups were hardly conscious of the need for each other. Over the years some reflective scholars and responsible journalists made occasional pleas for cooperation, but their voices were often drowned out by the shouts of those who seemed to have little interest in interaction between the two fields other than exchange of insults.

The relationship has improved remarkably. To be sure, the gap between the world of behavioral scientists and the world of journalists is by no means closed. But the academic is far more sensitive than before to the needs and problems of the press. At the same time, the mass media are far more anxious than before to have more adequate and more sophisticated reporting of developments and findings in the behavioral sciences, to have access to responsible consultants in the field, and to receive advice on utilizing behavioral science resources in dealing with issues in the news. There is at least general agreement that the behavioral sciences are far more than just a babel of alien technical tongues, that they try to seek new answers to old questions, that they have already influenced many views of man by man, and that they suggest a fresh, if not indispensable, approach to our understanding of social issues and human problems.

It is fair to say that both behavioral scientists and journalists are now willing, ready, and perhaps even eager to cooperate. But how the cooperation is to come about is quite another matter. This is going to take time and a lot of doing. It requires far more than just goodwill, although goodwill is definitely needed and helpful.

It was with these problems and a host of others in mind that the Russell Sage Foundation and the Graduate School of Journalism, starting at separate points, decided in 1965 to make a meaningful beginning toward what may evolve as a major program of inter-action between behavioral sciences and public communications. One part of this beginning was the launching of a special training program in behavioral sciences at Columbia University for experienced journalists with a generous grant from the Foundation. Another part of this beginning was the Arden House Conference.

About the Book

This book is divided into five parts.

Part I takes up the general problem of potential public uses of behavioral sciences and seeks to clarify some of the key problems in the field. Marvin Bressler, who delivered the keynote address at the conference, explains, in Chapter 1, what this single entity or "common culture" called behavioral science really is. He devotes a good part of his paper to those aspects of behavioral sciences that are especially useful in the public arena. He tells us how behavioral sciences assist men to decide what goals to pursue, what actions make their attainment more probable, and what are the profits and costs of success or failure. He discusses the limitations of behavioral

sciences and raises the question of whether the public has an un-
limited right to know material that is technical and potentially
dangerous to one without proper training in the field.

Richard Wald's paper (Chapter 2) represents a journalist's
approach to understanding society and social change. The piece
reflects the mood as well as the emotional load of many journalists
regarding the subject of behavioral sciences. He seeks in journalism
a new set of values for a kind of society, while Professor Bressler
tends to consider journalism as a crude exercise in behavioral
science—without license.

The two papers by Professor Bressler and Mr. Wald generated
considerable interest and much debate at the conference. Chapter 3
presents summaries of statements by two of the discussants: Ben
H. Bagdikian and John W. Riley. Mr. Bagdikian suggests that
journalism and behavioral science are two different fields trying
to do different things, though with obvious overlaps. He does not
see journalism as a shadow of behavioral sciences, as it is often
assumed, but a creative process of its own; he does not believe
that behavioral scientists always lead and journalists always follow; he is convinced that there can be a genuine dialogue between
the two fields; and he reminds us of the important fact that behavioral scientists always look for regularity and universality of
events while journalists who are normally interested in the unique
have a built-in resistance to hypotheses. Dr. Riley, on the other
hand, finds similarity in the Bressler and Wald papers. He suggests
that both behavioral scientists and journalists want to use the behavioral sciences in order to facilitate a better understanding of
people and society, that both see the times as being out-of-joint
(except that the newsman focuses more on individuals while the
sociologist looks at society and social problems), that each looks
to the other for a solution and that both have a willingness to
communicate.

In part II five leading social scientists report their research on
five critically important social issues. Robin Williams' paper on the
race question (Chapter 4) provides a historical perspective on race
relations, explains how racial prejudice is not an isolated attitude
but part of a functioning system, examines the conditions of the

so-called Negro revolt, and reports a whole series of research findings in the field. Melvin Kohn's chapter on social class and serious mental disorder (Chapter 5) is an example of how a social scientist works his way through a large body of research data, how he sharpens his tools of inquiry, how he gathers and utilizes his data, and how this thought process could be immensely useful to journalists. The last section of his paper makes considerable reference to the mass media. Alfred Kahn addresses himself to what is known empirically about the poverty phenomenon (Chapter 6) and has much to offer to both journalists and social scientists who are concerned with the problem. The chapter by Eli Ginzberg (Chapter 7) raises a series of critically important questions on automation and the impact of computers. It is his belief that the real thing that one learns from behavioral sciences is how to think about a problem, not what to think. The important point, as he puts it, is how to position yourself toward the problem area, and his chapter is a good example of how he follows his own formula. Stanton Wheeler's chapter on violence and crime (Chapter 8) covers a wide area of problems. It includes discussions on characteristics of crime, the problem of crime prevention and social policy, the matter of administration of justice, and the question of crime reporting and the mass media.

Part III explores the relationships between behavioral scientists and journalists. Leo Bogart (Chapter 9) examines the differences between journalists and behavioral scientists, describes the variations of social scientists and discusses the uses, misuses, and abuses of the behavioral sciences. Ernest Havemann takes up the question of jargon in his delightful piece (Chapter 10) on the barriers to communications between journalism and behavioral sciences. Emmett Dedmon's chapter (Chapter 11) represents another journalist's views on the subject of barriers to communications. Two social scientists, Ronald Lippitt and Edgar Borgatta, wrestle with the same problem in Chapters 12 and 13. John Mack Carter (Chapter 14) reports his perceptions of the mass market for behavioral sciences and suggests that the audience is willing to move up faster than editors will allow. Herbert Hyman and Joseph T. Klapper served as discussants at the session at which the above-mentioned papers were presented. Their statements are summarized in Chapter 15.

Part IV is devoted to some practical problems in cooperation between behavioral scientists and journalists. W. Phillips Davison, in Chapter 16, spells out the plan for the Columbia–Russell Sage Foundation Program in Behavioral Sciences and Journalism. He asks two basic questions: (1) how can news reporting of developments in the behavioral sciences be improved and (2) can journalistic writing about current social issues be deepened and enriched if journalists are acquainted with the behavioral sciences.

Wayne Danielson, in Chapter 17, has some specific suggestions on techniques for improving access to social science data and resources. Earl Ubell, in Chapter 18, speculates on the possibility of a behavioral science beat and offers some practical suggestions on the question. The report by Robert L. Jones, as a discussant, is summarized in Chapter 19.

Professor Daniel Lerner had the demanding task of presenting a summary and conclusions at the final session of the conference. There is no point to summarize his report (Chapter 20); it is only necessary to say that it is eminently well done. His report concludes this volume.

Acknowledgements

This volume was inspired by the leadership of Dr. Orville G. Brim, Jr., president of the Russell Sage Foundation, and Dean Edward W. Barrett of the Graduate School of Journalism of Columbia University. They served as co-chairmen of the conference.

I owe a warm and special debt of gratitude to Dr. Eleanor Bernert Sheldon, who participated in all the decisions which made the conference and this volume possible. She did an enormous amount of work as one of the coordinators of the conference. She chaired one of the sessions. In addition, she served as a friendly but firm adviser to me with a unique combination of enthusiasm and sensitivity.

I am deeply indebted to David Goslin of the Russell Sage Foundation for his friendly assistance and wise advice in the early stages of planning for the conference.

W. Phillips Davison helped and advised me at every stage of the conference, besides presenting one of the key papers in this volume.

Mrs. Lucy Simpson assisted me in arranging the conference, transcribed the discussion and did an enormous amount of typing. Miss Julie Kinnard, Mrs. Agnes Berger and Mrs. Patricia Stewart all typed and retyped various versions of the drafts of the papers and were helpful in many other ways.

Frederick T. C. Yu
New York, January, 1968

Conference Participants

The following roster lists all contributors, discussants and participants at the conference. It is with pleasure that we take this opportunity to express our genuine gratitude to this group of scholars and journalists.

Participants

Samuel L. Adams, *St. Petersburg (Fla.) Times*
Ben H. Bagdikian, *Saturday Evening Post*
Richard T. Baker, *Columbia University*
Edward W. Barrett, *Columbia University*
James G. Bellows, *New York Herald Tribune*
Leo Bogart, *Bureau of Advertising of the American Newspaper Publishers Association, Inc.*
Edgar F. Borgatta, *University of Wisconsin*
James Boylan, *Columbia Journalism Review*
Arthur H. Brayfield, *American Psychological Association*
Marvin Bressler, *Princeton University*
Orville G. Brim, Jr., *Russell Sage Foundation*
John Mack Carter, *Ladies Home Journal*
Peter B. Clark, *Detroit News*
Louis G. Cowan, *Columbia University*
Wayne A. Danielson, *University of North Carolina*
W. Phillips Davison, *Columbia University*
Emmett Dedmon, *Chicago Sun-Times*
Edwin Diamond, *Newsweek*
Irving Dilliard, *Princeton University*
Hyman A. Enzer, *Hofstra College*

Eli Ginzberg, *Columbia University*
David A. Goslin, *Russell Sage Foundation*
Edwin O. Guthman, *Los Angeles Times*
Phillip E. Hammond, *University of Wisconsin*
Ernest Havemann, *Writer*
Herbert H. Hyman, *Columbia University*
Harold R. Isaacs, *Massachusetts Institute of Technology*
Norman E. Isaacs, *The Louisville Times*
Robert L. Jones, *University of Minnesota*
Alfred J. Kahn, *Columbia University*
Penn Kimball, *Columbia University*
Joseph T. Klapper, *Columbia Broadcasting Company, Inc.*
Melvin Kohn, *National Institute of Mental Health*
Daniel Lerner, *Massachusetts Institute of Technology*
Ronald Lippitt, *University of Michigan*
Kenneth MacDonald, *Des Moines Register & Tribune*
Gordon Manning, *CBS News*
Herbert McClosky, *University of California*
Ralph McGill, *Atlanta Constitution*
C. A. McKnight, *Charlotte Observer*
J. Edward Murray, *Arizona Republic*
William E. Porter, *University of Michigan*
John W. Riley, Jr., *The Equitable Life Assurance Society*
Arville Schalenben, *Milwaukee Journal*
Eleanor Bernert Sheldon, *Russell Sage Foundation*
Hazel Brannon Smith, *Lexington (Miss.) Advertiser*
Earl Ubell, *New York Herald Tribune*
Richard C. Wald, *New York Herald Tribune*
Mary Lou Werner, *Washington Evening News*
Stanton Wheeler, *Russell Sage Foundation*
Robin Williams, *Cornell University*
James Q. Wilson, *Harvard University*
Frederick T. C. Yu, *Columbia University*
Leonard Zweig, *Trans-action*

Observers

Natalie Jaffe, *New York Times*
Fred Powledge, *Russell Sage Foundation Fellow*
Dorothy Barclay Thompson, *Chicago, Illinois*

Table of Contents

xv

Session One:

PUBLIC AND MASS MEDIA USES OF THE BEHAVIORAL
SCIENCES

1

The Potential Public Uses of the Behavior Sciences

Marvin Bressler
PRINCETON UNIVERSITY

The amenities of scholarly exchange during any colloquium dealing with the mass media require at least some passing reference to a "communication model." By fortunate happenstance, it is actually convenient in this case to explore the "potential public uses of the behavior sciences" by imagining a sequence beginning with *messages* (the substance, procedures, and ideology of the disciplines which study human action) that are relayed by *agents* (the spoken word, the printed page, the silver screen) to target *populations* (students, clients, and citizens). The message may be described as "useful" when it 1) refers to issues that are salient for substantial numbers of people, 2) assists them to understand or control the social world, and 3) is not garbled in the process of transmission or reception.

The purpose of this paper is to indicate to what extent these conditions now obtain and to speculate under what circumstances they could be satisfied in the proximate future. Since some of my colleagues at this conference will report on specific findings in a number of areas of social concern, my remarks will be sufficiently general to avoid trespassing on their domains. At the same time, I shall try to refrain from those flights into abstraction that have sometimes earned academicians the censure of men who prefer reality.

The Message of the Behavior Sciences

Bernard Berelson and Gary A. Steiner in their encyclopedic propositional inventory, *Human Behavior*, identify the behavior sci-

3

ences as the disciplines of "anthropology, psychology, and sociology
. . . minus and plus: *Minus* such specialized sectors as physiological
psychology, archaeology, technical linguistics, and most of physical
anthropology; *plus* social geography, some psychiatry, and the behavioral part of economics, political science, and the law."[1] The wide
range of interests encompassed by this term is evidenced by the
scope of the Berelson-Steiner volume, which includes chapters on:
1) methods of inquiry, 2) behavioral development, 3) perceiving, 4)
learning and thinking, 5) motivation, 6) the family, 7) face-to-face
relations with small groups, 8) organizations, 9) institutions, 10)
social stratification, 11) ethnic relations, 12) mass communication,
13) opinions, attitudes, and beliefs, 14) the society, 15) culture.

Formal definitions allocating these topics to particular disciplines—culture to anthropology, motivation to psychology, social
stratification to sociology, and so forth—are deceptive. Academic
disciplines, like most social products, are somewhat untidy, each
having been partly shaped by historical legacy, random accretion,
and the idiosyncratic preferences of its practitioners. Indeed, in my
own field, there is a charming ritual that requires every doctoral examination to begin with some variant of "What is sociology?" This
insultingly elementary query is addressed to the candidate in the
guise of putting him at his ease, but the real motives of the faculty
do us less honor. Quite simply, each of us clings to the vain hope
that one fine day some bright young man will define the precise
boundaries of our field, and thus remove our own perplexities. Since,
after many years, this savant savior has still failed to materialize, we
are beginning to suspect that he does not exist. Although we continue to pose the same cunning question with the same desperate
tenacity, we have abandoned any real expectation of enlightenment.
One escapes the most profound self-hatred and despair only by ob-
serving that his closest neighbors are similarly afflicted.

As each of the behavior sciences yields to expansionist ambi-
tions and expropriates concepts and substantive interests from the
others—a student may be enlightened about the political process,
for example, in as many as five instructional departments—the distinctions between them become increasingly blurred. These ecumenical tendencies are further sustained by a shared dedication to the

method of science, or at least to its ethos. This commitment requires within every behavior science a similar division of labor, which is itself a source of interdisciplinary unity. For example, although Paul Lazarsfeld and Talcott Parsons are both sociologists, each might be more appropriately grouped with some political scientists than with each other. The former has much in common with Angus Campbell, whose studies of voting behavior are quantitative and empirical, while the latter has an undeniable kinship to David Easton, who also constructs abstract theoretical models.

The endless polemic on the relative merits of these and still other strategies of inquiry—there is still a certain lingering validity to Poincaré's observation that natural scientists report their findings and social scientists debate their methods—has the curious effect of creating bonds of recognition that transcend distinctive substantive interests. A sociologist who is accustomed to spirited exchanges on the relative merits of "philosophizing" versus "card counting," and finds the doves and the hawks in psychology in acrimonious dispute over the claims of "clinical" versus "statistical" prediction, is confirmed in a favorite principle: In some respects, life is everywhere the same.

The behavior sciences, then, seem sufficiently homogeneous to warrant treating them as a single entity. By so doing we may inadvertently conceal important, but hopefully not crucial, differences. All justify their existence, in part, by the conviction that, although knowledge is its own excuse for being, behavior science has "uses" beyond understanding. Some of these are relevant for public policy. The term "public" has a relatively precise meaning in social science usage which need not detain us here. In the present context it refers to nothing more esoteric than large numbers of people who are obliged to choose among alternatives affecting their collective welfare.

The decision-making process (and its aftermath) is as familiar as it is inexorable. Goals are envisioned and sought; means are employed to achieve these goals; there are always disparities between the intended and the actual outcomes; the perception of these disparities generates tensions or strains, to which there are reactions, which then have consequences for the next stage of goal seeking.

Much of our discussion will take the form of illustrations dealing with a few selected aspects of this process, but it is important to realize that what is at stake are such questions as: What social aims do we most cherish? What other goals are we willing to sacrifice in order to achieve them? What are the most efficient means consistent with our values that we might employ to accomplish our objectives? What price are we prepared to pay in scarce resources—time, energy, and organizational ingenuity—to achieve our aims? What sectors of society shall bear these necessary costs of attaining our purposes? What shall be the sequence of successive approximations toward ideal goals? What strategies shall we adopt in stimulating consent to our proposals?

The most general use of the behavior sciences, their knowledge, methods, and implicit ideologies, lies in their capacity to make this entire sequence less problematic by rendering ends, means, and their interrelationships more intelligible. In brief, they assist men to decide what goals to pursue, what actions make their attainment more probable, and what are the profits and costs of success or failure.

The Potential Uses of the Behavior Sciences in Defining Social Goals

Paul Lazarsfeld once identified the polar points on the "uses" spectrum as "the idea, most clearly represented by Soviet opinion, that the only justified use of social research is social revolution . . . [while, at the opposite extreme] utility in the narrowest sense [refers to] studies for government agencies, for business firms, labor unions, or other voluntary organizations that pay for them in the expectation that they will advance their purposes."[2]

American behavior science mainly pursues technical rather than salvationist aims. The reasons for this choice are embedded in the nation's intellectual history and require, among other things, an explanation of why the American campus has so seldom been hospitable to the heresies of the right or the left. On the more superficial level, the *status quo* orientation reflects the triumph of the positivist doctrine of ethical neutrality in science.

Its fundamental theorem is that the only scientifically meaningful questions of value are those that can be reduced to statements of fact. The steps in this process consist of first recasting prescriptive statements into the same general form as scientific assertions and then of eliminating all surviving normative terms from the resultant proposition. Thus, for example, the contention, "no nation ought ever to wage war" is actually an elliptical version of an implied "if . . . then" sequence including antecedent ethical commitments (e.g., brotherhood, love, compassion) and expected outcomes (e.g., high noncombatant casualties, suppression of dissent, neglect of the domestic poor) which together create the basis for pacifist convictions. But science is ill-equipped to comment on the purely ethical aspects of any argument. It has no metric to distinguish the intrinsic morality of love vs. hate, compassion vs. cruelty, or brotherhood vs. fratricide. It may request a hearing only about such matters that are at least in principle subject to empirical verification, in this instance the probability that war would, in fact, entail the anticipated consequences.

A mature behavior science would presumably consist of a set of contingent propositions which furnished a "then" for every theoretically or socially significant "if" and a series of instructions for achieving a wide variety of sometimes antithetical goals. And since scientists would still lack standards for defining correct moral choice, they would have no direct official concern for the ultimate uses of knowledge.

This definition of function permits behavior scientists to "clarify" but not to "criticize" goals. In the tradition of Max Weber, they specify the probability that 1) men can achieve whatever aims they seek, 2) they would find success pleasing, and 3) they desire particular outcomes for the reasons professed.

The field of criminology offers an illustration of the first of these contributions. Advocates of the death penalty often repair to a principle of retributive justice that they derive from Genesis 9:6, "Whoso sheddeth Man's blood, by Man shall his blood be shed," and from Leviticus 24:17, "and he who killeth any man shall surely be put to death." "Whoso" and "surely" are crucial conditions in these biblical injunctions, and, as social research clearly indicates, neither is currently satisfied in the American system of criminal justice. As we advance in procedural time from undetected murders in the first degree, to offenses "known to the police," to the apprehension of the offender, to the courts, and finally to commutation of sentence, a predictable process of attrition rescues more than 95 per cent from execution. Criminologists can also demonstrate that, of those who are convicted, a disproportionate number of those executed are male, Negro, and poor. In short, the "whoso" and "surely" desiderata are each violated, and it is unlikely that justice is, or, given current conditions, could ever be truly retributive. Such evidence has no bearing on the ultimate morality of the principle, but it might nevertheless persuade an advocate of capital punishment to reconsider his position.

A second type of clarification of goals is exemplified by the numerous studies of large- and small-scale organizations which indicate that "success" for one part of a system may entail "failure" for another. Peter Blau's research on efforts to render a public welfare agency more efficient showed that the introduction of statistical records increased productivity, enhanced supervision, permitted the introduction of rapid changes, and improved relations between interviewers and supervisors. At the same time, such records had the unintended consequence of threatening the supervisor's status by reducing him to the level of a file clerk; antagonized interviewers when the supervisor disregarded records and used discretionary powers in assigning rewards; undermined the organizational goals by encouraging a good record at the expense of real achievement; and stimulated "cut-throat" competition among interviewers.[4] Under these circumstances, the client might wish to balance the blessings of efficiency against all the unpremeditated and unsought additional consequences.

It is probably useful to be aware of potentially contravening values even when the sustaining evidence is less secure. For example, I am not at all prepared to advocate the adoption of a crash program to combat what I am told is the rising ulcer rate of women. Aside from my customary stoicism in the face of other people's tribulations, I am cheered by the assurances of some behavior scientists that the incidence of peptic ulcers is in part related to the anxiety that results when people are free to choose—and perhaps fail—from among a wider range of available alternatives. If the obverse is true and women can purchase serenity only by surrendering to the constraints of ideal *Gemeinschaft* existence—*Kinder, Kirche, Küche*—then my only regret is that so few women give their stomach linings for their country. These shaky data and sadistic musings aside, the principle remains: By directing attention to the price that must be paid in some values in order to achieve others, behavior research and theory may result in a reconsideration of originally cherished goals.

Finally, behavior science can help people arrive at a better understanding of why they reach certain of their decisions. A recurrent theme in all social investigation is distrust of initial appearances. This spirit of intellectual exposé frequently calls into question rationality of behavior and purity of purpose. Voting behavior is unmasked and revealed as a function of group interest, laboratory studies demonstrate the unreliability of perception, the theory of relative deprivation asserts that the most rewarded may be the least content —the message, in short, is that reality is elusive and we are not what we seem to be. This *caveat*, if taken seriously, should result in a heightened self-consciousness and a richer and more complex notion of personal motivation. Such self-awareness might well introduce greater rationality into human effort.

These examples of goals—"justice," "morale," "rationality" —may seem strangely unidirectional if they are to serve as illustrations of actual and potential modes of goal clarification by scholars who daily celebrate their value neutrality. They have not been selected arbitrarily. For although most of my colleagues are pleased to speak in the muscular rhetoric of positivism, they do so without genuine conviction. They are, as a group, decent men and could not be persuaded knowingly to undertake researches that threaten human freedom or dignity. They try to discover strategies for dealing with poverty, not merely as an interesting exercise in social engineering, but also because misery offends their sense of decency and justice. Those social scientists who become involved in morally ambiguous pursuits such as direct services to the military establishment find themselves the centers of much controversy and the objects of frequent censure. Most "value-free" behavior scientists avoid the friction between their "neutrality" and their private convictions because their moral commitments are consonant with those of the dominant liberal ethic. They may thus escape the more troubling dilemmas of the doctrine of acquiescence.

A lesser number of behavior scientists regard "mere clarification" as opposed to the "criticism" of goals as a default of scholarly responsibility. They argue that the positivist retreats from moral choice behind the shield of modesty and the strategy of silence. Since he eagerly denies any expertise that is not borrowed from empirical science, he is able to parry with a "no comment" all questions that fall within the realm of social ethics. But by refusing to choose among competing social aims—e.g., the extension of the franchise to all citizens versus the maintenance of state rights—he implies that all goals are morally equivalent, thereby asserting much more than he had intended. Neutrality, then, becomes a value position like all others. If choice is unavoidable, value preferences should be made explicit, ranked, and ultimately assigned weights. Behavior science should expend its resources only on those goals that satisfy the requirements of a valid moral calculus.

Unfortunately, this call to our sense of duty is not ordinarily accompanied by a set of directives about the standards we might apply in assessing ends as well as means. An examination of classic and current definitions of the "good" in social philosophy is not reassuring. Barrows Dunham has identified eight such guides: 1) egocentric hedonism—"pleasant to me"; 2) utilitarianism—"pleasant to most people"; 3) moral intuitionism—"approved by me"; 4) culture relativism—"approved by society"; 5) conforming to the moral law; 6) conforming to the divine law; 7) a supreme good; 8) moral skepticism.[5] If behavior scientists are called upon to advocate particular systems of prescriptive ethics, they will need value standards that are at minimum 1) *social* in that they refer to the interrelationships among people and 2) *binding* in that they are not a matter of private definition. Existing positions fail to meet one or both of these criteria.

The most heroic attempt to find a value standard that is both social and obligatory is found in theories such as nonrelativist pragmatism that derive their mandate from history. They profess to discover that over time mankind has sought such ends as "plenty" or "truth" or "moral good" or "freedom," but history also includes Torquemada and Auschwitz and the Treblinka.

The absence of standards clearly differentiating vice from virtue seems to leave the field to the positivists. Their triumph is, however, almost entirely verbal. They do not contend, after all, that social criticism is trivial intellectual activity, but only that it is inconsistent with their conception of the scientist's role. But if a self-imposed role definition destroys part of their usefulness, then so much the worse for the definition. They could elect to think of themselves as "scholars" or "intellectuals" as well as scientists and expand the range of their legitimate activities.

The great merit of the salvationist tradition is that it insists that we pay attention to goals as well as means, to ultimate objectives as well as temporary expedients. Surely, we stand in need of the utopian visions of a B. F. Skinner and the jeremiads of a C. Wright Mills. Skinner assaults contemporary society in the name of a society yet to be; Mills, for all of his militancy, was primarily engaged in celebrating the durable values of Western civilization. If Skinner invites us to the brave new world, Mills reproached us for our infidelity to the promise of our past. It is easy to pretend condescension toward Skinner, to find him merely interesting, and to dismiss Mills as a scold because he refused us permission to be cynical about our own most cherished values. History is often unkind to those who are discourteous to prophets.

We have been spared the necessity of arriving at any definitive solution to the "value problem" because, despite the endless prattle about "manipulation," the behavior sciences do not yet know enough to be very dangerous. But our knowledge is greater than it was a decade ago, in another decade it will be greater still, and it is folly to rely on ignorance to protect us from philosophy. Meanwhile, utility is served by those who "criticize" and those who "clarify," by those who direct attention to a wider and sometimes better agenda of human possibilities, and those who, lacking apocalyptic vision, sustain the daily exertions of a complex society.

The Potential Uses of Behavior Science in Developing Means to Implement Social Goals

The task of specifying conditions and developing programs for the achievement of social goals is ordinarily known as applied social research. Such activity may be addressed to issues of the greatest national importance or to relatively modest questions of public convenience. Alvin Gouldner's summary of the activities of applied research organizations gives some indication of their scope.

1) the reduction of various forms of social deviancy as exemplified in efforts to rehabilitate criminals or juvenile delinquents, 2) improvement of the efficiency or effectiveness with which diverse lay goals are pursued as exemplified in the work of some industrial sociologists or applied anthropologists, 3) the reduction of tensions or conflicts such as in the work of some race relation specialists, 4) the reduction of tensions that a group experiences in relation to its environment such as those found in personnel testing, market research, and public relations surveys.[6]

The ideal-typical sequence of an action research goes somewhat as follows: 1) a moral principle is asserted; 2) its institutional base is identified; 3) social goals are derived; 4) descriptive studies test the correspondence between aspiration and reality; 5) the social and individual consequences of the disparities are specified; 6) behavior research suggests means for narrowing the gap; 7) programs are developed that incorporate the proposed solution; and 8) evaluation procedures indicate the "success" or "failure" of the program. We may illustrate this pattern by alluding to the problem of "equality of educational opportunity."

1. *Moral principle:* All citizens in a democratic society should have equal initial advantages in seeking the good things in life. If the race belongs to the swift, the starting line should be the same for all.
2. *Institutional base:* Free public education is the main instrument of public policy for providing some modicum of equality of opportunity.
3. *Social goal:* High-quality schooling should be equally accessible to all American children regardless of creed, color, national origin, social class, or differences in talent.
4. *Correspondence between goal and reality:* Research on the problems of the poor, Negroes, and Puerto Ricans leaves little doubt that the school system magnifies the inequities of a stratified society by offering some children superior education while

denying it to others. Moreover, many such children suffer from environmentally induced disabilities before entering school and throughout their educational careers.

5. *Social and individual consequences of the disparities:* The individual child experiences anxiety, hostility, and a deflation of self. At the societal level, lack of educational opportunity severely restricts the positive functions of education as a mechanism for recruiting and discovering talent, as an agent for economic growth, as a vehicle for social mobility, and as an instrument for peaceable social change.

6. *Research clue:* According to some scholars most of the growth or decline in tested intelligence occurs in the preschool years. A child who is the product of an intellectually impoverished environment is severely handicapped by the time he enters first grade.

7. *Program:* "Operation Headstart" establishes preschool programs as part of the war against poverty.

8. *Evaluation:* It is too early to make a definitive judgment, but such programs appear to be valuable. However, there is already sufficient evidence to indicate that they are unlikely to reduce cumulative social and psychological deficits unless they are articulated with subsequent school programs, effectively interpreted to parents and the school systems, and taught by instructors who find gratification in teaching "slow" children.

All of the resources of the behavior sciences—their theories, findings, and techniques; the methods that produce them; the ethical system that sustains the process of discovery—are implicated in the "action" process: 1) "pure" research in the purest sense, i.e., the development of conceptual schemes, measurement devices, and the like, that are substantively vacuous; 2) empirical generalizations about the nature of society and the individual at reasonably high levels of abstraction; 3) investigations of narrowly defined and circumscribed problems; 4) middlemen practitioners who can establish programs.

The unifying features of behavior science that link all of these echelons as they select appropriate means to achieve desired ends include: 1) its methods of arriving at truth, 2) its emphasis on the concept of "system", 3) its quest for valid generalizations, 4) its contribution of specific techniques, and 5) its virtue.

As the conference progresses, someone will doubtless wonder out loud whether or not the behavior sciences are "really sciences." This is a harmless way to pass the time of day. I am content to relinquish the glowing symbolism of "science" so long as it is understood that behavior research has distinctive properties which separate it from other ways of arriving at truth. One of these is organized skepticism, a kind of institutionalized paranoia. Scientific method, properly understood, consists of a series of procedures which maximize the opportunities for revealing the errors in a plausible conjecture. This is the purpose of experimental logic, sampling, replication —the entire cumbersome apparatus of behavior science.

The Cambridge-Somerville Youth Study, which began in 1939, is a dramatic example of the utility of scientific procedure. A group of 325 boys judged to be "delinquent risks" in these two Massachusetts communities received, for a period of five years, the full benefits of the standard repertoire of social science rehabilitation techniques. These included psychological counseling, religious exhortation, and the guidance of the police. Three years after the conclusion of the project, a follow-up study indicated that neither the seriousness nor the frequency of the offenses committed by the boys in the intervening period were as high as had originally been anticipated.

If matters had stopped at this point, the project's personnel would have had occasion for justified self-congratulation. However, unluckily for their equanimity, but fortunately for knowledge, they had taken the precaution of recording the progress of a control group of similar size and characteristics. Powers and Witmer, who directed the experiment, were unable to discover any appreciable differences in the subsequent behavior of the treatment and control groups.[7] A later study by Joan and William McCord tracing the experiences of both groups up to 1956 yielded substantially similar results, and the authors conceded that "using the standard of 'official' criminal behavior, we must conclude that the Cambridge-Somerville Youth Study was largely a failure."[8]

The point to be noted is that the investigators would never have discovered that this was the case if the routine skepticism of the scientific method had not been reflected in their research design. This quality of mind is a welcome antidote for those programs that invest hope and energy without making any systematic effort to evaluate the results. Surely, the yearning for precision, the barriers which are created against innocence, the refusal to acknowledge superficial proofs are themselves public resources.

Methodological sophistication has its theoretical counterpart in those concepts of all the behavior sciences that emphasize the interrelatedness of parts to each other and to more comprehensive wholes. This idea is incorporated or implied in such notions as *Gestalten*, "configurations," "context," and above all in the notion of "system." A fairly standard treatment of this idea, in this case as it appears in the literature of organization theory, is the following: "Organizations are systems of individuals and groups which act upon one another. Changes in the behavior of one status group within an organization must affect the behavior of other groups, which in turn may have consequences feeding back to the group which changed first."[9]

The concept of system means that behavior scientists are alert to the possible consequences of any change for the total unit in which it is implicated. Thus, for example, the contraction in the differential birth rate among socio-economic classes may also mean reduced opportunities for social mobility, which may in turn have consequences for voting behavior, which may in turn . . . . This continued awareness of interrelatedness, when brought to the attention of policy-makers, can protect against the assumption that problems may be solved in isolation.

Beyond these gifts of attitude and style, behavior scientists contribute the isolated facts, empirical generalizations, and the "middle-range" theories that are indispensable to public policy. Their capacity to generate increasingly abstract propositions is their greatest source of power. They diverge, in this respect, from the stereotype of crusading journalism which does heroic personal battle against the evils that beset us. Behavior science takes a rather more "cool" view of existence. It does not view life as a series of private triumphs or failures. It wishes, instead, to comprehend human behavior in most abstract categories, and it is in this respect vulnerable to the charge of "dehumanization" which is sometimes leveled against its intellectual style.

But the habit of mind that deliberately renounces the effort to describe behavior in its full complexity and cherishes particular events only because they may eventually yield general propositions is nevertheless invaluable for some kinds of social understanding. Robin Williams, for example, painstakingly culled the literature of intergroup behavior almost two decades ago and produced the following instructive generalizations:

1) Militancy, except for sporadic and short-lived uprisings, is not characteristic of the most deprived and oppressed groups, but rather of those who have gained considerable rights so that they are able realistically to hope for more;
2) A militant reaction from a minority group is most likely when a) the group's position is rapidly improving or b) when it is rapidly deteriorating, especially if this follows a period of improvement.[10]

Much that has seemed puzzling to some could have been anticipated if these propositions had been consulted. They might have stimulated more responsive social action if the public had been able to foresee that the civil rights movement would become increasingly militant rather than obligingly passive once it had seen some major victories. The peculiar strength of general propositions is that they are relevant not only for the population to which they refer but also for understanding other situations with similar conceptual elements. Williams' generalizations rather suggest that, now that college students and the organized poor have experienced some initial successes, neither is likely to fade painlessly away. The time for suppression, if it was ever a realistic strategy, has long since passed.

The behavior sciences are not only capable of aiding the public to anticipate and respond to events; they often provide the means to control them. Kenneth Boulding has recently contended that internal developments in the science of economics leading to greater theoretical power, the availability of extensive information, and the development of imaginative concepts have had profound repercussions throughout the entire Western world. His comments deserve extensive quotation:

> If one were to look for the most important single reason for the striking contrast between the twenty years after the First World War and the twenty years after the Second, in terms of economic development and the avoidance of great depressions, at least in the developed world, I would nominate the development of national income statistics as the most important factor. The whole concept of the gross national product, for instance, was almost unknown in political discourse before the Second World War. It is true also that certain conceptual changes in the theoretical image of the system, due mainly to the powerful insights of Keynes, went hand in hand with the new information system to create an image in the mind of economic policy makers of a controlled market economy, which means that the Second World War represents a real "system break" in the economic system of the Western world, with a very profound shift in its fundamental patterns of behavior.[11]

The intellectual power of the behavior sciences is linked with more virtue than is common in our society. Jacob Bronowski has eloquently stated the case for science as an ethical system:

> The men and women who practice the sciences make a company of scholars which has been more lasting than any modern state, yet which has changed and evolved as no church has. What power holds them together? In an obvious sense, theirs is the power of virtue. By the worldly standards of public life, all scholars in their work are of course oddly virtuous. They do not make wild claims, they do not cheat, they do not try to persuade at any cost, they appeal neither to prejudice nor to authority, they are often frank about their ignorance, their disputes are fairly decorous, they do not confuse what is being argued with race, politics, sex or age, they listen patiently to the young and to the old who both know everything. These are the general virtues of scholarship, and they are peculiarly the virtues of science. Individually, scientists no doubt have human weaknesses. But in a world in which state and dogma seem always either to threaten or to cajole, the body of scientists is trained to avoid and organized to resist every form of persuasion but the fact.
> The values of science derive neither from the virtues of its members, nor from the finger-wagging codes of conduct by which every profession

reminds itself to be good. They have grown out of the practice of science because they are in the inescapable conditions for its practice.[12]

This ode was not dedicated to behavior scientists, and they probably do not merit quite so much lyrical energy. But they, too, are the beneficiaries of scientific training, and they are mostly situated in universities which, all things considered, can usually boast of a bracing moral climate. This is an embarrassing claim and one that will not be confirmed by reading academic novels. These ordinarily convey the impression that universities are more bookish versions of Peyton Place, that their inhabitants are mainly preoccupied with bureaucratic scuffling, and that surface civility is a disguise for corruption. This description of the campus is not devoid of appeal, but at the risk of relinquishing my credentials as a certified cynic, I should like to maintain that the community of scholars has great respect for truth and little tolerance for mendacity and that those attitudes could be absorbed at great public benefit.

After this recitation of the exemplary merits of the behavior sciences, it would be less than candid to conceal that the behavior sciences, as they are now constituted, suffer from severe maladies that restrict their usefulness. Berelson and Steiner concede that they suffer from "too much precision misplaced on trivial matters, too little respect for crucial fact as against grand theories, too much respect for insights that are commonplace, too much indication and too little proof, too little genuine cumulation of generalizations, too little regard for the learning of the past, far too much jargon."[13] This indictment could be extended. The potential public uses of the behavior sciences are restricted by three major limitations: 1) some of their conclusions often turn out to be demonstrably erroneous; 2) others are disputed within the profession; and 3) data and techniques for inducing sponsored change are conspicuously meager.

Demography is among the most mature of all branches within the behavior sciences, and the late P. K. Whelpton was one of its most able practitioners. Yet his widely accepted population projections were consistently in error. At various times, he forecast that the "population of the United States . . . was scheduled to reach a maximum of 144.6 million by 1970 and to decline rapidly thereafter"; "the maximum during the century would not exceed 150 million"; "the population will reach its maximum of about 160 million soon after 1980, and then begin to dwindle numerically"; and "a maximum population of some 165 million would be reached about 1990 after which a decline would occur." Harold F. Dorn was prompted to ask, "Demography, is it science or literature?" and did not stay for an answer.[14] It is clear, to understate the matter, that social bookkeeping based on these projections would have gone far awry.

It is further true that many issues in the behavior sciences remain unsettled. During periods of recession, is the economy better served by massive governmental spending or by reduction in taxes? Do Protestants exceed Catholics in the achievement ethic? Is there a power elite, or is it more accurate to refer to an intricate network of "veto" groups? Is the "positive reinforcement" of the teaching machine more effective for stimulating learning than the variable and sometimes irascible real-life teacher? Is the cause of economic development in transitional societies better served by elite or mass education? If there were malice enough and time, the instances of ambiguities in fairly central issues in the behavior sciences could be almost indefinitely multiplied.

Another severe limitation on the uses of the behavior sciences is their absence of concrete knowledge about the processes of change. It is true, as Wilbert Moore has noted, that "several social scientific disciplines, and notably economics and sociology, do provide some fairly high-level, empirically-based, and interdependent propositions concerning social change."[15] However, high-level propositions are not the same as specific techniques for the transformation of individual men or their communities. The most publicized of these are "role playing," the psychodrama, and other such devices associated with the group dynamics movement. However, all would concede that, as measured against the magnitude of the challenge, these are frail instruments indeed.

The Populations

The principal audiences for the knowledge of the behavior scientists may be identified as 1) the captive population of college students, 2) strategic elites that make decisions in the society, and 3) the general public. It is difficult to ascertain to what extent the first of these groups has received the message. Their earnestness and performance on examinations seem to suggest that some knowledge has been absorbed; but, since there does not now exist a single study on the retention of information beyond graduation, it is difficult to tell whether any permanent damage has occurred. The research on differential effects of the academic "major" on values does not gladden the heart. There are no consistently large differences in political liberalism, ethnic tolerance, internationalism, etc. between those who concentrate in the behavior sciences and those otherwise occupied in the academy.

The prevailing evidence, then, gives us no warrant for assuming that persons other than the professional consumers of the behavior sciences—government officials, city planners, social workers, teachers—are much affected by them. There is, however, reason to believe that decision-makers, including congressmen, have a great deal of faith in their potential uses. Research funds from such sources as the National Institutes of Health, the National Science Foundation, and the Office of Education are ample, if not lavish, and fellowship assistance for graduate students is now available from a variety of governmental and corporate sources. An even more significant development is the reliance on behavior science experts at every level of society. As Henry Kissinger, himself a veteran of many Washington skirmishes, has written, "many organizations, governmental or private, rely on panels of experts. Political leaders have intellectuals as advisors. Throughout our society policy-planning bodies proliferate, research organizations multiply. The need for talent is a theme of countless reports."[16]

There is no satisfactory evidence indicating to what extent the general public is aware of behavior science findings. It would seem to follow, from all that has been said thus far, that they should be disseminated as widely as possible. The diffusion of such knowledge is, however, of a different order than other scientific information regularly carried by the mass media and involves perplexities that are inapplicable to, let us say, reports about space exploration or even medicine. The unhappy consequences of faulty perceptions of these fields are cushioned by the fact that any action that results from such distortions is subject to effective veto by a professional, responsible, and technically proficient intermediary. A reader of a medical feature in *Newsweek* may not be able to differentiate the aorta from the cerebellum, but it is not he who will prescribe drugs or perform surgery. The situation with respect to social knowledge is, of course, quite different. The layman's views become part of "effective public opinion" with all the action consequences implied by that uncertain phrase.

What, for instance, do we wish to convey to readers of the New York *Daily News* about racial differences in intelligence? What do we really know? The average test performance of Negroes is inferior to whites; there is, nevertheless, considerable statistical overlap; and an undetermined proportion of the variance may be attributed to environmental circumstance. Unfortunately for human decency, the equivalence of conditions that would permit confident interpretation do not obtain in contemporary America. When selected indices of social class are held relatively constant, differentials in measured intelligence customarily contract, occasionally expand, and sometimes remain unaffected. This being the case, most responsible scholars have concluded that there is "insufficient evidence to demonstrate intrinsic racial differences in intelligence." Moreover, the overwhelming majority of behavior scientists believe that evidence compiled under optimum conditions would reveal that the distribution of intelligence is the same among all races.

But since faith is not proof, it is altogether conceivable that whites are indeed "superior" to Negroes, the races are inherently equal, or, for that matter, Negroes are "superior" to whites. It seems highly arbitrary to assume that intelligence tests and environmental deficits are so perfectly calibrated as to account for the precise number of I.Q. points that Negroes differ from whites. This assumption may well underestimate the importance of the social milieu and the native intelligence of Negroes.

What shall we make of these findings, and how shall we transmit them to the general reader? Race relations are currently, to put it mildly, "delicate," and history affords much testimony that the doctrines of biological superiority have often been the last refuge of scoundrels. In the name of social responsibility, shall journalists then refrain from contradicting the widespread impression that "social scientists have demonstrated that all races are equal," or shall they indicate the unsettled and ambiguous state of knowledge in this sphere? There are questions which cannot be answered by easy reference to clichés about the "right of the public to know." At the very least, the phrase "to know" must be distinguished from unadorned "fact." Information does not become knowledge, nor does knowledge reach "understanding," until it is placed in context and its scientific and ethical consequences are defined.

Journalists might do well to inform their readers of the current state of the art in testing, to place the cognitive dimensions in proper perspective, to cite the intolerance of democratic theory for discriminatory behavior based on group averages, and above all to indicate the irrelevance of interracial comparisons for most issues of public policy. The problem is not whether Negroes are equal to whites, but whether they are equal to the ordinary burdens and privileges of contemporary life. And there is no evidence that Negroes are inherently unable to benefit from education, hold jobs, live in decent houses, and otherwise participate as full citizens in a free society. The hazards of exhibiting sensitive behavior science materials for public inspection may be those that are encountered in all aspects of democratic life, but they can be unduly magnified by journalists who, in the name of time-honored distinctions between "news" and "editorializing," refrain from morally relevant interpretation.

The Mass Media as Agent

At present, scholars speak to scholars, professors speak to students, experts speak to clients, but only the mass media can speak to the public. They could elect to report on the behavior sciences on the basis of criteria that are faintly analogous to familiar journalistic categories, 1) "for background only" and 2) "for direct quotation." In the first instance, the journalist uses knowledge to understand events and to interpret them for the benefit of his readers. However, he would not regard the behavior sciences as his "beat" but simply as one of many sources of information that increased his own craftsmanship. He might instead spend full time or less at the behavior sciences desk in much the same fashion as his colleagues who cover the drama, music, medicine, and other departments that regularly appear in the mass media. These are, of course, not mutually exclusive choices, and a particular publication or television outlet could very well decide to do both. Either course would seem to argue for the inclusion of behavior science training in the curricula of schools of journalism. All of the relevant disciplines are now far too complex, too specialized, and too technical to permit easy access to findings by means of the usual techniques of journalistic investigation.

He will need to develop scientific competence if for no other reason than the necessity for emancipating himself from uncritical reliance on professional informants. Much behavior science leaves a great deal to be desired, as is evident to any novice in the field, and a journalist needs sufficient immersion in the literature of economics, anthropology, sociology, political science, and the law to exercise independent judgment. The need for professionalism is here fully as great, say, as it is in the case of the National Association of Science Writers. Nor would it be amiss to expand the number of programs such as those supported by the Sloan, Rockefeller, Ford, and Russell Sage Foundations. Any behavior science beat should include, among other things, some concern for the institutional aspects of the behavior sciences, their sources of support, the conditions under which they produce knowledge, and their relationship to national policy.

Journalists may be deterred from learning more about behavior science because of its deficiencies as an art form. Behavior scientists are not famous for the distinction of their prose, and on all sides we are admonished, "Talk to us in English." Now it is obviously desirable to write with simplicity and grace, but, having granted this point, I am not at all sure that the injunction to "talk to us in English" is always a reasonable demand. The natural science editor is willing to learn the language of mathematics, to master technical terms, and to relax literary standards in order to confront the secrets of the physical universe. It is reasonable to require that a sentence should be no more obscure than its content warrants. But if the problems are complex and the analysis subtle, we sacrifice too much if we fail to use technical language and style. A specialized vocabulary not only promotes parsimonious communication; it often has the additional merit of intellectual precision. Journalists who wish to introduce readers to our findings will be obliged to learn and then translate the language in which they are expressed.

There are, to be sure, problems involved in determining how this tutelage can best be accomplished. Who shall preside over the behavior science department—a scholar who can translate his professional language into English, or a prose stylist who is willing to obtain the requisite professional education? In either case, he should be sensitive to the fact that linguistic elegance must sometimes be sacrificed in the process of converting a plausible intuition into a near certainty.

The alleged inscrutability of behavior scientists poses no insuperable obstacles to fruitful collaboration. A more troublesome difficulty is the pressure exerted on the media to sacrifice serious reportage for the sake of audience appeal. Journalists are still to some degree the captives of the public demand for high drama, "human interest," and "easy reading." These criteria could lead to excessive concentration on inconsequential trifles and induce the editor to ignore studies that are supported by quantitative rather than case history data.

It is, for example, impossible to describe the behavior of individuals in groups without using words such as "more" or "less," or "majority," or "minority," or "greater proportion," or "smaller proportion," and other words of this type. Now the word "majority," for example, can be translated to mean more than 50 per cent, and 50 is a number; when we begin to use numbers, tables cannot be far away, and for many people, neither can tedium. But the exclusive emphasis on "human interest" in the conventional sense will deprive readers of some of the most significant findings in the behavior sciences.

The commitment of behavior scientists and journalists to different aesthetic standards and canons of reporting suggest that they are in some respects two distinctive cultures. These differences should not be exaggerated. They have more in common than the mandate to publish or perish. Journalists are commonly engaged in a primitive form of behavior science that we call, in our spritely way, "participant-observation" and that reporters know as "getting the story." Some of the most celebrated studies in our literature, such as William Foote Whyte's *Street Corner Society*, are actually journalistic works that are sharpened by the concepts of the behavior sciences. Such studies are very valuable. They are especially useful in suggesting hypotheses which may later be confirmed by more sophisticated methods. My feeling is that journalists are ordinarily better participant-observers than are behavior scientists. They cannot be deflected by the intervening conceptual barriers that sometimes distort perception. When a newspaper reports a suicide, I am left with some palpable sense of waste and terror. A sociologist who reflects on the same incident feels the immediate need of enlisting Durkheim as an ally, and Max Weber cannot be far behind. At the level of "getting the story," we would do well to pay more attention to journalistic standards of salience, immediacy, and clarity.

Journalists are, moreover, at least the equal of behavior scientists in dealing with "the story behind the story" of major national and international events. In commenting on Amitai Etzioni's conviction that "the overwhelming majority of social commentators, editorial writers, etc. who are uninitiated to sociology have a poor record of understanding social issues from race relations to the radical right," Robert Bierstedt answers that "few if any sociologists are superior in social analysis to such publicists as Walter Lippmann and James Reston." He adds that "it is useful if embarrassing to recall that both of them are innocent of sociological training. . . . It is my own impression that most of us, as sociologists, tend to denigrate [as 'mere' journalism] the enterprise and accomplishment of publicists in general. . . ."[17]

Science claims no monopoly in understanding the world. The moon belongs to the astrophysicist and to the poet as well as to those who systematically study the marriages that result from lunar madness. Behavior science is itself only a grand hypothesis. We are wagering that, if we proceed according to methods that have some points of resemblance to those that have been successful in the natural sciences, these strategies will also yield benefits to us. Thus far our aspirations considerably exceed our achievements. Furthermore, even our best efforts tend to be somewhat disrespectful of the juices of life. One of my colleagues once heard a young graduate student explain that "human beings are residuals in my theoretical system."

Permit me to relate a brief parable. Some twenty-five years ago I entered the Army, together with a goodly number of fellow sophomores. Our drill sergeant answered to W.K.; his despairing mother did not trouble herself to endow him with a full name. He was a wit, a kind of illiterate Noel Coward whose ignorance was equal to the grandeur of his malice. From time to time, he would inquire solicitously, "Where the hell do you guys think you are—at the senior prom?" and dissolve in self-congratulation.

I had a friend with whom I exchanged little speculations about our sergeant's ancestry and his native intelligence. One day an officer interrupted our drill, said a few words to our nemesis, and gave him an assignment that made it necessary for us to return to our barracks without his benevolent guidance. As luck would have it, W.K. appointed my friend as his deputy. Now I was in the presence of a buddy, and I prepared to march back serenely with my usual dispirited shuffle. Suddenly, out of the foggy dew of Mississippi, I heard a voice no longer friendly asking, "Where the hell do you guys think you are—at the senior prom?"

The moral of this tale is, of course, that personality may well reside in the sergeancy rather than the sergeant. Speaking as a sociologist, this anecdote pleases me. It reveals the fact of order and predictability and does not require intimate knowledge of real people. But what is good for sociology may be bad for the country. A society without idiosyncracy would, of course, be intolerable. If I may paraphrase W. H. Auden: When social scientists fully understand human beings, it will be their duty to teach them how they might once again become incomprehensible. No such prospect need haunt us. When all of the behavior sciences reach full maturity, there will still be wonder and enigma aplenty for poets, journalists, and philosophers. In this company of men who wish to understand and guide other men, the behavior scientist will make significant contributions, but he will be only one among many.

---

1. Bernard Berelson and Gary A. Steiner, *Human Behavior*, New York: Harcourt, Brace & World, Inc., 1964, p. 11.

2. Paul F. Lazarsfeld, "The Sociology of Empirical Social Research," *American Sociological Review*, Vol. 27, No. 6 (December 1962), p. 765.

3. The late George Lundberg remains the authentic voice of positivism in American social science. An excellent account of his position may be found in George A. Lundberg, "Semantics and the Value Problem," *Social Forces*, Vol. 27 (1948), No. 1, p. 116.

4. Peter Blau, *The Dynamics of Bureaucracy*, Chicago: University of Chicago Press, 1955.

5. Barrows Dunham, *Giant in Chains*, Boston: Little, Brown and Company, 1953. See Ch. 5.

6. Alvin Gouldner, "Theoretical Requirements of the Applied Social Sciences," *American Sociological Review*, Vol. 22, No. 1 (February 1957), p. 93.

7. Edwin Powers and Helen Witmer, *An Experiment in the Prevention of Delinquency*, New York: Columbia University Press, 1950.

8. Joan and William McCord, "A Follow-Up Report on the Cambridge-Somerville Youth Study," *Annals*, March 1959, p. 322.

9. Allen H. Barton and Bo Anderson, "Change in an Organizational System: Formalization of a Qualitative Study," in Amitai Etzioni (ed.), *Complex Organizations*, New York: Holt, Rinehart and Winston, Inc., 1961, p. 401.

10. Robin M. Williams, Jr., "Racial and Cultural Relations," in Joseph B. Gittler (ed.), *Review of Sociology*, New York: John Wiley & Sons, Inc., 1957, p. 453.

11. K. E. Boulding, "Reality Testing and Value Orientation," *International Social Science Journal*, Vol. 17, (1965), No. 3, p. 410.

12. Jacob Bronowski, *Science and Human Values*, New York: Julian Messner, Inc., 1956. See Ch. 3.

13. Berelson and Steiner, *op.cit.*, p. 12.

14. Harold F. Dorn, "Pitfalls in Population Forecasts and Projections," in Joseph J. Spengler and Otis Dudley Duncan (eds.), *Demographic Analysis*, Glencoe, Ill.: The Free Press, 1956, pp. 69–90. Dorn is apparently not overly impressed with the distinction between "prediction" and "projection." He thinks the latter serves to conceal the intent to do the former.

15. Wilbert E. Moore, "The MacIver Lecture: Predicting Discontinuities in Social Change," *American Sociological Review*, Vol. 29, No. 3 (June 1964), p. 333.

16. Henry A. Kissinger, "The Policymaker and the Intellectual," *The Reporter*, March 5, 1959, p. 30.

17. See Amitai Etzioni, "Social Analysis as a Sociological Vocation," and comments by Robert Bierstedt and reply by Etzioni, *American Journal of Sociology*, Vol. 70, No. 5 (March 1965), pp. 613–624.

2

Newspaper Journalism and the Behavioral Sciences

Richard C. Wald
NEW YORK HERALD TRIBUNE

"The art of editing has advanced; it shows greater discrimination, a broader point of view. . . . To print the debates . . . in full, as the old-age newspapers would have done, avails less with busy people than to print the general drift of the speeches, the general sentiment of Congress. . . . All technique has advanced. Our newspapers are sharper, quicker, more moderate, nearer to the truth and to sound principles of sociology than the newspaper of twenty or thirty years ago. We may have less genius, but we have more trained and specialized talent."

Although the quotation sounds, except for some of the phrasing, like something that might have been written for the last issue of a journalism school review, it was actually written in 1911 for *Collier's Magazine* by Will Irwin. It is as true today as it was then, as descriptive of editors' ideas and attempts. And it is, of course, totally wrong.

The art of editing has not advanced. Lord only knows what sound principles of sociology are, but the problems of American journalism today are that newspapers look too much and sound too much like newspapers of twenty and thirty years ago. They are at times indistinguishable from their parents, and in too many cases what does distinguish them is a simple matter of wider columns, bigger type, or new type faces: new cosmetics on the same old ladies.

But we live in a new era. Our society changes in geometric proportions, and we cling to what someone else invented a long time ago as the purported mirror of what actually happens now.

Recently W. H. Auden was talking about the "anxiety caused when the techniques a society has invented for coping with life, which hitherto have been successful, no longer work." He said:

The Roman Empire had evolved legal, military and economic techniques for maintaining internal law and order, defending itself against external enemies, and managing the production and exchange of goods. In the third century these proved inadequate to prevent civil war, invasion by barbarians and depreciation of the currency. In the 20th century, it is not the failure but the fantastic success of our techniques of production that is creating a society in which it is becoming increasingly difficult to live a human life. In our reactions to this one can see many parallels to the third century. Instead of Gnostics we have Existentialists and God-is-dead theologians; instead of Neoplatonists, "humanist" professors; instead of desert eremites, heroin addicts and Beats; instead of the cult of virginity, do-it-yourself sex manuals and sado-masochistic pornography.

Something is wrong. Something is wrong with the world and something is wrong with us and the newspapers go on day after day telling us that everything is stable and intelligible and correct. Above all, they tell us everything is, somehow, impersonal—and that's where the fault lies.

I think we are suffering through a crisis of individual dignity, of personality, of the "I-ness" of me, that was caused by the huge extension of our lives into a mass society and by all the awareness that Freud has thrown at our feet the way someone has thrown that bomb at our feet and us aching with hope to be able to use it with what we think will be intelligence and aching with fear that we are doing the wrong thing and aching with the knowledge that somehow we are missing the boat. Where is that happy land all my prosperity is going to buy?

We live in a mass. Everything is too big, and nothing grows smaller. This country is the disease of the world's future and possibly, in its antibodies, the hope of its salvation. In the appearance of things we remain the same, and the newspapers help maintain the façade. We talk about our problems and the historical process as though nothing had changed for us as individuals. We all know that there is an irrational basis to the voting process as it in fact occurs, but the papers deal with it and with themselves as though we were still a sturdy band of farmers on our way to the ballot box, only now we're observed by television and the box has been automated.

What is an election but sudden shafts of passion in a morass of dead issues? When Senator Goldwater claims, as a presidential issue, the war against crime in the streets, suddenly everyone is drawn into the net. General Eisenhower comes to his side, people actually respond, a little knowledge is gained because he is talking about something recognizable and human and personal. But soon the personal relationship is lost in fuzzy thought. President Johnson will somehow manage to encompass that view also. The newspapers will make that comment equal to some weightless abstraction about possible future welfare schemes envisioned for another world. Two years later they will report a behavioral study of midwestern voters that indicates any Democrat could have beaten Nixon and the only issue that made any impact in Milwaukee was urban redevelopment on the west side and the possibility that the head of the household might get mugged on a street full of saloons, but people thought that defoliation sounded like an interesting idea even though they couldn't see what it had to do with them. "Sociologists See Pocketbook Issues Determining Vote"

And the voters figure that the distance between their personal troubles and the issues of the nation is too great to be bothered with. As far as the newspapers are concerned, they are in different worlds. Personal troubles are considered stuff for feature stories, and the issues of the nation, unfortunately, involve only processes and not people.

Yet everybody knows that people, as single, individual humans, are as troubled as the times are. It is the business of all of us here to find the intertwining process and explain it, or at least show it. We ought to consider some of the difficulties of today's men and our era.

We have annihilated time, and we celebrate the fact. The traveler who once arrived in Europe from the New World with a knowledge of ocean and passage now arrives at the identical airport he left, theoretically as safe as that sea-shell that bore Venus, every

Botticelli curl in place, every apparent ruffle ironed out. Except that, inside, the traveler is suffering from spatial dislocation and doesn't know it.

Everything is speeded up. The insurance company clock tells you the world is overpopulating itself apace, the cars go faster, and the age of the helicopter is upon us. All the little products of the day speed us to an early rest. Where is the time we save? Where is the time for all the things that crowd in to be seen or done?

Maybe that's why people take drugs. We're in a wild dislocation of sensibility; Einstein joggled the clock of history and there doesn't seem to be any orderly sense of process to things any more. Maybe the addict is telling the truth when he appears before the irate magistrate who has a public life built on a barely remembered Blackstone and tells him, "It does kill time. Lord yes."

What is the common factor that links the Harlem junkie and the Westchester high school girl? Maybe they both want to proceed at a pace of their own choosing. Maybe the sense of time and no-time, real speed-up and phony leisure has caught them by the arm. The musicians who are junkies all have different reasons, but one and all they say the rhythm is clearer and you can compose beautiful things in a second or pass an hour on one note. They don't hear a different drummer; they are the different drummers. They want to rearrange the world to suit themselves—and why not, if they think the world is an illusion fostered by "them"?

There is an enormous pressure against being an individual. Everybody knows that. Nobody makes anything any more as an idea that might be sold to people. A manufacturer would have to be crazy. What we do now is investigate the market need to determine if a new fluoride toothpaste might be sold; then pre-test acceptability by opinion sampling on names and colors; then spot-test the market in sample areas; then produce it. Everyone knows that Edsel failed because the marketing concept was faulty. There's a little sneaking joy in the thought of the Ford Motor Company losing that quarter of a billion dollars and carrying on a flirtation with Marianne Moore; everyone seems to think that's the way it should have been done. They just did their market conceptualizing poorly. Nobody thinks they should have tried simply to put out a good car. That might not sell.

The real message of *Editor and Publisher* is for the world to remember that a proper media buy in Easton, Pa., will give you a perfect test market. There isn't a single human in it, but it's one hell of a test market.

I don't know what the dropout figures are in the universities of the nation. I happen to know by accident that one out of every four freshmen entering this year at Yale will *not* get a degree in four years. We are in the midst of a massive wave of dropping out such as the country has never seen before. And not all the dropouts leave school. They simply drop out of the life we have prescribed for them.

Maybe we are trying too hard to persuade our students that fiction is real. We are offering a society that tells the young over and over again that if you drop out of high school you will lose x thousands of dollars in the course of your earning lifetime; if you don't complete college you will lose y thousands of dollars and all these great careers will be closed to you. Listen to the principal, listen to the teacher, listen to the President. Go to school. Get good grades. Make money. We are running a huge training system as an arm of our economy.

Then we tell thousands upon thousands of young people at liberal arts colleges that there are values in those books that will make them wiser and better, if not wealthier. We tell them to become whole men and women, to pick up the ideals another generation has lived by and, with a little bit of rearranging, to live by them too. That's what you're really in college for, boy.

And in the meantime? In the space between the attitudes, the unwary slip and they drop out. To be an intellectual is to know that it is understanding, not sensation, that is the best of the world. To be a dropout is to feel the sensations cannot be understood.

Berkeley was a tiny riot in a big university. It was all mixed up, if I read the reporting right, with a little bit of politics and a little bit of dirty speech and a little bit of all those tag ends of things campuses always have. But just from hearing recordings of what the crowd was yelling when they surrounded the police car on the campus, they were furious with Clark Kerr for telling the truth and saying he was running a factory to turn out minds for industry. They got worked up because they felt the place was too big to recognize that they had dignity and rights of their own.

I have done one painful, personal, impossible, in-depth interview with a young man who left college. He didn't find any meaning in it. Totally and for all time at the age of nineteen and to the present day, he said that Aristotle was like, dead, man. What was he to Hecuba or Hecuba to him? Where was the direction to it? Where were they all going? I was supposed to be on the side of the deans and I couldn't tell him. I can only speak in parables and prophecy because all the rhetoric is being used up the wrong way.

But the dropouts who seek for the "me" hidden and almost unseen in the great pressure of being a mass "you" don't all simply wither like the drug-takers who also seek a personal salvation. They drop out from the old attitudes to campaign for dirty speech, for Negro rights, against Vietnam, for university reform.

They try to find a new rhetoric for a new ferment, and their chance is almost nil because most don't even know what's bothering them.

Marshall McLuhan is right, maybe. We're in a new world, and our techniques are such that we have given ourselves a new form of communication, but we haven't figured out yet the way to use it.

Oh, we use television, but without knowing what we do. The young are our television generation. In all the ages of man there has never been such a thing. It abets the annihilation of time by giving you instantly in New York what is really tomorrow in New Delhi. It annihilates space. And it talks. All the time, incessantly. Just touch it and it springs to life ready to serve its function; to flap-flap-flap before you a sliding, glistening surface that involves and lets free in subtle ways no man has yet described. The medium is the message indeed.

The broadcaster thinks he is wicked and adventurous to conclude that his function is not really to educate or even entertain, but to sell. A huge national network pulsing with power, drenched in cash, pushing out merchandise at every hour of the day. That's true. By reaching an audience it creates a market; by creating a market it makes goods possible. It flattens speech and regularizes taste. It creates, instantly, clichés that once needed years to form and chews up whole areas of thought and leaves them behind like Milton Berles of memory.

Possibly, the broadcaster's real function is to create a cohesive, self-reinforcing, self-renewing, growing mass. It is providing the basis for modern life.

The thrust of the medium becomes a way of life even as its literal message becomes a rule. Clearly, its emphasis is on numbers. There is nothing immoral in that. To reach the numbers, the programs must seek the lowest common denominator. That denominator is what is within a man that is most like the things that are in every other man. It doesn't matter whether your theory is that the commonness of each of us is given by God or society; it is there and it is being sought out by television. The effect is to emphasize and strengthen in each of us what is common to all. But we were born one, not many, and our need is to find that one and cleave to it lest it be lost, and we with it.

And what of the dropouts from television? The most immune to television advertising are the young who whistle the jingles. It is all the same and it all cancels out. We live in a society of plenty that has given up catering to our needs and now curries our desires. But the desires are hard to rank in order, and the advertising pitch becomes part of the mass of things, and the greatest of all invention is to be Doyle, Dane, and Bernbach and find a way to differentiate.

Meanwhile the style of life grows more luxuriantly different. The old epigram was that youth was so precious it was a shame it had to be wasted on the young. That was in a day when the young were imagined as unreflective and age had its charms.

But now youth knows it's young and doesn't want to lose that quality. Television has taught the scholar that he has now the most precious thing on earth. On the West Coast, where our styles in being young are made, the pump-house gang thinks death comes at twenty-five, and the slightly older generation, carrying around fears its parents imparted during the Depression, lives in another climate of mind from the sunny, careless, rootless way of the new young. Television doesn't just teach happy endings. Television teaches things more subtle: change, easiness, swiftness, the irrelevance of time and space, the public impermanence even of stars, the personal indestructibility even of bad guys, and above all—flap-flap-flap— speed that dissolves everything in a wink.

So the dropout from the official culture and the official society picks up the television culture and is yet dissatisfied, because it does not lead to an individual "me"; it leads to an "us" where the common denominator is youth, its style is to be on the road, its attitude is to expect of life the same ease of dropping away from involvement that the little screen teaches. Individual dignity seems to come only in a kind of striving against some difficulty, whether that difficulty be the red-neck of myth and fact who would deprive the Negro of his rights, or the foreign land that would offer adventure and service to the Peace Corps, or some existential attitude that's harder and harder to find without becoming the cliché of "Beat."

Why do we have such a fascination now with the hollowness of success? Why does Norman Mailer write about the American dream while millions nod "yes"? Why should *Darling* be understood widely as a fine movie? When debunking and protest were done in the thirties, the predominant cast of mind was political or economic. Except for the best of poets, the insight of the time was that the failure of public success was private hypocrisy: the pious rich man who really wanted to exploit the workers or was unfeeling about their sufferings; the selfish actress who found redemption in good works; the scientist who left his rich wife to go back to the laboratory. These were private failures directly related to a public point. The thing that was wrong with their success was that it got them off the good, the true, and the beautiful path of somehow contributing to the greatest good. It was a failure of action.

But the failure of success in modern terms is a failure of passion—individual, personal, incommunicable. Indeed, its greatest irony is that in the midst of the greatest clatter of media, it cannot be put into words. It is the failure that has no exit. It is the marriage wherein the husband and wife are not so much unfaithful as incapable of talking to each other or hearing if there were talk. And there is no salvation of any public kind. It is the self-realization that we are hollow men and that the attainment of mass ends is really individual tragedy. Today we all know that the movie actress desired by every virile man can commit suicide—and not over some unhappy love affair. She commits suicide for aching reasons that we all know and cannot state. And so we love her for it and we understand a little of what the new French philosophers mean when they talk about suicide being—but not quite being enough—a personal affirmation in the face of the absurdity of existence. We knew in the old days that it did not profit a man to gain the world if he lost his soul, and we knew that this meant you should live a godly life even if you had a lot of money. What do we know of it today? I think we know that your soul is harder to keep than we used to think.

We are in the middle of a great paradox, apparent to all and a comfort to none. The paradox is that we are in an age of enormous possibilities of communication. It is possible to talk to the moon, and we think we hear patterns of thought from the stars. But we are beginning to suspect we cannot talk to each other. We are being overwhelmed by the hugeness of life to feelings of individual insignificance, and this is enforcing our isolation. It is not a failure of television. Television talks *at* us, not to us. It is a failure, among other things, of newspapers, which are supposed to talk to us and do not.

There is always a *Zeitgeist* and there is never a *Zeitgeist*. Never, because we are all born of Adam's sinful knowledge; we live our lives in the midst of death and trouble and joy; and we die, each in his time, as men. For so much of the basic human condition, we are all joined and alike. Always, because other times have other ways; cultures and civilizations change.

I think we are now witnessing in this country the growing awareness that something is awry with men's souls, something that shouldn't be wrong. I think that the spirit of our time will prove to be a care for individual souls under whatever tags we will use: civil rights, human rights, peace, or, as in the third century, a Failure of Nerve.

Why is it that the sixties have produced the revolution in civil rights? It's a hundred years since the end of the Civil War. True, it takes time for the idealism of the few to become the inheritance of the many, but if it took this long, why not another decade or two? If we are so ready and ripe now to force a change, why was it not so in the late thirties and the early forties? Surely then, when we knew the world of economics had let us down, there was enough feeling that the Negro was getting a rotten deal. Surely the riots right here in New York in the early forties were as violent and passionate as anything since? Surely the racial hatred that stalked the streets of Chicago in Studs Lonigan's youth ought to have provoked the idealism of the young and the consciences of the Eastern Establishment. But it didn't.

The Supreme Court not only reads the election returns; in 1954 it began to influence them. With its decision against separate-but-equal, because such a concept meant different and unequal, meant a denial of individual dignity, the court provided us with a great act of political intuition.

The real reason Negro civil rights has become an issue now is that the country now is troubled by its thoughts about individual life, dignity, whatever you call it. This is the real idea whose time is now arriving; this is our *Zeitgeist*.

Nothing nonviolent has been more shocking, more of an affront to the nation and its habits than these scruffy people doing silly things to enforce their own singular ideas on the community. The nerve of some of these people to dress so queerly! and to sit-in at lunch counters like that! and to demand that society answer to them alone or else they'll damn well fast to death, or something. Who do they think they are? Somebody?

But we, as a society, let them get away with it. We have changed our laws and our attitudes to accommodate them. Why? Because secretly we have joined them in the belief that there is some release, some communication in knowing that I am but one, but I am one and that this black, poor, uneducated minority is yet human and deserving of some of our concern.

And allied to this is a great malaise in our nation about Vietnam.

This is the mark of our half of the century. We all know that we are going to be remembered in history for what we are doing now in Southeast Asia. We are embarked on a strange kind of war, for which the Korean episode was but training and initial bloodletting. We are embarked on a vast imperial enterprise in the course of which, willy-nilly, we have become involved by little steps in the enormous jump to a war of attrition. We have never fought such a war before.

The President says that he seeks a consensus. He says it in his words and in his actions. And we think that he does not have one because we see a debate going on whose terms are pro- and anti-administration. Let us reason together, the President says, and we think we are not reasoning together.

This is not so. There is a consensus and we are part of it.

The wellspring of opposition to the present policy is a real feeling that we are doing something terrible to the people of Vietnam; that we are wreaking on the heads of the innocent the horrors of a conflict that began long ago and in another country. The wrongness we see is a wrongness to people. The response is compassion that finds its outlet in arguments of legality, morality, and expediency but is at base a sense that men ought to live the lives they can with the minimal guarantees of being left alone.

That same wellspring of feeling actually informs the comments and decisions of the administration. I do not think it is lip-service the President and his secretaries pay when they talk of the horror they know they are visiting on these people and their willingness to pay for a better life.

The point is that our argument is really over methods, not ends, even though we have not articulated the ends. In our own life here and now in this country we find no inner completion from outer wealth. There is a gnawing beginning awareness of that. All of us are involved, and our argument over a strange war of attrition in an unfriendly world is really the different expressions of some basic agreements.

Suddenly we all accept the fact that it is proper to argue a war on the question of humanity. It is an acceptance that grew from the first questionings of those looking into themselves to find a reason for individual dignity; it was joined by the clean-shaven who are tormented by the same question and don't know how to formulate it; it has managed to penetrate the Congress, where the whole process of thought is set along lines of majorities, not of individuals.

That is our consensus. Maybe we are even beginning to understand that we do something to ourselves when we do terrible things to others.

You would think it is the business of newspapers to report this, and so it is. But they do not. From our problems as a society we develop problems as individuals. From our doubts as individuals we develop actions as a society. But newspapers miss out on the individuals and report only on the stereotypes of action or public event, always the same and seldom enlightening.

This, it seems to me, is the central problem of our time and my trade. The only sociologist I knew at all well was C. Wright Mills. I worked for him briefly years ago. He used to come thumping into the room in those clodhopper boots and checked shirts and tell unintelligible stories about his grandfather Wright, who invented a currency and distributed and enforced it among the Mexicans who worked on his ranch. I didn't know what he was talking about half the time and the other half of the time I couldn't figure out what it had to do with real life in a university. For part of the time he was talking about the difference between a mass—the ones who get talked to and don't or can't or won't answer back; the ideal television audience—and a public—the ones who no sooner get an opinion or a fact than they set about discussing it and arguing it and variously worrying it to death; the noisy newspaper audience. He wrote something I have only recently begun to believe is true:

The knowledgeable man in the genuine public is able to turn his personal troubles into social issues, to see their relevance for his community and his community's relevance for them. He understands that what he thinks and feels as personal troubles are very often not only that but problems shared by others and indeed not subject to solution by any one individual but only by modifications of the structure of the groups in which he lives and sometimes the structure of the entire society.

Men in masses are gripped by personal troubles, but they are not aware of their true meaning and source. Men in public confront issues, and they are aware of their terms. It is the task of the liberal institution, as of the liberally educated man, continually to translate troubles into issues and issues into the terms of their human meaning for the individual.

This is part of an argument about a power elite that often seems beside the point. But it speaks to me poignantly of newspapers and indeed of what I suspect are behavioral sciences.

The newspapers of today are really not much different from what they were a generation or two ago. There are the ones you believe and the ones you don't. The ones you believe are frozen into a mold of "objectivity." They address themselves to the public of discussion by talking issues as if they were spouting equations. The ones you don't believe are frozen into a mold of entertainment. They address themselves to a mass of beliefs and clichés in which cops are hard-boiled, scientists fuzzy, and starlets lissome. And the DPL plates always park in terrible places. The two mix. In the ones you do believe, if you read the sports pages, baseball seems frozen in the image of Paul Gallico, and the finance pages almost choke on a jargon that makes the new economics even harder to follow.

But times have changed and needs have changed. We are not now all caught up in that one world of economic blight and political response. We are redefining our world into a crisis of personal relations, and the newspapers don't deal with people.

A newspaper really is supposed to mirror its time and its community. It's supposed to be a little ahead so that it can lead or prod or whatever the best editorialist's phrase is; it's supposed to be close enough so that it is identified daily with the lives of its readers. I know how powerful the reading habit is because my paper wants to take readers away from others. That habit comes from identification. And yet, it also comes from availability and frequency, so that the monopoly paper becomes a habit despite almost anything. I don't think monopoly papers are necessarily bad. I think that maybe A. J. Liebling was wrong about that. I don't know what they had in Milwaukee before the *Journal* built itself up, but I doubt it was better than the *Milwaukee Journal* because I doubt if they had the excess of cash that allows for specialists, correspondents, and the best things in a paper.

But newspapers all together form an unconscious monopoly that *is* bad because it has no new models.

We like to say that newspapering is an art or a profession or something like that, but probably it's just a trade. In all the arts I can think of, there has been a revolution caused by introspection. Picasso and Braque and Pollock and Rauschenberg keep saying there have to be new forms, new modes, new materials, new outlets to conform to my eye, my vision, my personal dignity. And they

insist that the audience has to work to understand because acceptance is too easy and too meaningless. The tone scales keep changing in music; sculpture starts to destroy itself; dancers find new
forms; and novelists seek wilder and odd ways.

The newspapers go on, though.

Their great end once was to let you know what happened at
the battle of Antietam or San Juan Hill or Belleau Wood or Guadal-
canal. Now television can do that faster and better. And you know
it must be right because, after all, it's there. You know the television
debate must be the right thing because there's that pudgy-looking
senator talking to the other guy and those arguments certainly
sound familiar. The interviewer never asks an embarrassing question, but we've lost the habit of that because the newspapers seldom
ask one. Television has not yet decided to provide as many details,
and no one has figured out how to put a crossword puzzle on the
little screen, but these are all legitimate ends for television and television will figure out a way to do it. And then what? What is the
role of the newspaper?

I think it is to talk to the public, not the mass. It is to be useful
and serviceable in giving every day the etceteras that have to be
printed in agate and in lists, plus the announcements and warnings
and statements that life is full of, but most of all to talk to people.
It is the newspapers' job to render events intelligible to the man who
reads, on the level of what events mean to him. It is their job to provide a common currency of idea and rhetoric that should be the
concern of every citizen. Their job of education is not just to explain
but to provide the information on which explanation is based. And
their job is to be talked back to.

It isn't enough to go on day after day reporting the back-and-
forth talk about the mayor and the police department. There has to
come that point at which the relevance of it all is explained or at
least attempted. And its relevance has to be to the individual. The
commonest way is to his pocketbook—the new school bond issue is
going to cost a penny in the hundred on the real estate taxes. But the
hardest way is to his soul, to his involvement in the community, to
the way in which he as a man is caught up in the social problems that
are caused by bigness and drift.

The worst thing a paper does is to make clichés out of people.

Senator Morse becomes a common scold and the sit-ins become bearded youths of questionable cleanliness. Yes, there's the scold, and yes, there's the unwashed hair, but that loses the major in the minor.

Men make the events of our times and men are bound up in them, but we talk about issues and events and not about men.

I don't know how to change it. I don't know what is the formula by which this new thing should be done. I haven't the vaguest idea of how that next newspaper genius is going to catch the world and make it listen to its true thoughts. But I know it's coming and it has to be done.

I know too that when T. S. Eliot comes on the scene nobody understands his poetry and his audience has to be educated. I think maybe we have to educate our audience. Or maybe we ought simply to force everyone to listen to the radical professors. (I don't know what's happened to professors these days, but they all seem to be in the business of goading their students. Maybe they ought to teach by negatives and start good, formal academies from which the young can learn by articulate and purposeful rebellion.)

I don't really know what's wrong with the behavioral sciences, but I'm perfectly willing to tell you. I don't understand half of the articles I see because I can't read them and for the most part everyone seems in the descriptive dodge, telling me what the numbers add up to, and too few people seem in the prescriptive one, telling me what ought to be done or at least giving me a chance to argue about it.

An Aside for a Moment to Cher Lecteur

This is a speech you are reading, meant to be spoken. It was delivered at Arden House along with an interpolation that my requirement of the behavioral sciences is that they speak to me "and you gotta speak to me in English."

Too much of the output is too narrow, too obvious, or too opaque for me. I need the help of the sciences, and I know I must educate myself to understand them, but we don't deal in the same medium. My medium is the English language.

I thought I had spoken charmingly and found I had opened a

deep vein of annoyance or resentment. My education was undertaken directly and forcefully and, to my surprise, effectively. I agree now that there are some things written that are not for me and needn't worry me as a reader. I think the scientists agreed that their study was of men and not of the beauty of numbers, abstractions, or concepts that come together under the title of mankind.

But essentially, still, I think that I don't talk to the universities and they don't talk to me. I need what they have. I need to be educated. My newspaper and I need the vision of other ways of doing and telling so that we may be able to do what we are supposed to do, to tell the world what it's really like today, here, now.

It is not good enough to say that all the insights and refinements of science need a special vocabulary and therefore the sciences need an intermediary between the practitioners and the crowd. Special vocabulary they may indeed need, and it is rash for a layman to declare otherwise. But we are in a world whose special vocabularies increase aboundingly. Each one is a barrier to general understanding, and it is incumbent on scientists—on behavioral scientists in particular—to think as well as to speak: to think of an exact word for an easy barbarism; to think of English instead of sociologese.

Language is the connective tissue between thought and communication and it must not be laid waste. We ruin our forests, we putrefy our rivers, we litter our landscape, and with a profligate hand we throw away the natural resources it took centuries to provide. Our language is younger but more precious. It changes and it must change. It needs the special terms of definition that men need for new thoughts.

What it doesn't need is a mindless rephrasing of terms common in the trade so that casual conversation sounds like a parody of the formal monograph and little children ultimately take up the foolishness of grown men.

So much for getting in another word.

The real relationship between the behavioral sciences and journalism is that they meet in the audience. In a sense, the scientists go to the audience and bring back studies; journalists use the studies to go back to the audience. To the extent that one is usable to the other, each is more valuable. An accurate newspaper clearly trying to portray the world as it is, is a tool for a scientist. A meaningful behavioral study clearly explaining something about how men work in their society is invaluable to a newspaper. I suppose, though, that we get what we deserve. Television, in the main, restricts itself to audience surveys and media penetration analyses, each tainted from time to time. Newspapers, in the main, think that the real use of behavioral science is to get a personality test that will tell you whether you match up against Joel Kupferman twenty years later or whether you are happily adjusted in your job, the way some totally fictitious lobotomized model is.

If we want to look at men; if we want to draw them into this world and not let them drop out; if we mean that they really have a place in this polity of our devising, then we have to talk to them in the ways the time needs and we have not yet invented. Somebody has to help us invent it. And somehow we have to worry out what happens when it's invented—will anybody out there be listening, or reading? If I begin to sing the right song, will all the ears be gone?

If I had all the money in the world and I wanted to start a newspaper right now in New York, what should I do? I'd have volunteers in plenty because all the best people on all the best newspapers are uneasy now. That's fact. They want something different.

But how should I employ them? Someday soon that television tube on my porch is going to start spitting out reams of paper that add up to a newspaper. It will have the etceteras of my life neatly included, the stock of Fairchild Camera will go up another hundred points, and what will my newspaper do then, poor thing?

I think it will do what it must. It will apply intelligence always where before a simple recital of events was sufficient. It will attempt to report the particulars of action, so that it is seen as a thing that happens to men. It will attempt to explain by being personal, by being engaged in affairs, by relating individual concern with social concern.

There has to be a formula for that, because there aren't enough geniuses to invent it new each day and a formula lets the rest of us know what to do. I don't know what the formula is.

3
A Review of Session One

*Editor's note: The two keynote papers by Marvin Bressler and Rich-
ard C. Wald generated a good deal of interest and much discussion.
Space permits only summaries of reports by Ben H. Bagdikian and
John W. Riley, Jr. as discussants.*

Ben H. Bagdikian
SATURDAY EVENING POST

The two fields—behavioral sciences and the mass media—operate on
quite different levels, trying to do quite different things, though with
obvious overlaps. This is one of the problems involved when we start
talking about the press and the behavioral sciences.

One of the other problems is that we are not sure what sort of
relationship we're talking about. Do we want the press to cover the
behavioral sciences as it would education? Or should newspapers,
papers and the press generally, use the behavioral sciences to organ-
ize themselves in a corporate way? Or do we mean that the news
apparatus should use these sciences more in perceiving news? Mr.
Wald has suggested the possibility also that the newspaper can be
used to give the audience itself insights with which to understand
what is going on.

I am impressed by how this began with a rather egocentric
view, with the two fields not coming together at the same level at
all. I get the feeling from Mr. Bressler's presentation that in a sense
he looks upon journalism as a crude exercise of behavioral science,
without a license at that. I get the feeling from Mr. Wald that journalism is seeking a new set of values to speak with some relevance
to a new kind of society, a society with greatly changed values.
These are really two quite different things, which don't come to
grips.

Dr. Bressler described the method and disciplines of the behavioral sciences and the fact that these are obviously of commanding

45

importance in understanding society, and that therefore they are of commanding importance to the mass media. But there's an element here which is overlooked. Journalism is not just a crude exercise of the behavioral sciences; it has a different function. The press represents a discovery and creative process of its own, which includes some of the insights of the behavioral sciences but also other things—an intuition that is quite separate. In the exercise of these things, the mass media are slovenly, even by their own lights. There are 1,700 papers, and there are even more broadcasting stations, operating with a tremendous variation in values, competence, and seriousness; but on the whole the communications media's process is not just a counterpart, not just a shadow of behavioral sciences.

There can be a genuine dialogue between behavioral scientists and journalists, and much can be learned both ways. I don't think it is true that the behavioral scientists always lead and that the perceptive journalists always follow. In 1957 a Negro reporter and I went to the South to various towns; he would talk to the Negro community, I would talk to the white community, and late at night we'd integrate the lousiest flea-bag in town. We discovered some very interesting things about community relations, about intergroup relations, and about ourselves. Now, we would have been greatly benefited if we had been able to talk to a Robin Williams, to a Kenneth Clark, to a number of people who first of all had some fundamental insights into this generalized field but who may also have had some personal experience. But in talking to some social scientists three or four years later, I discovered that most of their work followed the news events—which is perfectly natural. I think there is a great deal that the press creates by its process of discovery, which provides knowledge that may be incompetent social science but is something beyond that, too.

So now, to the practice of politics. I don't think politics as practiced in the United States or probably any place is just crude behavioral science. I think it encompasses a number of things, including a sensitivity to a very complicated set of circumstances to which a disciplined science can't always be expected to bring order in time to be useful. I think that the press at its best has better contact with surface events than do the social sciences. I do think—if I may now put off my benevolent hat—that there are barriers in the press against using the general insights and the disciplines of the behavioral sciences.

One of these is the vestige of anti-intellectualism, which I think is disappearing. It probably comes from the social make-up of the working press 30 or 40 years ago, when most working reporters came from lower middle-class backgrounds and found themselves intruders in the world of power and propriety, where they felt the need to defend themselves and tended to be anti-intellectuals. Most of them hadn't gone to college. This is largely changed; the new generation of reporters is remarkably sophisticated in comparison, and not anti-intellectual.

There are other barriers. There is the inherent and ultimately helpful prejudice within journalism in favor of the concrete and the immediate, which may mean that it will ignore even proven theories in order to report or detect a dramatic physical event, even at the risk of misconstruing it. A friend of mine was one of the whiz kids who went to the capitol with John Kennedy, and he entered Washington bureaucratic, political life with a kind of amiable contempt for the press. After he had dealt with some of the best men in the business—the best correspondents, and some of the better columnists—he came to see that some of them had first-class minds, that they had a respectable body of knowledge, that they knew what he was saying when he talked, but that somehow things never quite jibed, not only in their conclusions but in how these men wrote. One night we were having a drink, and he announced a discovery with excitement. He said, "You guys don't have any hypotheses!" And I think that's true. While the scientist is looking for regularity and universality, the journalist is often looking for just the opposite. He's looking for the different, he's looking for the concrete. I think almost every journalist has a strong built-in resistance to hypotheses. As viewed by the trade, the ideal reporter is the one who seems to reproduce fact, visible events, documented statements, in a succession which looks very innocent but of course is not, in which the reader finishes with his own hypothesis. This is the pervasive model, I think, of the good firsthand reporter. He does not present a hypothesis. He must appear not to have one. And while this, of course, is not literally the case—we all have our hypotheses at varying strengths, at varying places in the process of reporting—I think the prejudice against it is a good one. I think it's a poor presumption for the reporter to report by saying, "My theory of how this works is this." Some do exactly this—some of the worst and some of the best—and with these we depend entirely on how knowledgeable and insightful they are. But I think that the working reporter has a built-in prejudice against this, and I think on the whole it's a very good thing—just as I think it's probably a good thing that most politicians are pragmatic.

Another barrier is the fact that institutionally the press is economically and socially conservative, not in any rational way, but merely in a nostalgic sense. This has been a great inhibition in a number of ways, first of all, in detecting what is going on in society. Whole subcultures have arisen in society which have no respectability in the press until they force themselves into the open with great drama. We've had persistent poverty, even knocking off 30 per cent from the official figures, long undetected largely because the press did not have the kind of nervous system, and the kind of vocabulary, to become sensitive to these things, and if they did, to know how to express them. The press has been hostile to change precisely in a period when the most significant process in society is rapid change. The press has resisted the fact that we are no longer seventeenth-century folk; it has been nostalgic at a time when it really should have been out there reporting on what was happening and has, as I say, lacked a vocabulary of words and ideas. As a consequence the country itself, until very recently, has lacked a vocabulary to describe accurately or significantly the process of social change.

It was a remarkably short time ago that the word "planning" was an editorial taboo. All kinds of planning were bad *per se*. Now there's a change. But this is, I think, an example of the kind of stricture which the press had and which inhibits it in reporting what are now reliable signs of change, though now it is catching up fairly quickly.

Still another barrier is a very great difference in the functioning of the press and the functioning of the behavioral scientists. I don't agree that the press is less able than the behavioral scientists to speak to the general public. I don't think that's true. I think the press is wretched in this way: it's inadequate and frequently irresponsible; but on the whole I think the press has a better idea of what the general public will absorb and understand than have academics.

Another big difference is that the scientist may attack the old pieties within the protection of his discipline and of his colleagues. He feels some pressure, but on the whole he has a tradition which rewards him for this. When the press does such a thing, it does so in a terribly public way—among the people who hold these pieties partly because the press installed them. But in any case it does this in a very public way. The press cannot just say, "We have believed that these things are true, and they *were* true up until last Tuesday; these were parts of our American heritage that every red-blooded American held dear and it would have destroyed us if we ever adopted anything different. But now try to understand we're going to adopt something different." The press is something like the Church or any large traditional institution that depends on conservatism but is also geared to the general public, with all of the "subpolicies" and the pressures involved. So the press is neither as free nor can it be as unconcerned with impact in attacking the old pieties and announcing new truth as the behavioral scientists. It has to do it in an empirical way.

So the press has some built-in inhibitions against the use of the behavioral sciences. But I think it is peculiarly suited not only to transmit but to absorb what's going on in the social scene, some important social phenomena in which the social scientists frequently follow rather than lead the press.

John W. Riley, Jr.
THE EQUITABLE LIFE ASSURANCE SOCIETY

One remarkable thing about the papers by Marvin Bressler and Richard Wald is their basic similarity.

First, the newspaper man states the essential problem of this conference much as the sociologist states it. The newspaperman wants to use the behavioral sciences—he freely admits this—in order to facilitate a better understanding of the relationship between people and society. The sociologist, to use his own phrase, is concerned with the impact of the behavioral sciences on decisions and politics in the public sector. But the sociologist goes on to say that this interest is contingent on affecting the lives of substantial numbers of people. Now these statements quite naturally flow from their different perceptions of the real world. And I suspect that since any practical consequence of this conference will ultimately call for a closer collaboration between journalists and behavioral scientists, perhaps the first thing to do is to compare their perceptions of the real world.

Now how does each see the contemporary world? The newspaperman observes that we live in a new era; we are suffering through a crisis in individual dignity; we live in a mass—everything's too big. We talk about our problems and the historical processes as though nothing had changed for us as individuals. Similarly, the sociologist talks about the "problems of our times." He asks, What social aims do we most cherish? What price are we prepared to pay in scarce resources for achieving these aims? What sectors of society will bear the costs? Clearly, both the newspaperman and the sociologist see the times as being somewhat out of joint. One simply focuses more on individual problems, whereas the other is concerned more with society and with social problems. The newspaperman goes on to specify what this means for his profession. He says, "Personal troubles are considered stuff for feature stories, but the issues of the nation unfortunately involve social processes." Similarly, the sociologist observes that while the culture of journalism is dependent on the adventitious human interest story, the behavioral sciences are almost exclusively in search of regularities which recur.

There are similar components in the basic problem of the conference as these two highly articulate representatives of two different fields see it. However, in the last analysis each wishes to maximize the utility of the behavioral sciences in explaining and communicating the infinitely complex relationship between people and their times.

But the convergence does not end with their statements of the problem. There is also a surprising identity in their estimates of the potential contributions of their respective fields. To use social science jargon, there is a remarkable overlap in their picture of what we would call the "ideal type."

Let me illustrate. The newspaperman sees his medium as providing an honest currency of idea and rhetoric—that's his phrase —which should be the concern of every citizen. Almost at the same time, the sociologist takes note that his responsibility is to resist every form of persuasion except fact and to appeal neither to prejudice nor to authority. The newspaperman takes on the job of rendering events intelligible to the man who reads on the level of what events mean to him. The sociologist similarly assumes the responsibility of protecting against naiveté and gullibility, premature generalization. The newspaperman sees his job as lying well beyond the simple reporting of the isolated fact. The sociologist sees the same obligation. He wishes, however, to call our attention to the importance of the system reference. He wants to emphasize the interrelatedness of the parts of society, to protect against the assumption that any one problem can be solved in isolation. Finally the newspaperman sees his medium as something which must be useful and serviceable. Its announcements, its statements, its warnings must be addressed to people, not just to the mass. And the sociologist also sees his obligation as pragmatic, despite the fact that we obviously are suffering from severe maladies in pinning down our utility.

In short, both the sociologist and the newspaperman are willing to share the responsibility of providing the public with a common language of ideas which should be based upon fact rather than on mere opinion. And both seem to agree that the substantive content for this common language should be free of premature generalization, yet characterized by explanations which transcend interpretation of isolated facts. Whether or not this language is the English language, I think, is petulant. And finally, they seem to concur in the belief that their respective outputs are directly or indirectly useful and serviceable, certainly at the decision-making level of everyday affairs.

With so much basic agreement in these two statements of the problem and indeed in the convergence of their perceptions of the actual and potential contributions of their respective fields, we might have predicted a comparable similarity in their proposed remedies. But at this point, we are confronted by two quite different points of view. The newspaperman, following his estimate of the changing times and his full confession that newspapers go on day after day, that everything is stable, intelligible, and correct, calls, in effect, upon the behavioral sciences for what he chooses to call a model. He does insist that the model be written in English, which will enable his medium to apply a new kind of intelligence that the times demand. Previously, simple recitation of the fact was sufficient. He suspects that this model should be based upon sound principles of sociology, but you can almost hear him sigh, "Lord knows what sound principles of sociology are." But he does not despair. He concludes that there must be a formula, and the journalist simply cannot afford on a daily basis to invent a new formula.

The sociologist calls for quite a different remedy. While he, too, is equally aware, painfully so in some cases, of the limitations and shortcomings of his own discipline, his proposed remedy is to place the responsibility on the journalists. They must, he insists, develop professional competence in the behavioral sciences. And his overarching reason for this is, if for no other, the necessity for journalists to emancipate themselves from this uncritical reliance upon informants.

So there we have it. The newspaperman looks to the sociologist for a solution to the problem as he sees it; and the sociologist in turn looks to the newspaperman to take the initiative and set things right.

There is more potential agreement than difference. Perhaps the difference is one of means rather than of ends. In any event, there seems to be at least a latent willingness to communicate. I suspect that the central issue here is to find ways and means of clearing away the intellectual underbrush which may be currently inhibiting such communication.

In closing, I want to leave you with two rather exciting possibilities for facilitating better communication and for creating a better mesh between these two cultures. Let me illustrate them very briefly.

Most immediately, it would seem neither an unlikely nor unattainable goal, certainly not an undesirable one, to articulate some mutually agreed-upon theory or theories which would stimulate more imaginative public and mass media uses of the behavioral sciences. Here I would take issue with Ben Bagdikian. I think we do need hypotheses. Now, on the other hand, I would take issue with Marvin Bressler: I do not think we need to go quite as far as Talcott Parsons. Such an effort need not be very definitive nor even very formal. What I have in mind is some elementary theory, let's say, of deviant behavior, a theory which could conventionally be used in reporting events having to do with crime, with race relations, with mental disorders or drug addiction. Certainly the current reporting on problems of this sort leaves much to be desired. Similarly, I have in mind some theoretical notion of the meaning of experimental method, which could also be used conventionally in the reporting of events and their consequences. I suspect that editors and social scientists are equally distressed by the kinds of unimaginative stories which simply report striking correlations but which almost inevitably carry strong implications of causal relationships. How can I best illustrate that? The many dramatic accounts of such events as the recent blackout in the Northeast or the consequences of the New York transit strike are examples. Newspapers were full of stories in which no control was even hinted.

A far more basic and longer-range possibility for a better meshing of these two cultures rests upon mounting a new research effort toward a more adequate understanding of the revolution which is certainly raging in communications technology today. The newspaperman, I think, was quite right to call our attention to the seminal work of Marshall McLuhan. But it was almost ten years ago that Wilbur Schramm correctly observed that this revolution is essentially centered in man's relationship to the machine—

a changing relationship—beginning with his very perceptive account of its starting with Gutenberg's converted wine press, which simply was a mechanical device for enabling man to duplicate messages. It was not until much later, in the nineteenth century, that a series of remarkable inventions—the telephone, the telegraph, the motion picture, the vacuum tube—enabled man to use a machine not only to send and receive messages with great rapidity, but indeed to use the machine to do some of his listening and some of his seeing for him. Then came World War II, which produced a machine with which man could communicate and which in turn would send messages back to him. The principle of radar, the most recent chapter, is just beginning to open up the use of the computer as an integral part of the technology of communications. Now, not only can man build machines which can communicate with each other, but the consequences, for example, of computer-controlled communications satellites seem certain to be so profound as to bring about great changes in our relationship to men in other parts of the world. Here, surely, is a problem which calls for joint effort.

Similarly, but on a different level, the sociologist was quite right: We need a far more sophisticated model of communications than the behavioral sciences have thus far been able to construct. The old paradigm, "Who says what to whom with what effect?" was a useful one and needs far greater specification and elaboration. I suspect we would all agree that there is more than a germ of truth in the saying that men still do more to messages than messages do to men.

Session Two:

SOCIAL ISSUES AND THE MASS MEDIA

4

Implications for the Mass Media of Research on Intergroup Relations and Race

Robin M. Williams, Jr.
CORNELL UNIVERSITY

Our mandate here is to present some of the concepts and findings of social science concerning intergroup relations (especially "race" relations) that are particularly pertinent for mass media dissemination to the public. Since this task calls for many judgments in deciding what to leave out from among a very large number of quite disparate studies, it will not be surprising if some of the choices seem arbitrary. We hope, however, that some of the items chosen will be useful and reasonably important for considering the place of mass media in intergroup relations in the United States today.

Introduction

As recently as fifty years ago much of the so-called social science literature dealing with race and race relations was heavily tinged with ideas derived from the biological thinking of the nineteenth century. Notions of innate racial traits were influential, and racial prejudices were often thought to involve some kind of "instinct" or "innate repulsion." At that time, there were only the beginnings of scientific understanding of the depth and strength of social and cultural factors in determining attitudes and behavior in this area. Three hundred years of European expansion, conquest, and colonialism had provided a massive body of presuppositions and prejudices that easily combined with the heritage of slavery in the United States to encourage seizing upon any biological notion that could be interpreted as lending support to white dominance and superiority. The popularization of neo-Darwinian conceptions of "survival of the fittest" worked in this direction, even as did the various theories of instincts that attempted to explain all behavior as the outcomes of inborn propensities. The vogue of so-called intelligence tests after the use of the Army Alpha in World War I probably greatly reinforced the popular belief in racial differentials in general intelligence.

It is difficult for us today to appreciate how unquestioned were the assumptions that made up the racial ideology of most white Americans only a half-century ago. Abroad, colonialism had come to seem a natural and inevitable system of governing the "little brown brothers" who made up the "lesser breeds without the law." At home, the position of Negro Americans at the bottom of the economic and political structure daily reinforced those stereotypes that to many white Americans seemed to explain and justify the existing system of race relations. Most Negroes were poor, uneducated, rural, concentrated in the South, politically disenfranchised, terrorized, unorganized, inarticulate, and very nearly powerless to change their condition. Long before this time, in the Compromise of 1876, the North had in effect turned back to the white South the privilege of dealing with race relations in its own way. Since the Supreme Court's decision in *Plessy* v. *Ferguson* in 1896, establishing the doctrine of "separate but equal," a pervasive system of racial segregation had been institutionalized, with the blessing of the highest law of the land. To the great masses of the Negro population then struggling to exist from day to day, the future events of the 1950's and 1960's surely would have seemed so strange as to be almost wholly incredible.

Today, of course, most of the picture we have just sketched has changed dramatically. For all practical purposes the old-style colonialism is dead. Resurgent nationalism and social revolutions have swept across Asia and Africa. The vast shift in world power to the "new nations" forcibly calls the attention of the white minority to its position in a world population most of which is nonwhite. On the domestic scene, the new aspirations and claims of Negro protest movements highlight demands for important shifts in the national social structure.

In a society now overwhelmingly industrial and urban, race relations take place within a context of exceedingly rapid technological and economic change. As we have said elsewhere:

... tremendous forces have been moving the social system of the United States rapidly toward an integrated mass society, i.e., dissolving and breaking down segmental local structures, particularistic subsystems, and categorical ethnic-racial divisions. The movement has been toward highly differentiated and centralized economic and political structures. The population is mobile, both geographically and socially, in an urban and rapidly urbanizing society. High levels of aspiration and of mass consumption increase the social demand for an increasing flow of goods and services to wider and wider sectors of the population. In reaction to unsettling change, especially in relation to claims to social status and security, various segments, strata and groupings of the white population feel themselves under imminent threat of loss of prerogatives or of closure of advancement. Meanwhile, many members of racial and ethnic collectivities that are relatively deprived have come to feel increasingly hemmed in and frustrated in their aspirations.[1]

Migration has shifted millions of Negroes from the rural areas and the South into the cities and into the North and West. The Negro population has gained in education; has developed an articulate middle-class leadership; has gained access to nationwide means of communication; has developed effective organizations and an increasing measure of political skill and power. As the whole society has increased in scale and power, vastly enhanced economic productivity has created undreamed-of affluence for upper- and middle-class whites—only a small portion of which has "trickled down" to the still radically disadvantaged majority of the Negro population.

Over the almost two centuries of its national existence the United States has changed from a loosely organized agricultural society, based on small family enterprises and the social controls of local communities, to a massive urban and industrial world power. Our understanding of intergroup relations clearly must be based upon our understanding of these basic changes and of the kind of total social system to which they have led. As American society has grown in scale and in technological power and economic productivity, it has become a highly differentiated, specialized, and hence interdependent system. Both economically and politically it comes increasingly close to being a seamless web of interdependence. At the same time it is also a society of vast concentrations of political and economic power in the large-scale, complex formal organizations—corporations, government, unions, trade associations, and so on—within which occur the crucial acts of decision that direct the course of societal development. It is an *organizational* society. Correspondingly, the diffuse informal social controls of the family and the local community have been more and more superseded by the explicit formal controls of law and law enforcement, of the "private" or "public" bureaucracies, and of the special interest associations. Communication through direct informal personal interaction has been increasingly overlaid by the formalized communication of the large-scale organization and of the mass media.

If we look back only so far as the turn of this century, we see that race relations then existed in a total social context more radically different from that of today than is generally appreciated even by the relatively well-educated American public. No longer can intergroup relations be defined and regulated in the particularistic terms of pseudopaternalism. No longer can state and local officials regard themselves as wholly free to ignore the effects of their policies and actions elsewhere. As our whole society increasingly operates through formal organizations and political and legal mechanisms, it is no surprise that relations among racial, ethnic, and religious groupings likewise come more and more to be formalized and politicized.

With specific regard to our most important racial minority, a complex set of interrelated processes have transformed Negro Americans since 1900 from an unorganized population into a social collectivity that is more and more capable of unity and concerted action. Marked increases have occurred in group pride, in awareness of collective aims, and in a sense of social solidarity. During this period, as migration shifted the Negro population more and more from farm to city and from South to North, attitudes of hopelessness and apathy began to give way to militancy and to a more purposive awareness of blocked opportunity. Common fate reinforced a sense of group identity and an awareness of conspicuous and chronic deprivation and a sense of moral outrage vis-à-vis white society. As rising aspirations collided with rigid discrimination and segregation, dissatisfaction grew. As efforts to gain equality of opportunity encountered the intransigence and apathy of much of the dominant population, alienation and disillusionment likewise grew.

The pace of organized protest startled many white persons who had still remained unaware of the "social dynamite" that had long been accumulating and who did not understand the depth and intensity of American Negroes' feelings of hurt, resentment, bafflement, and moral indignation. This massive gap in comprehension between white and Negro Americans repeatedly revealed during the miscalled Negro Revolt of the 1960's is all the more striking when we recall that the bases for the "revolt" had been apparent to serious students of race relations for more than twenty years. In this single observation there is more than ample reason for the attention we now turn upon research in this field.

Selected Conclusions from Research on Intergroup Relations[2]

The relevance of findings from social science research to the tasks of the mass media obviously depends heavily upon the existing knowledge, beliefs, and values of the populations to whom messages are directed. Perhaps the most salient initial facts here are, first, the widespread presence in the white American population of stereotypic beliefs and negative evaluations concerning Negroes, and second, the quite rapid changes in the prevalence of such beliefs and evaluations since World War II. For example, the proportion of white persons in the North endorsing a belief in equality of intelligence as between Negroes and whites rose from only 50 per cent in 1942 to 82 per cent in 1956; in the South the figure increased from 21 per cent to 60 per cent during this period. (Between 1956 and 1964 these proportions did not change appreciably.)[3]

No studies have dealt directly with the sources of such changes in the beliefs of individual persons. It is plausible, however, to attribute some substantial influence to the dissemination of the conclusions of the biological and social sciences concerning human racial similarities and differences, especially in the context of reactions against the racism of Nazi Germany. Anthropological evidence of the diversity and overlap of physical characteristics within and between conventional racial categories was made more salient by rapid world-wide changes in the position of nonwhite populations. Meanwhile, the limitations and distortions of so-called intelligence tests became clearer and more widely known. Several academic generations of college students have come to know how greatly "test intelligence" depends upon cultural and social factors. More recently the conclusions of psychological and sociological research have been complemented by new genetic and biochemical knowledge concerning the great specificity and complexity of the determinants of physiological and neurological functioning, e.g., sickle-cell anemia, or phenylketonuria, or the importance for normal development of the intra-uterine and neonatal environments. Among well-educated persons considerable influence has probably been exerted by sheer exposure to the continuing accumulation of evidence that the physical and psychological characteristics of animals and men represent exceedingly complex interactions of very large numbers of genetic and environmental determinants.

Whatever the sources of past changes in racial stereotyping, the long-run effects of information from the continuing research may be expected to be substantial. Just within the one field of the study of psychosocial development of infants and children, for example, numerous studies are showing that many specific capacities and performances are to be best regarded not merely as manifestations of such global attributes as general intelligence but rather as *profiles* of levels of many different kinds of functioning. Similarly, research data continue to explicate the crucial proposition that human psychosocial development (regardless of "race") represents sets of complex processes so operating that each point in the life history is continuous with later developments, with the consequence that complex psychosocial abilities are greatly dependent upon cumulative-sequential learning. Likewise, special interest attaches to the indications from recent studies that cultural and social deprivation in early childhood may have massive effects upon later capacities and performances.

Although a full understanding of the findings to which we have sketchily alluded makes nonsense of historically received racial beliefs,[4] such beliefs do not necessarily disappear merely because they have been shown to be scientifically invalid or inadequate. In fact, during the last ten years, the counterattack of neoracism that has been going on in the United States probably reinforces the tenacity of ideas of racial superiority. Continuous education over a considerable period of time undoubtedly would be required were popular beliefs to be brought somewhat nearer to our best scientific knowledge. (The main conclusions are simple and basic: man is a single species; there are no "pure races"; genetic inheritance is a matter of specific family lines, not of a racial "blood"; distinctive racial differences in innate generalized intelligence have not been demonstrated.)

But many of the most interesting social science findings and well-grounded hypotheses do not concern these biosocial matters but rather deal directly with the phenomena of prejudice and discrimination.[5] In turning to the large body of research on these topics, it is obviously necessary in the interests of brevity drastically to select and simplify the findings. For convenience, main conclusions are stated in numbered paragraphs.

1. It has long been well established, of course, that reactions to social groups and categories are learned, not "inborn" or "innate." It is likewise well established that development of unfavorable attitudes and stereotypes in the individual—contrary to some commonsense impressions—is not dependent upon unpleasant, personal experiences;[6] rather prejudices may be learned from parents, from peers, from reading, or listening and viewing, without any direct contact with the object of prejudice.

2. In current American society, racial, ethnic, and religious stereotypes and ethnocentric attitudes are widely prevalent. Few exact data exist, but it is a safe estimate from the many different studies that an important degree of some kind of prejudice affects well over two-thirds of the adult population.

3. However, many—perhaps most—members of the prejudiced population hold their beliefs and attitudes at a low level of intensity and salience, subscribing to cultural clichés and con-

forming to the perceived social climate with only moderate emotional involvement or firmness of conviction.

4. Strong, actively hostile intergroup attitudes typically are most frequent when established beliefs are being challenged and established relationships suddenly changed, especially when actual or anticipated changes are perceived as threats to important vested interests.

5. "Prejudice" is not an undifferentiated single entity. Although there are tendencies for various types of prejudices to cohere in a global attitude, and although prejudiced individuals tend to be prejudiced toward several objects (not just one or a few), there is nevertheless an important degree of specificity both in the type of attitude and in its object.

6. Some prejudices are learned responses to social indoctrination and may not involve strong resistances to change in basically altered circumstances. In some other kinds of prejudices, great resistance may be encountered.

7. Some prejudices serve individuals as important means for dealing with psychological need-dispositions. In the absence of alternative mechanisms and gratification, attempted changes in such prejudices will be strongly resisted.

8. Some prejudices stand as supports for social privileges and advantages concerned with wealth, income, sex, power, prestige, and other scarce values and interests. In the absence of access to alternative satisfactions, direct attempts to remove such prejudices will meet strong resistance.

9. Established systems of racial discrimination and segregation tend both to actually generate prejudices and to powerfully reinforce those that have already become established.

10. Those prejudices most difficult to change by education and propaganda combine these properties: (a) they serve strong psychological needs; (b) they support important vested interests; (c) they represent a high degree of consensus in the population; (d) they are promulgated and sanctioned by persons of high prestige and authority in economic, political, educational, and religious life.

11. Racial prejudices are not the attitudes of isolated human atoms, each of whom develops and maintains his beliefs and evalua-

tions separately from other persons; rather such beliefs and evaluations are developed, shared, and supported within active systems of social relationships.

In hundreds of studies the systematic quality of social belief-systems has been documented, and other research has greatly deepened and made more specific our understanding of the power of social groups to evoke conformity from individuals within them. We know that under specified conditions unsupported individuals will in a substantial proportion of cases publicly conform to a unanimous group judgment that contradicts the evidence of their own eyes.[7] We know that when people as individuals shift from one social environment to another, they tend over time to take on the attitudes and beliefs prevalent in the new groups within which they interact.

12. Prejudice is an attitude. Discrimination is overt behavior. Although prejudicial attitudes tend to lead to discriminatory behaviors, the relationship often is loose and unreliable. Many prejudiced persons do not discriminate in particular situations; some relatively nonprejudiced persons do discriminate.

13. Prejudice almost always is related to and constrained by other attitudes and values. As expressed in discriminatory behavior, its consequences are cast up against, e.g., the values of business profits, a peaceable community, local notoriety, the proper education of one's children, the threat of repressive police or military action, or the likelihood of new legal regulations. Knowing only the initial racial prejudices, indexed "in isolation," gives only an insecure basis for predicting behavior when such basic choices of values are confronted.

14. Different social situations have profoundly different effects upon intergroup behavior. It is not necessary in every instance to change the "hearts and minds of men" prior to legal and administrative actions designed to reduce racial discrimination.

15. Legal and administrative changes aimed at the removal of discrimination can actually lead directly to changes in prejudices; such changes in the rules and sanctions for overt behavior, under appropriate circumstances, can constitute powerful "propaganda of the deed," evoking important educative effects.

16. Direct personal interaction between Negro and white persons is

most likely to dissolve stereotypes and to lead to friendly relationships when the participants meet as functional equals in a noncompetitive situation and engage in complementary activity leading to the successful attainment of goals mutually accepted as worthwhile. The effects will be especially marked when the interaction reveals the sharing of important beliefs and values.

17. Under conditions of widespread racial discrimination, the naturally occurring social interactions across the lines of categorical distinction in American communities have only slight net effects, at most, in reducing prejudice. Voluntary contacts tend to select persons of both groupings who are already low in prejudice; intensive and continuing interaction is rare; and most situations of contact bring together whites and Negroes acting within restrictive and conventionalized roles.

18. However, community surveys show that under natural conditions, on net balance, the white and Negro persons who most often interact across the racial line are most likely to be nonprejudiced and friendly. Although self-selectivity is important, the evidence suggests that in the long run and on the average social interaction reduces rather than increases prejudice. (Naturally it is important also to keep in mind that certain kinds of interaction do increase prejudice.)

19. Although certain types of personalities are especially prone to prejudice, interracial interaction can reduce prejudice even among some so-called authoritarian personalities.

20. Favorable attitudes among whites toward Negroes are most likely to be found among persons who are young, well-educated, active participants in community organizations,* and experienced in a wide range of social roles and situations. The same generalization apparently holds for the attitudes of Negroes toward whites.

21. Reactions of Negro Americans to discrimination and segregation during the last generation have shifted away from passive

---

* Of some special interest is the finding of several studies that prejudice is least among persons who attend religious services *very* frequently and among those who do not attend at all; the moderate participator apparently is highly conventional and is strongly affected by pressures for social conformity.

adaptation and withdrawal toward organized resistance and reform. Sociological studies have supported the prediction that maximum organized pressure for change comes from a numerically and proportionately large urban, partially segregated, and internally stratified minority that has been increasing in power and absolute economic position but that continues to be disadvantaged relative to a dominant population that nominally shares beliefs in equality of opportunity, in political democracy, and in universalistic ethics.

22.   Militant protest is most likely to occur, not under stable conditions of maximum poverty and social oppression, but under conditions of rapid change and relative deprivation.[8]

Severe relative deprivation plus social humiliation may result in accommodation and outward apathy in a fragmented, weak, and overpowered minority. But the same combination is explosive when conjoined with: (a) a high level of intragroup communication, resulting in a widely shared and intense sense of collective fate; (b) a recent history of rapidly rising aspirations; (c) a strong sense of legitimacy of these aspirations; (d) a strong sense of the arbitrary or immoral character of the blockages to these aspirations; (e) awareness of power or potential power of the minority in the political arena; and (f) failure of the dominant grouping to evidence realistic action to remove the basic sources of grievance.

Clearly it is an easy prediction that conflicts over segregation and group discrimination are certain to emerge as Negroes increase their education, income, and occupational status without at the same time securing a reduction in barriers to full participation in the society at large. The situation of the greater part of the American Negro population over the last decade has been that of conspicuous and chronic relative deprivation. Although absolute gains have been made," . . . in each interrelated realm—health, employment, business, income, housing, voting, and education—the absolute gains of the 1950's pale when contrasted with current white standards. . . . The resulting relative deprivation is the fundamental basis of mass Negro American dissatisfaction today."[9]

23.   Extensive documentation now supports the proposition that

*proposed changes in particular parts of a system of intergroup
dominance are initially resisted with a vigor disproportionate
to any immediate calculation of narrow or "material" self-interest.* As Allen Grimshaw has summarized my own interpretation here:

> Discriminatory behavior is an outcome of numerous and diverse
> motivations and brings an equally varied set of gratifications. Mo-
> tivations to which actors refer in explaining their behavior are only
> a partial accounting of actual motives and gratifications involved;
> discrimination may in part be a latent by-product of apparently
> quite unrelated processes. Strong vested interests support institu-
> tional arrangements which legitimize needs and provide rational-
> izations for uncomfortable value conflicts. Thus, there is an inter-
> locking and mutual support from two varieties of overdetermination
> —psychological and social. Resistance to change is not solely a con-
> sequence of individual personality predispositions but involves in-
> terests, opportunities, norms, ethical values and a variety of other
> diffuse sources of social conformity interacting in a variety of ways.
> However, one correlate of these observations is that it is not neces-
> sary to alter basic personality structures in order to change specific
> patterns of segregation and discrimination. [These data suggest to
> us] . . . the priority of social structure over personality in actual de-
> termination of behavior and suggests, moreover, that attitudes will
> change to become consonant with behavior.[10]

24. To the extent that intergroup relations come to involve large
collectivities, they become highly consequential for the distribution of power, the exercise of authority, and the modes of
resolving conflicts. Social control at macrosocial levels operates through four major sanctions: retaliation compensation,
withdrawal of reciprocity, supernatural sanctions, and legal
sanctions.[11] As a society becomes more highly differentiated
and interdependent, under an exchange economy, withdrawal
of reciprocity between individual persons tends to lose force.
If secularization accompanies differentiation and mobility, as
it does today, supernatural sanctions decrease in importance.
To the degree that consensus decreases, retaliation compensation will no longer work, for the parties fail to agree upon the

rules. For all these, and other reasons, a society like that of the United States will come to place greater reliance upon legal sanctions. Then, as local communities in a political democracy become less autonomous economically and less insulated from two-way mass communication, local conflicts cease to be local in consequences. *In a permeable, interdependent, centralized political democracy, intergroup conflicts, therefore, inevitably become politicized.* In other words, as person-to-person informal social controls in race relations diminish in frequency and effectiveness, the greater is the likelihood of impersonal political and administrative control.

25. When white persons become aware that segregation and discrimination of Negroes entail high costs to them *personally*, the likelihood grows that prudence may overweigh prejudice. Currently, gains in income and occupational upgrading among Negroes often are regarded by white observers solely from the standpoint of the competition and threat these may offer to whites. What is sometimes thereby overlooked is the increased potential thus created for rewards going from Negroes to whites. The most obvious example is the increased purchasing power Negroes can now send to—or withhold from—white business establishments. (In ten metropolitan areas of the South in 1961, Negro purchases amounted to almost two billion dollars, or almost one-fifth of retail sales.)[12]

Relations of economic interdependence constitute an area in which desegregation and civil rights may be favored by what may well be the stronger rather than merely the higher motivations of the white population or its leadership. Successful resolutions of current conflicts in favor of universalism and an open, equalitarian order depend, to a high degree, upon finding effective ways of presenting the powerful elements of white society with a choice in which the values represented by segregation and discrimination are pitted against values of a higher priority—greater profits, political power, peaceable labor relations, an orderly and prestigeful community, protection of civil and political rights of whites as well as Negroes, ethical convictions, and others.

26. Neither equality of economic opportunity and political rights nor abolition of segregation in public accommodations and facilities leads directly to increased Negro-white interaction in informal recreational, "social," or familial contexts.

27. (a) The extent and intensity of resistance to increased rights (or privileges) of any ethnic (racial, religious) segment of the society will increase directly with the degree to which the present or prospective change is perceived by persons in other ethnic categories as a direct threat to their own long-term future prestige ranking, as determined by the evaluations of other persons who are in a position to importantly affect that ranking.

    In short, resistance will increase directly with perceived threat to prestige status.

    (b) More specifically, resistance will vary directly with the perceived threat from the reactions of others within the dominant ethnic segment who have economic or political power, religious authority, or other indirect sanctioning power (for example, the ability to influence community evaluations of the person). That is, anticipated sanctions from persons of power and authority are especially threatening.

    (c) Whatever the perceived threat to status, it will be the more powerful, the less possibility there is for alternative ways of maintaining status, once the prospective change has occurred. Feeling trapped tends to produce panic.

    Although prestige status is the subject of these three propositions, they are expected to apply to any other threatened values.[13]

28. Lack of continuous, fine-grained communication among the subgroupings of a social system exposed to rapid changes, especially from outside, means that when changes finally *are* communicated the new information is likely to be unexpected and massive and correspondingly difficult to accept and cope with rapidly. If members of each segment of a community are in touch almost exclusively with a communication net confined to that segment, even changes arising from local sources will

become known belatedly and fitfully in other portions of the social structure. If the changes are of a character to pose problems of adaptation, the more erratic and delayed the communication, the more difficult the subsequent coping behavior is likely to be.[14]

29. Large and increasing proportions of the Negro population share with many persons in the white population aspirations for high school and college education and for middle-class occupations, suburban living, and a generally sober, respectable style of life. Also shared are a great many specific patterns of family behavior and child rearing. (The very existence of this "black bourgeoise" is almost totally unknown to many, perhaps most, white people.)

30. American Negroes overwhelmingly reject political radicalism of the extreme Left or Right. Radical influence has been slight in the major protest organizations. Militancy has grown directly out of native aspirations, not new systems of political ideology.

31. The greater the similarity of values and beliefs of Negro and white persons the more likely it is that relatively full communication will reduce prejudice.

This incomplete listing must be closed. It represents one quite limited inventory, and other students of the field would question some of the choices and would have many reservations concerning the precision of statement and adequacy of evidence. It is our hope only that to a reasonable approximation it suggests the main thrusts of the evidence and thinking generated in the research efforts of the last two or three decades. In the next section, we examine a few possible implications for the mass media.

Mass Communication, Race Relations, and Modern Society
Our society can no longer rest so much as in the past on the modes of consensus characteristic of a localistic agrarian republic. It is our contention here that both social science and mass communication are increasingly in the position to act as "honest brokers" between the diverse segments of a mass society. What is the case for

this assertion in the particular instance of Negro-white relations today?

First, the common culture of American society cuts powerfully across the increasingly problematic and arbitrary "color line." Both whites and Negroes are caught up in rapid technological and economic changes. Both are subject in varying ways and degrees to the effects of high geographic mobility. Both live in the shadows of unprecedented international threats. Both share thousands of items of common experience.

But, second, under conditions of urban residence, class differentiation, and *de facto* segregation, the web of personal communication and friendships between Negroes and white is thin and weak. To the extent that personal interaction diminishes, shared experiences decrease, mutual role-taking becomes more difficult, and vivid and concrete personal understanding fades. Communication about racial and ethnic groups carried on by word of mouth within any one ingrouping tends to be highly selective, restricted, simplified, incomplete, and inaccurate. The stereotypic quality is likely to represent greatest distortion when close contact with persons in the outgroup is least. In our present mass urban society the likelihood of incomplete and distorted information is, therefore, exceedingly high. Some important correctives possibly can be supplied to the extent that the mass media can convey to whites and Negroes alike an accurate and vivid portrayal of the essential facts of the contemporary situation, together with some of the historical context.

It seems reasonable to believe that if there is to be a realistic and viable working consensus concerning intergroup relations in this country, the mass media have an essential part to play, at two quite different but crucially related levels, namely, the level of a basic intellectual framework and the level of specific facts, values, beliefs, and symbols. Without an intellectual framework of concepts and generalizations, messages concerning race relations easily become disconnected and incoherent; they easily degenerate into unrealistic exhortation, ineffective sentimentality, and empty slogans and images. Without specificity and vividness, on the other hand, the conceptual framework loses contact with the audience and becomes alien abstraction and incomprehensible jargon. What we have tried to indicate in the present review is only that substantial research findings do exist, and that a wider knowledge of them probably would enhance interracial understanding.

Now, as we all know, it has been repeatedly shown that exposure to mass media is highly self-selective; people tend to pay attention to that which is congruent with their predispositions and to evade or interpret the message to bring it toward their own initial view or set. It has been demonstrated in some detail how response is affected by the recipient's initial attitudes,[15] group membership, and personality characteristics, as well as by the character of the message, its source, and the mode of presentation. When all has been said and done, however, the media do have effects, and in the long run, in my opinion, quite substantial effects. Consideration of the manner of programing and presentation is outside the scope of this paper. We wish only to remind ourselves that the audience of the mass media does not consist only or even predominantly of separate and isolated human atoms. Of course, the audience does consist partly of, and is for many purposes treated precisely as, such an audience—as an aggregated mass of individuals who will or will not buy a particular brand of shampoo or tune in on a particular station or channel. For many other purposes, however, the individual viewer-listener-reader acts as a member of social groups in relaying information and opinions, in deciding how to vote in an election, or in forming an opinion about school integration or civil rights demonstrations. This simple point is recurrently misunderstood in the most fundamental way. It may therefore deserve reemphasis. The point is not that individuals having certain characteristics tend to cluster and to react similarly, although this is obviously important. The crucial facts, however, are *the facts of interaction and interdependence.*[16]

What, then, are the social science findings most suitable for presentation to the enormous, complex, diverse, interactive set of audiences of the mass media? Here we leave the ground of research and sociological interpretation to record a few personal reflections upon possible implications of our present understanding of intergroup relations in this society. Leaving aside qualifications and reservations, we believe it is broadly true that:

1. Anxiety, fear, and generalized or specific sense of threat are of primary importance in intergroup hostility and conflict. Realistic messages that are *reassuring* are therefore of primary importance. The facts often justify such messages with regard to school desegregation, voting, employment, housing, delinquency and crime, political beliefs, and public accommodations.

2. Negro and white Americans of comparable education and economic position share a large number of very important values, beliefs, hopes, fears, and ordinary human experiences. Communications that convey a sense of this commonality may be expected to enhance favorable prospects for orderly social change in race relations.

3. The Negro revolt is thoroughly "American" and predominantly institutional, legal-minded, and basically conservative rather than revolutionary. Up to the present time it has sought to work within the main frameworks of the preexisting political and economic systems rather than to radically change them. It has consistently appealed to the spirit of the Declaration of Independence and the Bill of Rights rather than to a new political ideology. Although American Negroes are pressing and will continue to press for abolition of forced segregation and of arbitrary discrimination, and although the changes they demand certainly are not trivial, the major demands fall easily within the range of values nominally accepted by the great bulk of the white population.

4. Recent laws and court decisions have not ended discrimination or segregation, and largely leave untouched the massive problems of unemployment and disproportionately low incomes. In this field the facts do not "speak for themselves"; they stand in special need of context and interpretation.

5. At the risk of repeating the obvious, we reemphasize that special care probably is needed in presenting materials related to race relations to avoid even the appearance of unduly one-sided treatment. However, continuous effort is necessary to present materials that unobtrusively help to correct exaggerated stereotypes.

6. Out of the large body of research on the effects of communica-

tion, nothing has appeared to contradict seriously the generalization that personalized appeals typically are more effective than impersonal messages.

7. Responsible dissemination of social science materials dealing with intergroup relations will have to deal with real differences in typical beliefs and behaviors of members of ethnic, religious, and other categories, and it need not fall into false sentimentality or excessive exhortation. In the long run, however, by repeated coverage of a wide spectrum of materials, it may turn out that the mass media will have contributed greatly to mature social perspective, clarity of understanding, and even to respect for differences and conflicts of values in our pluralistic and changing society.

---

1. "Social Change and Social Conflict: Race Relations in the United States, 1944–1964," *Sociological Inquiry*, Vol. 35, No. 1 (Winter 1965), p. 8.

2. No attempt will be made here to give extensive citations; the large body of literature is partially summarized in such works as: Gordon W. Allport, *The Nature of Prejudice*, Boston: Beacon Press, 1954; Bernard Berelson and Gary A. Steiner, *Human Behavior: An Inventory of Scientific Findings*, New York: Harcourt, Brace & World, Inc., 1964 (Ch. 12); Thomas F. Pettigrew, *A Profile of the Negro American*, Princeton, N.J.: D. Van Nostrand Company, Inc., 1964; Arnold M. Rose, "Race and Ethnic Relations," in Robert K. Merton and Robert A. Nisbet (eds.), *Contemporary Social Problems*, New York: Harcourt, Brace & World, Inc., 1961; George E. Simpson and J. Milton Yinger, *Racial and Cultural Minorities* (3rd ed.), New York: Harper and Row, 1965; Robin M. Williams, Jr., *The Reduction of Intergroup Tensions*, Social Science Research Council Bulletin No. 57, New York, 1947; Robin M. Williams, Jr., "Racial and Cultural Relations," in Joseph B. Gittler (ed.), *Review of Sociology*, New York: John Wiley & Sons, Inc., 1957; Robin M. Williams, Jr., *Strangers Next Door*, Englewood Cliffs, N.J.: Prentice-Hall, Inc., 1964.

3. Herbert H. Hyman and Paul B. Sheatsley, "Attitudes Toward Desegregation," *Scientific American*, Vol. 211, No. 1 (July 1964), p. 20.

4. We make no attempt to cite the vast literature. For historical perspective, however, special attention may be called to: Louis L. Snyder, *The Idea of Racialism*, Princeton, N.J.: D. Van Nostrand Company, Inc., 1962.

5. Simple working definitions for present purposes are: (1) prejudice = an inaccurate categorical prejudgment that is rigidly held when exposed to new knowledge; (2) racial discrimination = treatment of an individual to his disadvantage solely because of his membership in a racial category.

6. Prejudiced persons are, indeed, more likely to recall such unpleasant

experiences," . . . but this seems to be more of a rationalization after the fact of prejudice than a cause of it" (Berelson and Steiner, *op.cit.*, p. 507).

7. The most frequently cited experimental demonstrations of such effects are those of Solomon E. Asch (*Social Psychology*, New York: Prentice-Hall, Inc., 1952, Chs. 15 and 16).

8. Cf. Williams, *The Reduction of Intergroup Tensions*, p. 60.

9. Pettigrew, *op.cit.*, p. 191.

10. Allen D. Grimshaw, "Research on Intergroup Relations and Conflict: A Review," *Journal of Conflict Resolution*, Vol. 8, No. 4 (December 1964), pp. 496–497.

11. Robert T. Holt, "A Proposed Structural-Functional Framework for Political Science," *The Annals of the American Academy of Political and Social Science*, Monograph 5, (February 1965), pp. 103–104.

12. Vivian M. Henderson, *The Economic Status of Negroes*, Southern Regional Council, Atlanta, Georgia, 1963.

13. Williams, *Strangers Next Door*, p. 387.

14. *Ibid.*, p. 308.

15. It surely is plausible—and comes as no surprise—that "The more strongly people feel against ethnic minorities, the less likely they are to be changed in attitudes or behavior by formal communications or propaganda, and especially by the mass media" (Berelson and Steiner, *op.cit.*, p. 518).

16. Cf. Marten Broumer, "Mass Communication and the Social Sciences: Some Neglected Areas," in Lewis Anthony Dexter and David Manning White (eds.), *People, Society, and Mass Communications*, London: The Free Press of Glencoe, Collier-Macmillan Ltd., 1964, p. 557.

5
Social Class and Serious Mental Disorder*

Melvin L. Kohn
NATIONAL INSTITUTE OF MENTAL
HEALTH

In this essay, I shall attempt to assess the evidence suggesting that social class somehow is related to the incidence of serious mental disorder, particularly to the types of disorder we call schizophrenia. The evidence is inconclusive, but tantalizing, and since we have no better leads about the dynamics of schizophrenia, this one is worth pursuing; therefore, I shall go on to consider what this might suggest for our understanding of the dynamics of the disorders. Finally, I shall touch on some of the much less equivocal evidence that social class importantly affects how people suffering from serious mental disorder are handled.

By serious mental disorder I refer, loosely, to what are more precisely called the functional psychoses and the more serious forms of neurosis—in general, the incapacitating disorders, excepting only those that have a demonstrated biological basis. (If we confine our attention to disorders occurring in young adulthood and middle age, the exception is not important.) I shall focus on schizophrenia, the most frequently occurring of the serious mental disorders. The emphasis on schizophrenia is because of its singular importance as a public health problem, because so much of the relevant research has been focused on schizophrenia, and perhaps most of all because I happen to think of schizophrenia as the most theoretically chal-

---

*This paper is adapted from Melvin L. Kohn, "On the Epidemiology of Schizophrenia," *Acta Sociologica*, Vol. 9 (1966), pp. 209–221.

lenging of the mental disorders. But whenever the data force me to do so, and in fact whenever they allow me to generalize that far, I shall broaden the discussion to talk of the serious mental disorders in general.

As I use the term "schizophrenia," I shall be following the American practice of including within that rubric several disorders, all characterized by a "loss of contact with reality" or, more simply, by an inability to understand, at however minimal a standard of accuracy, what other people are doing. The European usage of the term is narrower. I follow the American usage not because I think it superior, but because any attempt at comparability requires one to use the more inclusive term. One can reinterpret the European data quite easily by adding the relevant smaller categories that make up our more global term.

Social classes will be defined as aggregates of individuals who occupy broadly similar positions in the hierarchy of power, privilege, and prestige. In dealing with the research literature, I shall treat occupational position (or occupational position as weighted somewhat by education) as a serviceable index of social class for urban society.

One further prefatory note: Much of what I shall do in this paper will be to raise doubts and come to extremely tentative conclusions from inadequate evidence. If you wonder why this is worth doing, the reason is that we know so little and the problem is so pressing. Genetics does not provide a sufficient explanation,[1] and, I take it from Kety's critical review,[2] the biochemical and physiological hypotheses that have been advanced have so far failed to stand the test of careful experimentation. So, inadequate as the following data are, they are the best that are available to us.

I

It seems to me that most of the important statistical studies of schizophrenia can be viewed as attempts to resolve problems of interpretation posed by the pioneer studies—Faris and Dunham's study of rates of schizophrenia for the various ecological areas of Chicago[3] and Clark's study of rates of schizophrenia at various occupational levels in that same city.[4] Their findings were essentially as follows:

Faris and Dunham: The highest rates of first hospital admission for schizophrenia are in the central area of the city, with diminishing rates as you move toward the periphery.

Clark: The highest rates are for the lowest-status occupations, with diminishing rates as you go to higher-status occupations.

Let us consider the issues that arise in trying to interpret these findings.

1) The first, the simplest but nevertheless a strangely perplexing one, is whether or not the findings are somehow peculiar to Chicago. This much we can say with certainty: they are not unique to Chicago. The essential finding of the Faris and Dunham investigation, on ecological distribution, has been replicated or partially replicated in a number of American cities—Providence, Rhode Island; Peoria, Illinois; Kansas City; St. Louis; Milwaukee; Omaha, Nebraska[5]—and in Oslo, Norway.[6] The essential finding of the Clark investigation, on the occupational distribution, has been confirmed again and again, in these same investigations, in Hollingshead and Redlich's study of New Haven,[7] in the research by Srole and his associates in midtown New York City,[8] and in several other investigations.[9] Svalastoga's reanalysis of Strömgren's data for northern Denmark is consistent,[10] as is Leighton's for "Stirling County," Nova Scotia,[11] and Ødegaard's for Norway.[12]

But there are some exceptions. Clausen and I[13] happened across the first when we discovered that for Hagerstown, Maryland, there was no discernible relationship between either ecological area or occupation and rates of schizophrenia. On a reexamination of past studies, we discovered a curious thing: the larger the city, the stronger the correlation between rates of schizophrenia and these indices of social structure. In the metropolis of Chicago the correlation is large and the relationship is linear: the lower the social status, the higher the rates. In cities of 100,000 to half a million, the correlation is smaller and not so linear: it is more a matter of a pile-up of cases in the lowest socioeconomic strata, with not so much variation among higher strata. When you get down to a city as small as Hagerstown—36,000—the correlation disappears. This proved to be the case not only for Hagerstown, but for the tiny city of "Bristol," Nova Scotia, in the Leightons' investigation,[14] and for the rural area of Scania, in Sweden, that Hagnell and Essen-Möller have been investigating.[15] So one must conclude that although there is overwhelming evidence for a correlation of both ecological area and occupation to rates of schizophrenia, it has been demonstrated only for larger cities. We are dealing then with the social structure of the larger urban environment.

2) The second issue is, depending on how you look at it, either a trivial technical issue or a substantive issue of great importance. As a technical issue, it is generally referred to as the "drift hypothesis"; as a substantive issue, it is the issue of mobility.

The drift hypothesis was first raised as an attempt to explain away the Faris and Dunham findings. The argument is that in the course of their developing illness, schizophrenics tend to drift down into lower-status occupations and lower-status areas of the city. It is not that more cases of schizophrenia are produced in these strata of society, but that schizophrenics who are "produced" elsewhere end up at the bottom of the heap by the time they are hospitalized, and thus are counted as having come from the bottom of the heap.

There have been odds and ends of evidence for and against the drift hypothesis, none of it definitive.[16] The best-designed studies in this country seem to indicate that schizophrenics have been no more downwardly mobile than other people coming from the same social backgrounds. Furthermore, Srole and his associates have recently found, in their study of midtown New York, that rates of mental disorder correlate nearly as well with their *parents'* socioeconomic status as with patients' own socioeconomic status. Certainly the parents did not drift downward because of the patients' disorder.

But there is contrary evidence from Britain. Goldberg and Morrison[17] found that male schizophrenic patients admitted to hospitals in England and Wales show the usual pile-up in the lowest social strata, but their fathers' occupations do not. So the issue is still in doubt. I think the weight of evidence lies against the drift hypothesis, but I should prefer to defer a final evaluation until there is more definitive evidence.

Mobility as a substantive issue is another thing. Ever since Ødegaard's classic study of rates of mental disorder among Norwegian migrants to the United States,[18] we have known that geographic mobility is a matter of considerable consequence for mental

illness, and there is increasing evidence that the same is true for social mobility. We have not known how and why mobility matters
—whether it is a question of what types of people are mobile or of
the stresses of mobility—and unfortunately research has failed to
clarify this issue. The question is one of considerable importance,
but since it takes me afield from the main theme of my discussion,
I shall not pursue it here.

3) The third issue in interpreting the Faris and Dunham and the
Clark investigations is the most serious of all: the question of the
adequacy of hospital admission rates as a measure of the incidence
of mental disorder. Faris and Dunham tried to solve the problem by
including patients admitted to private as well as to public mental
hospitals. This was insufficient because, as several subsequent studies have shown, many people who suffer serious mental disorder
never enter a mental hospital. Subsequent studies have attempted
to do better than Faris and Dunham by including more and more
social agencies in their search for cases; Hollingshead and Redlich
in New Haven, and Jaco in Texas,[19] for example, have extended
their coverage to include everyone who falls into any sort of treatment facility—Jaco going so far as to question all the physicians in
the state of Texas. This is better, but clearly the same objections
hold in principle. And Srole has demonstrated that there are considerable social differences between people who have been treated,
somewhere, for mental illness and severely impaired people, some
large proportion of them schizophrenic, who have never been to any
sort of treatment facility. So we must conclude that using treatment
—*any* sort of treatment—as an index of mental disorder is suspect.

The alternative is to go out into the community and diagnose
everyone—or a representative sample of everyone—yourself. This
has been done by a number of investigators, for example Essen-
Möller in Sweden, Srole and his associates in New York, Leighton
in Nova Scotia. They have solved one problem, but they have run
into two others, perhaps equally serious.

One problem is finding a reliable and valid criterion of mental
illness.[20] For all its inadequacies, hospitalization is at least a reliable
index, and you can be fairly certain that the people who are hospitalized are really ill. But can one really be certain that the Leightons'

estimate that approximately 48 per cent of their population suffer at least 10 per cent impairment,[21] or Srole's that 23.4 per cent of his are impaired, are meaningful? Psychiatric diagnoses, even of hospitalized patients, are notoriously unreliable. Psychiatric diagnoses of people in the community, usually based on secondhand reports, are likely to be even more unreliable.

Personal examination by a single psychiatrist using presumably consistent standards is one potential solution, but applicable only to relatively small populations. Another is the further development of objective rating scales, such as the Neuropsychiatric Screening Adjunct first developed by social scientists in the Research Branch of the U.S. Army in World War II[22] and later used in both the Leightons' and Srole's investigations, but not developed to anything like its full potential in either study. Meantime, we have to recognize that the community studies done so far have been based on indices whose reliability and validity are at any rate suspect.

The other problem with community studies is even more serious. In most of these studies we are no longer dealing with the *incidence* of mental disturbance, but with its *prevalence*.[23] That is, we are no longer measuring the number of new cases arising in various population groups during some period of time, but the number of people currently ill at the time of the survey. This reflects not only incidence but duration of illness. And, as Hollingshead and Redlich have convincingly shown, duration of illness is highly correlated with social class. Various approximations to incidence have been tried, and various new—and often somewhat fantastic—statistical devices invented, to get around this problem, but without any real success. Clearly, what is needed is *repeated* studies of the population, to pick up new cases as they arise and thus to establish true incidence figures. (This is what Hagnell and Essen-Möller are attempting in Scania, and it is a very brave effort indeed.) The crucial problem, of course, is to develop a reliable measure of mental disorder, for without that our repeated surveys will measure nothing but the errors of our instruments. Meantime, we have to recognize that the many prevalence studies of communities—including all the recent large studies in the United States—are using an inappropriate measure that exaggerates the relationship of socioeconomic status to mental disorder.

So the results are hardly definitive. They may even all wash out—one more example of inadequate methods leading to premature, false conclusions. I cannot prove otherwise. Yet I think the most parsimonious interpretation of all these findings is that they point to something real. Granted that there isn't a single definitive study in the lot, the weaknesses of one are compensated for by the strengths of some other, and the total edifice is probably much stronger than you would conclude from knowing only how frail are its component parts. A large number of complementary studies all seem to point to the same conclusion: that rates of mental disorder, particularly of schizophrenia, are correlated with various measures of socioeconomic status, at least in large cities, and this probably isn't just a matter of drift or duration of illness or who gets hospitalized or some other artifact of the methods we use. In all probability, more schizophrenia is actually produced at lower socioeconomic levels. At any rate, let us take that as a working hypothesis and explore the question further. Assuming that more schizophrenia occurs at lower socioeconomic levels—Why?

II

Is it really socioeconomic status, or is it some correlated variable that is operative here? Faris and Dunham did not take socioeconomic status very seriously in their interpretation of their data. From among the host of variables characteristic of the high-rate areas of Chicago, they focused on such things as high rates of population turnover and ethnic mixtures and hypothesized that the really critical thing about the high-rate areas was the degree of social isolation they engendered. John Clausen and I later produced more direct evidence that seems to refute the social isolation hypothesis.[24] But there are any number of other possibilities. Ethnic composition is a possibility, and one recent study in Boston suggests that the reason why large cities show strong correlations of social class to rates of mental disorder, and small cities do not, is that the small cities do not have the right mixtures of lower-class ethnic groups.[25] Perhaps. Or perhaps genetics provides an explanation. If there is a moderately strong genetic linkage in schizophrenia, then one would expect a higher than usual rate of schizophrenia among the fathers and grandfathers of schizophrenics. Since schizophrenia is a debilitating disease, this would be reflected in grandparents' and parents' occupations and places of residence. In other words—it could be the drift hypothesis after all, in a rather complex version.

There are several other possibilities, but in the absence of any compelling evidence, it hardly seems worthwhile reviewing them. All we can say for now is that some correlated variable might prove critical for explaining the findings; it might not be social class, after all, that is the truly operative variable. But until that is demonstrated, the wisest course would seem to be to take the findings at face value and see what there might be about social class that would help us to understand schizophrenia.

III

What is there about the dynamics of social-class position that might affect the probability of people becoming schizophrenic? How does social class operate here, what are the intervening processes? Is it stress, or childhood experience, or something else about the conditions of life in different social classes that really matters for the differential likelihood of developing schizophrenia?

The stress hypothesis is in some respects the most appealing, in part because it is the most direct. We have not only our own observations as human beings with some compassion for less fortunate people, but an increasingly impressive body of scientific evidence, to show that life is rougher and rougher the lower one's social status. The stress explanation seems especially plausible for the very lowest socioeconomic levels, where the rates of schizophrenia are the very highest.

There has to my knowledge been only one empirical investigation of the relationship of social class to stress to mental disorder, that by Langner and Michael in New York.[26] This study, as all the others we have been considering, has its methodological defects—it is a prevalence study, and many of the indices it uses are at best questionable—but it tackles the major issues head-on, and with very impressive and very intriguing results. It finds a strong, linear relationship between stress and mental disturbance; specifically, the more sources of stress, the higher the probability of mental disturbance. It also finds the expected relationship between social class

and stress. So the stress hypothesis has merit. But stress is not all
that is involved in the relationship of social class to mental disorder.
No matter how high the level of stress, social class continues to be
correlated with the probability of mental disturbance; in fact, the
more stress, the higher the correlation.[27] Thus, it seems that the effect of social class on the rate of mental disorder is not only, or even
principally, a function of different amounts of stress at different
class levels, but of something else again. What else?

One possibility is that not only stress, but also reward, is dif-
ferentially distributed among the social classes. The more fortunately situated not only are less beaten about, but are better able
to withstand what stresses they do encounter because they have
many more rewarding experiences to give them strength. This idea
has never to my knowledge been studied empirically.

Another possibility, long popular with psychiatrists and clinical psychologists, focuses on childhood experiences. The basic idea
here is that their childhood experiences, particularly in their relationships with their parents, have somehow better prepared middle-
and upper-class than lower- and working-class people for dealing
with the hazards of life.

And now we enter what is perhaps the most complicated area
of research we have touched on so far, and certainly the least adequately studied field of all.

Allow me to speak for a moment about studies of family relationships and schizophrenia, leaving social class out of the picture
for a brief while. There has been a huge volume of research literature, most of it inadequately designed. One has to dismiss the majority of studies, because of one or another incapacitating deficiency.[28] In many, the patients selected for study were a group from
which you could not possibly generalize to schizophrenics at large
either because the samples were comprised of chronic patients,
where one would expect the longest and most difficult onset of illness with the greatest strain in family relationships, or because the
samples were peculiarly selected, not to test a hypothesis, but to
load the dice in favor of a hypothesis. In other studies, there have
been inadequate control groups or no control group at all. One of
the most serious defects of method, to which we shall return, has

been the comparison of patterns of family relationship of lower- and working-class patients to middle- and upper-middle-class normal controls—which completely confounds the complex picture we wish to disentangle. In still other studies, even where the methods of sample and control-selection have been adequate, the method of data collection has seriously biased the results. This is true, for example, in those studies which have placed patients and their families in stressful situations which are bound to exaggerate any flaws in their interpersonal processes, especially for people of lesser education and verbal skill who would be least equipped to deal with the new and perplexing situation in which they found themselves.

Still, some of the studies have suggested respects in which the family relationships of schizophrenics seem unusual, and unusual in theoretically interesting ways—that is, in ways that might conceivably be important in the dynamics of schizophrenic personality development. Some of the recent investigations by Bateson and Jackson, on communication processes in families of schizophrenics,[29] and by Wynne and his associates on emotional processes in such families,[30] for example, are altogether intriguing.

But—and here we must once again bring social class into the picture—there has not been a single well-controlled study that demonstrates any substantial difference between the family relationships of schizophrenics and those of normal persons *from lower- and working-class backgrounds.*[31] Now, it may be that the well-controlled studies simply have not dealt with the particular variables that do differentiate the families of schizophrenics from those of normal lower- and working-class families. My study with John Clausen,[32] for example, deals with only a few grossly measured aspects of family relationships and does not take up the very processes that more recent psychiatric case studies have emphasized as perhaps the most important of all. It may be that investigations yet to come will show clear and convincing evidence of aspects of family relationships definitely different for schizophrenic-producing families and normal families of the same social background.

If they do not, that still does not mean that family relationships are not important for schizophrenia, or that it is not through the family that social class exerts one of its principal effects. I have said that there is no evidence of any difference between the family relationships of schizophrenics and those of normal families of the lower and working classes. Another way of putting the same facts is to say that there is increasing evidence of remarkable parallels between the dynamics of families that produce schizophrenics and family dynamics in the lower classes generally,[33] which *may* indicate that the family patterns of the lower classes are in some way broadly conducive to schizophrenic personality development.

Clearly these patterns do not provide a sufficient explanation of schizophrenia. We still need a missing *x*, or set of *x*'s, to tell us the necessary and sufficient conditions for schizophrenia to occur. Perhaps that *x* is some other aspect of family relationships. Perhaps the lower-class pattern of family relationships is conducive to schizophrenia for persons genetically predisposed, but not for others. Or perhaps it is generally conducive to schizophrenia, but schizophrenia will not actually occur unless you are subjected to certain types or amounts of stress. We do not know. But these speculative considerations do suggest that it may be about time to bring all these variables—social class, early family relationships, genetics, stress—into the same investigations, so that we can examine their interactive effects. Meantime, we must sadly conclude that we have not yet unraveled the relationship of social class and schizophrenia, nor learned what it might tell us about the etiology of the disorder.

IV

However inconclusive the evidence that social class importantly affects the incidence of serious mental disorder, there is little doubt about the importance of social class for how mental disorder is handled. Hollingshead and Redlich conclusively showed that the lower a man's social class, the less he gets of the society's therapeutic resources, and the longer he is likely to remain incapacitated.[34] Higher-status patients are initially likely to go to private practitioners or to private hospitals; only if things go badly do they transfer to state hospitals. Lower-status patients are likely to go to state hospitals straight away, the proportion increasing dramatically with every drop in class level. Although few patients hospitalized for serious mental disorder are given psychotherapy, those few are concentrated almost entirely in the highest statuses. (This is true even in state hospitals. It is not simply a matter of richer patients paying private practitioners and private hospitals for therapies unavailable to the poor.) Lower down, patients may receive one or another form of somatic therapy. At the bottom, they get nothing but custodial care. There is, not surprisingly, a close relationship between social class and how long a patient is likely to be incapacitated in a mental hospital.

All this is based on Hollingshead's and Redlich's study of New Haven, but their conclusions have since been confirmed in other cities.[35]

The question of who gets psychotherapy was further studied by Schaffer and Myers in an examination of what happened to people who turned for help to the outpatient psychiatric clinic at Yale.[36] (Most of the people included in this study, it must be noted, were suffering less serious mental disorders than those we have been considering, but the results seem to apply to people suffering serious mental disorder, too.) The clinic treats only people who cannot afford private psychotherapy and charges fees so steeply graduated according to ability to pay that finances presumably do not enter into the question of who gets what type of treatment. Nevertheless, there is a startlingly close association between the social class of the would-be patient and the disposition of his case. Essentially, the highest-status applicants (of those eligible) are given psychotherapy by the best-trained members of the staff, those of intermediate status are given shorter-term psychotherapy by less-trained members of the staff, and the lowest-status applicants are turned away. This pattern is hardly unique to the Yale clinic, for it has since been found in clinic after clinic.[37]

It should be noted, in partial defense of psychiatric practice, that there is considerable question as to the efficacy of psychotherapy for lower-class patients. Psychotherapy is not only expensive; it is a tool fashioned for use in middle- and upper-class culture, where the idea of examining one's motives and feelings is not altogether alien.[38]

The solution would seem to lie either in the further development and application of more appropriate forms of psychotherapy —group therapy, for example—or in the development of new forms of treatment altogether. The restructuring of the mental hospital as a social institution would seem to offer one of the most promising possibilities. There has been a great deal of potentially useful exploration here, but as yet little systematic application. Another possibility, of course, is psychopharmacology.

The one major change in the treatment of mental patients that has occurred in recent years—the widespread use of tranquilizing drugs—has resulted in a marked reduction in social class inequities in the proportion of patients who are able to leave the hospital within a year of admission.[39] This has happened, interestingly enough, not so much because of direct physiological benefits to patients who received the drugs, as because the drugs have changed mental hospitals as places to live and work. Linn showed that the benefits, in terms of the probability of release within a year of admission, that came with the introduction of drugs, have been as great for the patients who did *not* get drugs as for the patients who did.[40] Apparently the drugs, by reducing noise, belligerence, messiness, and fear to tolerable proportions, have made civilized life possible even in the large state institutions. Whatever beneficent processes a mental hospital may encourage now have a real opportunity to work. And since the lowest-status patients had been the most disadvantaged, the most likely to be abandoned to the back wards, they have benefited the most from these changes.

Lest we too quickly applaud, however, it must be remembered that although class differences in rates of release from mental hospitals have been reduced, they still exist. We have not yet learned how to treat the mental disorders of the lower social classes even as well as we do the mental disorders of the middle and upper classes; which, it need hardly be emphasized, is far from an exalted standard of comparison.

---

1. See: David Rosenthal, "Problems of Sampling and Diagnosis in the Major Twin Studies of Schizophrenia," *Journal of Psychiatric Research*, Vol. 1, pp. 116–134; Pekka Tienari, "Psychiatric Illness in Identical Twins," *Acta Psychiatrica Scandinavica*, Vol. 39 (1963), Suppl. 169; and Einar Kringlen, "Discordance with Respect to Schizophrenia in Monozygotic Twins: Some Genetic Aspects," *Journal of Nervous and Mental Disease*, Vol. 138 (January 1964), pp. 26–31, and *Schizophrenia in Male Monozygotic Twins*, Oslo: Universitetsforlaget, 1964.

2. Seymour Kety, "Recent Biochemical Theories of Schizophrenia," in Don D. Jackson (ed.), *The Etiology of Schizophrenia*, New York: Basic Books, 1960.

3. Robert E. L. Faris and H. Warren Dunham, *Mental Disorders in Urban Areas: An Ecological Study of Schizophrenia and Other Psychoses*, Chicago: University of Chicago Press, 1939.

4. Robert E. Clark, "Psychoses, Income, and Occupational Prestige," *American Journal of Sociology*, Vol. 39, No. 5 (March 1949), 433–440, and "The Relationship of Schizophrenia to Occupational Income and Occupational Prestige," *American Sociological Review*, Vol. 13, No. 3 (June 1948), pp. 325–330.

5. The findings for Providence are reported in Faris and Dunham, *op.cit.* All the others are reported in: Clarence W. Schroeder, "Mental Disorders in Cities," *American Journal of Sociology*, Vol. 48, No. 1 (July 1942), pp. 40–48.

6. Per Sundby and Per Nyhus, "Major and Minor Psychiatric Disorders in Males in Oslo: An Epidemiological Study," *Acta Psychiatrica Scandinavica*, Vol. 39 (1963), pp. 519–547.

7. August B. Hollingshead and Fredrick C. Redlich, *Social Class and Mental Illness*, New York: John Wiley, 1957.

8. Leo Srole, with Thomas S. Langner, Stanley T. Michael, Marvin K. Opler, and Thomas A. C. Rennie, *Mental Health in the Metropolis: The Midtown Manhattan Study*, Vol. 1, New York: McGraw Hill, 1962.

9. See, for example, Robert M. Frumkin, "Occupation and Major Mental Disorders," in Arnold Rose (ed.), *Mental Health and Mental Disorder*, New York: W. W. Norton, 1955.

10. Kaare Svalastoga, *Social Differentiation*, New York: David McKay, 1965, pp. 100–101.

11. This study is reported in three volumes: Alexander H. Leighton, *My Name is Legion: Foundations for a Theory of Man in Relation to Culture*, New York: Basic Books, 1959; Charles C. Hughes, with Marc-Adelard Tremblay, Robert N. Rapoport, and Alexander H. Leighton, *People of Cove and Woodlot: Communities from the Viewpoint of Social Psychiatry*, New York: Basic Books, 1960; Dorothea C. Leighton, with John S. Harding, David B. Macklin, Allister M. MacMillan, and Alexander H. Leighton, *The Character of Danger*, New York: Basic Books, 1963.

12. Ørnulv Ødegaard, "The Incidence of Psychoses in Various Occupations," *International Journal of Social Psychiatry*, Vol. 2, No. 2 (Autumn 1956), pp. 85–104; "Psychiatric Epidemiology," *Proceedings of the Royal Society of Medicine*, Vol. 55, No. 10 (October 1962), pp. 831–837; and "Occupational Incidence of Mental Disease in Single Women," *Living Conditions and Health*, Vol. 1 (1957), pp. 169–180.

13. John A. Clausen and Melvin L. Kohn, "Relation of Schizophrenia to the Social Structure of a Small City," in B. Pasamanick (ed.), *Epidemiology of Mental Disorder*, Washington, D.C.: American Association for the Advancement of Science, 1959.

14. Dorothea C. Leighton *et al.*, "Psychiatric Findings of the Stirling County Study," *American Journal of Psychiatry*, Vol. 119, No. 11 (May 1963), pp. 1021–1026.

15. Olle Hagnell, "A 10-year followup of a psychiatric field study," mimeographed, 1963; Erik Essen-Möller, "Individual Traits and Morbidity in a Swedish Rural Population," *Acta Psychiatrica et Neurologica Scandinavica* (1956),

Suppl. 100, pp. 1–160; Erik Essen-Möller, "A Current Field Study in the Mental Disorders in Sweden," in Paul H. Hoch and Joseph Zubin (eds.), *Comparative Epidemiology of the Mental Disorders*, New York: Grune and Stratton, 1961.

16. See, for example, Mary Bess Owen, "Alternative Hypotheses for the Explanation of Some of Faris and Dunham's Results," *American Journal of Sociology*, Vol. 47, No. 1 (July 1941), pp. 48–52; Mary H. Lystad, "Social Mobility Among Selected Groups of Schizophrenic Patients," *American Sociological Review*, Vol. 22, No. 3 (June 1957), pp. 288–292; Rema Lapouse, Mary A. Monk, and Milton Terris, "The Drift Hypothesis and Socioeconomic Differentials in Schizophrenia," *American Journal of Public Health*, Vol. 46 (August 1956), pp. 978–986; Morris S. Schwartz, "The Economic and Spatial Mobility of Paranoid Schizophrenics and Manic Depressives," unpublished M.A. thesis, University of Chicago, 1946; Donald L. Gerard and Lester G. Houston, "Family Setting and the Social Ecology of Schizophrenia," *Psychiatric Quarterly*, Vol. 27 (January 1953), pp. 90–101; Srole *et al., op.cit.*; August B. Hollingshead and Fredrick C. Redlich, "Social Stratification and Schizophrenia," *American Sociological Review*, Vol. 19, No. 3 (June 1954), pp. 302–306, and Clausen and Kohn, *op.cit.*

17. E. M. Goldberg and S. L. Morrison, "Schizophrenia and Social Class," *British Journal of Psychiatry*, Vol. 109, No. 463 (November 1963), pp. 785–802.

18. Ørnulv Ødegaard, "Emigration and Mental Health," *Mental Hygiene*, Vol. 20 (1936), pp. 546–553. See also Christian Astrup and Ørnulv Ødegaard, "Internal Migration and Disease in Norway," *Psychiatric Quarterly Supplement*, Vol. 34, Part 1 (1960), pp. 116–130.

19. E. Gartley Jaco, *The Social Epidemiology of Mental Disorders*, New York: Russell Sage Foundation, 1960.

20. See Bruce P. Dohrenwend and Barbara Snell Dohrenwend, "The Problem of Validity in Field Studies of Psychological Disorder," *Journal of Abnormal Psychology*, Vol. 70 (February 1965), pp. 52–69.

21. Dorothea Leighton, "The Distribution of Psychiatric Symptoms in a Small Town," *American Journal of Psychiatry*, Vol. 112, No. 9 (March 1956), pp. 716–723.

22. Shirley A. Star, "The Screening of Psychoneurotics in the Army," in S. A. Stouffer, with L. Guttman, E. A. Suchman, P. F. Lazarsfeld, Shirley A. Star, and J. A. Clausen (eds.), *Measurement and Prediction*, Princeton, N.J.: Princeton University Press, 1950.

23. See Morton Kramer, "A Discussion of the Concepts of Incidence and Prevalence as Related to Epidemiologic Studies of Mental Disorders," *American Journal of Public Health*, Vol. 47, No. 7 (July 1957), pp. 826–840.

24. Melvin L. Kohn and John A. Clausen, "Social Isolation and Schizophrenia," *American Sociological Review*, Vol. 20, No. 3 (June 1955), pp. 265–273.

25. Norbett L. Mintz and David T. Schwartz, "Urban Ecology and Psychosis: Community Factors in the Incidence of Schizophrenia and Manic-Depression Among Italians in Greater Boston," mimeographed, 1963.

26. Thomas S. Langner and Stanley T. Michael, *Life Stress and Mental Health*, New York: The Free Press of Glencoe, 1963.

27. The latter finding is in part an artifact of the peculiar indices used in this study, and reflects differences not in the incidence of illness but in type and

severity of illness in different social classes at various levels of stress. At higher stress levels, lower-class people tend to develop incapacitating psychoses and middle-class people less incapacitating neuroses.

28. See John A. Clausen and Melvin L. Kohn, "Social Relations and Schizophrenia: A Research Report and a Perspective," in Don D. Jackson (ed.), *The Etiology of Schizophrenia*, New York: Basic Books, 1960.

29. Gregory Bateson, with Don Jackson, Jay Haley, and John Weakland, "Toward a Theory of Schizophrenia," *Behavioral Science*, Vol. 1, No. 4 (October 1956), pp. 251–264.

30. Lyman C. Wynne, with Irving M. Ryckoff, Juliana Day, and Stanley I. Hirsch, "Pseudo-Mutuality in the Family Relations of Schizophrenics," *Psychiatry*, Vol. 22, No. 2 (May 1958), pp. 205–220; and Irving Ryckoff, with Juliana Day and Lyman C. Wynne, "Maintenance of Stereotyped Roles in the Families of Schizophrenics," *AMA Archives of Psychiatry*, Vol. 1 (July 1959), pp. 93–98.

31. For a comprehensive review, see Victor D. Sanua, "Sociocultural Factors in Families of Schizophrenics: A Review of the Literature," *Psychiatry*, Vol. 24, No. 3 (August 1961), pp. 246–265.

32. Melvin L. Kohn and John A. Clausen, "Parental Authority Behavior and Schizophrenia," *American Journal of Orthopsychiatry*, Vol. 26, No. 2 (April 1956), pp. 297–313.

33. See, for example, Melvin L. Kohn, "Social Class and Parent-Child Relationships: An Interpretation," *American Journal of Sociology*, Vol. 68, No. 4 (January 1963), pp. 471–480; and, generally, Frank Riessman with Jerome Cohen and Arthur Pearl, (eds.), *Mental Health of the Poor*, New York: The Free Press of Glencoe, 1964.

34. Hollingshead and Redlich, *op.cit.*, Ch. 9. I am relying primarily on their data for psychotic, particularly schizophrenic, patients.

35. See, for example, Robert H. Hardt and Sherwin J. Feinhandler, "Social Class and Mental Hospitalization Prognosis," *American Sociological Review*, Vol. 24, No. 6 (December 1959), pp. 815–821.

36. Leslie Schaffer and Jerome K. Myers, "Psychotherapy and Social Stratification," *Psychiatry*, Vol. 17 (February 1954), pp. 83–93.

37. See, for example, Norman Q. Brill and Hugh A. Storrow, "Social Class and Psychiatric Treatment," *Archives of General Psychiatry*, Vol. 3, No. 10 (October 1960), pp. 340–344, and the references contained therein.

38. Relevant here is the increasing evidence that lower-class patients are resistant to psychotherapy, and are likely to discontinue treatment prematurely.

39. Erwin L. Linn, "Patients' Socioeconomic Characteristics and Release from a Mental Hospital," *American Journal of Sociology*, Vol. 65, No. 3 (November 1959), pp. 280–286.

40. Erwin L. Linn, "Drug Therapy, Milieu Change, and Release from a Mental Hospital," *AMA Archives of Neurology and Psychiatry*, Vol. 81 (June 1959), pp. 785–794.

6
Poverty and Public Policy

Alfred J. Kahn
COLUMBIA UNIVERSITY

If wars may be said to have honeymoon periods, the honeymoon of the war against poverty was over almost before it had begun. Moreover, by the time the effort had entered its second program year, claims of fiscal mismanagement, of political abuse, of the locking out of "normal" political participation, and of inadequacy in concept and implementation all served to emphasize that mayhem might well be committed or divorce proposed—unless, of course, the demands of the "other" war effort in Vietnam were in themselves sufficient to curtail the enterprise.

Most citizens confronted with possibilities such as these would know where they stood, without recourse to a review of what is known empirically about the poverty phenomenon and of theoretical perspectives offered. However, what is the situation for the analyst who chooses to develop his policy perspectives with a view to what is known and with some self-conscious effort to specify values? What, in fact, do we know, and what are the program and policy implications of what is known?

Adequate social science perspectives on the antipoverty effort probably require the knowledge and discipline of the economist, the political scientist, the historian, the sociologist, the psychologist, the anthropologist, the lawyer, and the social worker. Such a team of analysts might summarize a perspective in a volume, not in one brief paper. Indeed, several such volumes have already appeared.[1]

What is possible, then, is some selective review of significant knowledge and theories as these appear relevant to current policy and program considerations. Value issues will not be pursued to any significant degree, although the implicit assumptions will probably be apparent. Nor will we seek in any general sense to account for the current interest in a war on poverty except to note briefly that:

1. Whatever its specific dimensions, the poverty problem is significant, causes suffering, and is disturbing, and its dramatization has caused some Americans to favor more active amelioration or efforts toward its abolition.
2. The antipoverty program has been enhanced (if not generated) by the impetus given by the civil rights revolution to efforts to equalize opportunity, or at least to narrow inequalities.
3. The healthy performance of our industry has generated a growth in gross national product and a federal fiscal capacity sufficient to undertake and sustain a serious antipoverty effort (although there is some debate as to whether it can be sustained during the Vietnam escalation).

The general press has tended to highlight conflicts about excessive local political control of the poverty program or the freezing out of local governmental powers. The issue relative to the part to be played by "the poor" is defined as one of either admitting or not admitting them to a city-wide, local, or service-agency policy role. There has been some note taken of the threat to "the establishment," variously defined as made up of voluntary social agencies, social workers, community councils, and public officials. Federal-state and state-local conflicts have also had attention.

These are real conflicts, and serious issues inhere in them, but they are not the only conflicts or the only issues. For the social science and professional literature also highlight questions of concept, definition and cutoff point for poverty, issues of economic strategy, perspective on social change, and theories of coordination and planning in government and social affairs. A review of "facts" may serve to suggest a few of these issues, if only briefly.

How Much Poverty?

During the past several years, we have moved from the very

rough estimates of poverty which could be drawn upon immediately, when President Johnson proclaimed the "war" in 1964, to a series of much more satisfactory and precise analyses. Major contributions have been made in this field by Morgan and his colleagues, Orshansky (and her collaborators at the Social Security Administration), Lampman, Ornati, and others.[2] Less complete, but interesting, contrasting reports have been prepared in several European countries, particularly England.[3] Even more sophisticated work is expected in this country shortly. For the most part, since it is heavily relied on by most students of the subject, obviously respected by the Council of Economic Advisors, and generally noted, we shall concentrate on the Social Security Administration analysis.

First, however, it is necessary to comment on the "poverty line." By the standards under which Franklin D. Roosevelt referred to "one-third of a nation" in 1933, one-eighth are poor today.[4] In terms of 1947 standards, our poverty totals have declined from one-third to less than one-fifth. Present standards would have defined one-half the nation as poor—if applied in 1933.[5] A fixed $3,000 standard, applied in 1929, would have placed two-thirds of the nation in poverty.[6]

Obviously, there are elements of social definition in poverty which are somehow reflective of both a society's potential and its requirements; indeed, these two factors seem interrelated. Lampman notes that the poverty line is "set at pre-tax income levels at which most families of a given size do in fact purchase a nutritious diet."[7] However, both standards of nutrition and patterns of income disposal are highly variable over time and between places. A Japanese observer comments that in preindustrial traditional society the poor are surrounded by other poor and lack a yardstick. Their poverty is in a sense invisible even to themselves, just as it is taken as part of life by the others. In fact, poverty becomes a policy problem only as the stage of socioeconomic development begins to make it manageable.[8]

From this perspective, it is natural for an affluent society to recognize a widespread poverty problem and to undertake its eradication. An antipoverty war takes place only under advanced industrialization and relative affluence. It belongs to an "age of high mass consumption," to borrow Rostow's term.[9]

The following relationships may be hypothesized: the adequate functioning and survival of a society at a given stage of development demand assurance of social institutional arrangements to solve problems of production, distribution, socialization, motivation, internal and external defense, and so on (the sociologist's and anthropologist's "functional prerequisites"). Such arrangements, in turn, are dependent on assurance of adequate physical development and stamina (to pilot a jet plane or serve as a foot soldier, for example), adequate education and training (to work in a modern factory or to understand a wiring diagram for TV repair), related standards of housing, transportation, warmth, etc. The series of social mechanisms which translate the demands from institutions into expectations of individual modal performance eventually lead through a diverse series of paths to conceptions of need and of what a society might offer its members—indeed, to what it must offer its members and what their rights are. Definitions of the poverty line, by-products of the process, thus must be expected to change as technological, political, and resource variables influence basic institutional change.

Orshansky and her collaborators have reported on the U.S. poverty picture today in these terms.[10] The poverty line used, computed at what is described as a "stringent level of living" and assuming both relatively sophisticated shopping practices and enough mobility to permit some choice, is "drawn separately for each of 124 different types of families described by the sex of the head, the total number of other adults, the number of children under 18, and whether or not they live on a farm." The anchor point in the index is "the amount of income remaining after allowance for buying an adequate diet at minimum cost. . . ."[11] By this standard, the nonfarm poverty line (1963) for a family of four is placed at $3,130, whereas it is at $1,540 for a single person and $4,135 for a family of six. Some of the interesting findings may be summarized briefly:

1. The poverty total had declined to 32 million by 1965. From 1959 to 1964 the absolute total decreased from 38.9 million to 34.1 million despite the population growth. In 1964, the base

year for most of what follows, the poverty group included 18 per cent of the noninstitutionalized population.

2. Of the poor, 14.8 million were children, and of these, 4.4 million were in a family with no man at the head.

3. Of all youngsters in poverty, nearly half were in a home having at least five children. Households judged poor included nearly one-fourth of the nation's children. Income in the large poor families was so low that many would have been poor even if they had had only two children.

4. Thirty per cent of the noninstitutionalized aged (over 5 million individuals) were in poor households (1963).

5. The 15 million poor children and their $7^1/_2$ million poor parents (or adult relatives caring for them) accounted for three-fourths of the persons in poor families. Of the aged poor, 2.7 million were in families.

6. Teen-age youngsters among the poor had less educational attainment than those in better-off families and appeared to break away from their families more frequently than the others. Many were school dropouts and were not in the labor market, or were unemployed.

7. Among families with male heads, employed in March 1964, 7 per cent of the white families and 31 per cent of the Negro families were in the poverty group.

8. The poverty in farm areas affected 23 per cent of families, contrasting with 14.1 per cent of families with nonfarm residences, but most poverty was concentrated among nonfarm people.

9. Three out of ten poor people were nonwhite (1963), a rate of three and a half times that of whites. In fact, one of each two nonwhites was in the poverty group (three in five children).

10. Families headed by women accounted for one in three of the nation's poor but only one in ten of all families (1963).

11. Six per cent of the families headed by a male, year-round, full-time worker were nevertheless poor. (Almost half of these were farmers, service workers, laborers.) Heads of almost 30 per cent of all families called poor worked full time for the entire year.

12. Nearly 40 per cent of the children in poverty were in the family of a worker with a full-time job all through 1963.

13. Poor families experienced an unemployment rate three times the rate in nonpoor families, a higher rate of complete withdrawal from the labor force, more long-term and disabling illness.

14. The 1963 gap between the incomes of the poor and the poverty line was 11.5 billion dollars.

Major studies tend to converge in their findings about poverty-linked characteristics and the high-risk groups for poverty: farm workers, female-headed households, Negroes, the aged, those with less than eight years of education, the large family with young children (even if the father is present). Ornati has, in fact, calculated the greater likelihood of poverty for these and related types of families and has shown that the factors are highly predictive; most of these factors operate even when the economy does well.[12]

The generalization already made relative to the sociocultural determinants of the poverty line are supported by a series of preliminary analyses defining poverty levels in other countries well below the Orshansky income standards and yielding widely varied rates for population segments.[13] An Italian report talks of one-quarter of the population in poverty or distress, while a "rough" Norwegian hypothesis places the total at 6 per cent. A British report places 18 per cent in poverty, 30 per cent of those in such households being children (the comparable United States ratio, computed on a different poverty line, being 18 per cent and 43 per cent).[14]

There is extensive documentation of the consequences of poverty status for health, longevity, education, perspectives on life, and so on—but this material will not be summarized here. Most Americans apparently accept the general notion that extreme poverty should be coped with as an object of public policy; but the question is, What policy?

While the general discussion of policy issues must be deferred until additional background is presented, the summarized data certainly make it clear that no *single* antipoverty strategy will work if the phenomenon is defined operationally by the generalizations listed above. Thus, to talk only of economic growth is to ignore the aged and the handicapped. Employment opportunities will not necessarily be open to Negroes as the economy prospers. Some sectors of the economy might do well without helping the farm laborer or the poorly educated city teen-ager, for example. Nor can a policy be sustained which assumes that any "worthy" or well-motivated individual need not be in economic "trouble."

Poverty "Culture"

Oscar Lewis' *Children of Sanchez* publicized the notion of a "culture of poverty" and gave some insight into the social-psychological concomitants of a life of poverty which extends from generation to generation in a Mexican slum. His more recent work provides similar insight into Puerto Rican experiences. At the same time, social scientists have found that the poverty culture idea may serve a variety of purposes, some of them mutually contradictory.

Novels, social surveys, field studies, autobiographies, and agency case studies over the years have documented the fact that poor people may, and often do, differ from many other people in their value systems and perspectives on life, in their attitudes on social and political issues, in sexual behavior and child-rearing patterns, in the content of the aspirations they hold for their children, in the roles of husband–wife–teen-ager, in the priority accorded various house furnishings and amenities, in relationships with aged parents and other relatives, and so on. Other data have shown the persistence of poverty from generation to generation in certain sections, or regions, or parts of the city, in certain ethnic groups, in certain occupational strata.

The question naturally has arisen as to whether a group's style of life does not contribute to its poverty or, indeed, actually cause it. (In fact, this conclusion was part of the conventional wisdom until recently.) From this the transition has been made to the notion that in a period of general prosperity one must attribute pockets of poverty largely to intergenerational cultural transmission. Such a view tends to generate either a hopeless and somewhat punitive perspective (they were born that way and are destined to be that way), or a completely sociotherapeutic and individually rehabilitative antipoverty policy (education, retraining, etc. are the way to end the cycle).

A related problem has also developed. Some of the investigators of the life of the poor have concluded that in some senses the value-systems, relationships, and behavior patterns uncovered have much to commend them and should be protected. While this has appeared as a refreshing antidote to the assumption that upward social mobility and economic improvement must always point toward the middle-class suburban "ideal," it, too, has developed some potentially unsatisfactory consequences. Attention to what poor people are and how they live tells one a good deal about why and how they are closed out of the cultural mainstream and how services, facilities, and governmental mechanisms are unavailable to them. Such insight therefore tells public officials, planners, and administrators a considerable amount about how one must restructure education, health and social service techniques, and delivery modes if these are to become equally available to the most disadvantaged poor. In fact, it is unlikely that many people who are fully capable of grasping economic and social opportunities will be able to take the crucial first steps unless there is restructuring.

On the other hand, the need and desire thus to take account of preference and diversity at the point of a potential user's initial contact and entry into a service system may lead to the reshaping of certain crucial systems to serve the disadvantaged (those in "cultural poverty") and to offer something less than what everybody else gets. One might cite the "unequal" character of "separate but equal" education, the frequently unsatisfactory state of "clinic" medicine or slum schools, and so on. Thus, a romantic overenthusiasm for "life styles" of the poor, sincerely meant, may defeat the long-term objectives of the reformer.

Confronting some of these dilemmas and dangers, one must also note that they are compounded by a rather loose use of the phrase "the poor." "The poor," of course, may be all of those who at a given moment fall beneath the Social Security Administration's poverty line, but he who uses the phrase must recall that the group is not a fixed caste. In fact, Levitan reminds us that one-fifth of the group left the category in 1962 and one-fifth entered in 1963. Other economists document entry into and departure from this status within the course of one year both by changed circumstances and by virtue of minor definitional changes.[15]

The man on the street, the social scientist, and the policy-maker all often forget that "the poor," in the sense used by the various analyses, are nothing more than a statistical category. They are not members of an interacting social group. They are not necessarily always the same people as those described in the "cultural poverty" literature. Or, even more likely, the objects of the various cultural case studies probably constitute small subsections from the overall poverty category, as well as including some people whose incomes are above any given poverty line. To generalize from Oscar Lewis' or any other case studies to "the poor" is therefore reckless.

A number of authors have shown that, in fact, there has been in the course of the current poverty dialogue a dangerous tendency "to apply to all who are poor or who are manual workers" those characteristics "taken as typical of the more unstable bottom group."[16] Those who follow this path thus ignore the remarkable congruence of aspirations and values shared in many economic strata, the continuous social integration that accompanies economic mobility, and the readiness of many disadvantaged citizens fully to grasp opportunity as the barriers are let down. They also fail to ask whether some of the valued characteristics may not be ethnic and regional and capable of perpetuation "after poverty."

Recent work has suggested that the "culture of poverty" notion may be helpful, if utilized to a limited degree and carefully specified. Ohlin's review, among others, supports the following generalizations:[17]

1. Only some of the poor participate in "the culture," no matter where the line is drawn.
2. Much recent work (Harrington's, for example) thus overextends the concept.
3. The "culture" may contain advantageous as well as handicapping traits (helplessness and alienation, but also personal trust and mutual aid).
4. It is useful to distinguish the underpaid working class from the marginally located under classes.

5. A person who is part of the long-time poor in effect must learn certain social skills to survive in his disadvantaged status. However, "once this happens the chance of altering his condition by solving the original problem is no longer enough."[18]

6. Many social institutions (education, law enforcement, health, employment, etc.) tend to alienate, close out, become unavailable to, reject, discriminate against a society's most submerged elements. Since such institutions are the doorkeepers to opportunity, the most disadvantaged cannot escape and may give up. The "hopelessness" thus resides not in their "culture" alone, but in the mutual estrangement between such culture and the large society. (Schorr speaks of conditions which cause, affect, or perpetuate poverty as a "syndrome of mutually reinforcing handicaps."[19])

On balance, Ohlin calls for "a careful mixture . . . of financial aid, clearly defined opportunity, and skillfully administered social services to aid individuals and families *to escape* (emphasis added) from the culture of poverty." To those who see in this view a lack of respect for cultural differences and for the positive values in the culture of poverty, he cites recent research to the effect that "values of a culture regarded by the participants as desirable are cherished in this type of cultural change and harmful ones left behind."[20]

Theories and Strategies

These are not, of course, new issues. Even the early settlement houses coped with the question of what might be preserved and what people had to learn to give up as the price of mobility and social integration.

Before examining just what the Economic Opportunity Act of 1964 and its 1965 amendments offer in response to the facts and by way of strategy, it may be useful to look more generally at our twentieth-century approaches. The current concern, in effect, is the third discovery of poverty in the United States.

As I have noted elsewhere, it was during the Progressive Era that Americans began to renounce some Elizabethan Poor Law generalizations and to make a distinction between "pauperism" as a problem of personal defect and poverty as a social condition. Protective legislation in such fields as factory inspection, safety, child labor, housing, water pollution, public health generally, and so on were the most lasting outcomes. The distinction was not accepted fully nor permanently maintained. The traumatic dramatization of the poverty of the 1930's changed basic attitudes toward security in American culture and created the foundation of social insurance and large-scale federal support in health and welfare. Whereas it had once been assumed (by the ethic, if not by the man in the street) that the competent would always achieve success, a drive for personal security in any social status now ceased to be a sign of inadequacy. Society had to provide insurance against commonly experienced risks, and a floor of assistance was required for those not adequately insured—because any status carried uncertainties beyond the control of any individual.[21]

In effect, it was the poverty of the 1930's which settled the responsibility of our society to guarantee a minimal health-education-welfare underpinning. All modern industrialized states have followed the same pathway toward what is generally recognized as one of the components of a welfare state.

Not that the transition was complete or the Elizabethan Poor Law assumptions fully dropped. Much in the New Deal's social program was defined as appropriate only for the emergency. While a social insurance system was launched and an employment service created, some of the continuing need was assigned to a public assistance program (Aid to Dependent Children, Old Age Assistance, Aid to the Blind, etc.). Here, large elements of earlier deterrent, punitive policy and limited aid were built into law, administrative procedure, and professional orientations. The belief that need was a reflection of defective moral makeup or inferior heritage often continued as a hidden premise as states and cities translated enabling laws and federal grants-in-aid into operating programs.[22]

The more basic analysis of the causal factors in the economy behind the debacle of the 1930's also provided some of the leverage for introduction of countercyclical economic strategies and for the giant step taken by the Employment Act of 1946. It was the latter act and the gradual elaboration of its possibilities over the past twenty years which completed the available repertoire of poverty-war interventions. A government which has access to fiscal and monetary policies and a variety of related measures to affect aggregate demand is now recognized as in a position basically to influence employment—and thus poverty. Each choice, of course, has its advantages and price—but strategy may and must now be discussed with access to the total repertoire.

Before "locating" the Economic Opportunity Act of 1964, overall social policy trends should be somewhat more specifically defined and their philosophies characterized. It has been found useful, first, to distinguish *residual* from *institutional* approaches to modern social welfare.[23] The former perspective involves the assumption that, generally, the forces of the marketplace, the family, and other primary institutions (church, neighborhood, etc.) meet basic needs. Where temporary malfunctioning or crisis (depression, flood, epidemic) leave individuals in difficulty, welfare measures are developed. These are seen as temporary. The assumption is that, as interim measures, they should not become too comfortable or adequate and that systematic coverage is not needed. While residual services may be available as right and may formally be stigma-free, the very fact that they are defined as episodic and crisis-meeting seems to transfer to many such services the aura of blame and personal inadequacy which characterized all relief measures from the fourteenth to the early twentieth century.

Institutional approaches, by contrast, see certain new problems and needs as inherent in the industrial-urban system even when it works well (unemployment because of technological progress, health problems in the aged because we have increased longevity, more mentally retarded adults in need of care because medicine now keeps them alive, the need for playgrounds because there is more time for leisure, etc.). Institutional perspectives on intervention thus involve seeking to change or supplement the system to cope with new social realities as perceived. Social security, day care, medicare, new cultural resources, and many other programs associated with the Great Society or the welfare state are seen as realistic responses to social change, as relatively permanent, as needed by the total community, and as not carrying any stigma in their use.

Residual responses tend for the most part to create case services involving relief, treatment, rehabilitation of the deviant and disadvantaged individual. Institutional responses may be in several categories:

1. Efforts to affect the system by fiscal, monetary, or social policy (tax laws, interest rates, retirement options, for example), by regulatory legislation, or by change in institutions (new concepts of the school, for example).
2. Permanent creation of new social resources available to all as they wish to use such services or as they fit into categories or statuses which are eligible (public health, homemakers, public housing, clubs for the elderly, youth centers, vocational retraining). I have called such services "social utilities."[24]
3. Creation of case services which (whether medical, psychiatric, psychological, or social work) are available on a diagnostic basis, see the deviance as "illness," broadly defined, and do not introduce moral judgment or social disabilities into the "treatment."

While these categories are ideal types in the analytic sense, they do serve to remind us that the basic thrust in most industrialized countries has been from a residual to an institutional philosophy in social welfare. In the United States the ethic often demands a residual rationale, while the social reality takes us beyond it.

In these terms we may review the policy and program repertoire available to those who designed the antipoverty effort. In effect, they could:

1. seek new ways to improve the economy's performance and abolish unemployment on the assumption that money, goods, and "opportunities" would "trickle down" or "spill over" to the disadvantaged and thus end poverty;
2. find ways to give poor people enough additional money so as to take them out of the poverty group;
3. provide more goods, services, facilities (social utilities) generally, so that "the poor" would find their lives improved by access to resources "in kind";
4. give special help to individuals and groups unable to enter into

the socioeconomic system or take advantage of it for lack of
education, skill, motivation, access, location—or because of social discrimination—and create special protected jobs, all by
way of preparing people to enter the job market in the future;
5. give special help to regions, areas, cities, or industries not able
   to keep up with the general performance of the economy for a
   variety of reasons;
6. improve relief and social security grants and services.

It will be recognized immediately that the federal government
had some involvement in programs on all these levels before 1964
and that the involvement has increased since that time, apart from
the Economic Opportunity Act. However, it is useful, separately, to
characterize the act *per se* before looking at the total governmental
effort.

*The Economic Opportunity Act (E.O.A.) of 1964 and 1965 as an
Antipoverty Strategy*
It is not necessary for present purposes to distinguish the 1964
act from 1965 amendments or to review all administrative arrangements and current proposals. The following listing quickly conveys
the character of the "war" as defined in the act. The totals represent
quantitative *targets*.

1. *Administered by Office of Economic Opportunity*
   (a) Job Corps (Title I-A). Fiscal 1966 appropriation $310 mil-
       lion (10,000 young people for 1965, 64,000 young people
       for 1966)
   (b) VISTA (Title IV-A). Fiscal 1966 appropriation $15 million
       (2,000 in training or work in 1965 and 5,000 in 200 com-
       munities in 1966)
   (c) Community Action Program (Title II-A) (includes Head
       Start, Legal Services, and Migrant programs). Fiscal 1966
       appropriation $663 million (500 grants to 350 communi-
       ties in 1965, 650 grants to 600 communities in 1966)
2. *Administered with the Department of Health, Education, and
   Welfare*

   (a)   College Work-Study (Title I-C). Transferred in 1966 to United States Office of Education budget (45,000 students plus 64,000 for the summer in 800 institutions for 1966)

   (b)   Adult Basic Education (Title II-B). Fiscal 1966 appropriation $30 million (35,000 trainees in 1965, 70,000 trainees in 1966)

   (c)   Work Experience (Title J). Fiscal 1966 appropriation $125 million (88,000 people in 1965 and 112,000 people in 1966)

3. *Administered by the Department of Labor*

   (a)   Neighborhood Youth Corps (Title I-B). Fiscal 1966 appropriation $259 million (150,000 in part-time work in 275 sites and 70,000 more in summer work for 1965 and 215,000 in part-time work in 430 sites, plus 50,000 more in summer work for 1966)

4. *Administered by the Department of Agriculture*

   (a)   Loan programs for rural areas (Title III). Fiscal 1966 appropriation $35 million (7,000 small loans for 1965, 14,490 small loans for 1966)

5. *Administered by the Small Business Administration*

   (a)   Employment and Investment Incentive Loans (Title IV). Included in Community Action Program budget until fiscal 1967 (1,000 loans in 1965 and 3,000 in 1966)

While the act and the 1965 amendments have additional facets, and while additional changes were being introduced during 1966, from migrant programs to efforts to incorporate the aged into the effort, the drift is clear: This is essentially a "case" service strategy and is quite continuous with a basically residual tradition in American social welfare. Rhetoric aside, the emphasis is on changing people's attitudes toward work and school, equipping them with basic skills, giving them an economic toehold through loans (if they are poor risks), helping them remain in school—in short, on remedying defects in an individual or his immediate circumstances which stand in the way of his participating adequately in the economy and thus (presumably) emerging from poverty. The economy's decreasing need for unskilled workers is taken account of in provision for work training, and it is assumed that once better trained the no longer unskilled will find work. "Dropouts" are to be educated and counseled, and the economy is assumed to have places for them.

Yet, this is not the sum total of the EOA strategy. Note is yet to be taken of the Community Action Program and of the Economic Opportunity Council created by the act. The Community Action Program (CAP) clearly is the "venture capital" of the program and was budgeted for 32 per cent of the whole in 1964 and 44 per cent in 1965. While the concept is never fully spelled out, CAP is charged with facilitating an attack on the "roots of poverty" through self-help efforts in areas generally the size of a municipality, but to be varied in accord with the situation. On the basis of 90 per cent federal funding, these efforts of public or nonprofit agencies must "give promise of progress toward the elimination of poverty or a cause or causes of poverty. . . ." The Office of Economic Opportunity announced from the beginning that "the door is always open for new programs and new approaches. Since community needs and resources vary, considerable latitude is allowed in the development and conduct of a CAP." However, governmental and bureaucratic realities being what they are, the sums allocated had to be spent. While there may be debate about how to abolish poverty, the effects of local expenditure are visible. Small wonder, then, that during the first two years most communities took their cues from OEO about Community Action Projects:

They are designed to coordinate the fight against illiteracy, unemployment, poor health and poor housing. They aid the migrant farm workers and Indians on reservations . . . are focusing on early childhood development, remedial education, literacy courses, job development and training, day care, homemakers services, community organization, legal aid to the poor and health services.[25]

In short, with significant exceptions, Community Action Programs do more of what is done under other titles of the act, but are to a degree free to design service-delivery modes, priorities, and program focus in accord with local preference. (OEO exerts considerable pressure for Head Start, Legal Services, and Upward Bound

—a 1966 addition—and specific sums are now designated for each unit of the CAP budget.)

Despite the high-sounding phrases about the "roots" of poverty and its "elimination," the community of the Community Action Program is seldom of a size or potency adequate in the era of industralized megalopolis to eradicate poverty. Few Community Action Programs can affect industrial development or consumer demand sufficiently to assure jobs for their people, and none can offer transfer payments or other funds in sufficient sums and for long-enough periods for those unable to work.

What, then, of the much-quoted phrases indicating that, to be approved, a Community Action Program must be "developed, conducted and administered with the maximum feasible participation of residents of the areas and members of the groups served. . . "? The legislative intent is here far from clear. Most of the evidence suggests a democratic and sociotherapeutic intent, much like that in traditional community organization and community development: If people help design services, their needs will have increased attention and the very act of participation will increase their competence as members of the community. Under such circumstances, programs which are developed are more likely to be utilized and to be effective.

To a small minority, from the very beginning, and to a somewhat larger group subsequently, there was in the notion of "maximum feasible participation . . ." an additional concept. As put by Cloward, "the antipoverty program, precisely because of its mandate to 'involve the poor,' can help to bring about the political preconditions for major economic changes. But this can happen only if the forms of involvement lead to new bases of organized power for low-income people. Economic deprivation is fundamentally a political problem and power will be required to solve it. . . .

"The possibility that the antipoverty program can contribute to the growth of low-income power lies in delivering to the poor and their leaders control over the programs and the funds to be funneled into their slums and ghetto communities."[26]

From this perspective, but certainly from none other, the EOA was to be seen as a domestic prescription for a political and social

revolution legislatively inaugurated, taxpayer funded, and implemented by application to Washington. While such interpretations
persist and are fed by the several situations in which locally organized community action groups have in fact developed considerable
political consciousness, wrested control of the local apparatus, and
used their new-found power politically, it is clear that the long-term
trend is for the bureaucratization and absorption of the Community
Action Programs into the governmental system. As summarized by
two recent observers:

> ... we see no evidence that involvement of the poor by government will
> generate a force for social change by nurturing the political capabilities
> of the poor. Rather governmental programs for the poor are likely to di-
> minish whatever political vitality the poor still exhibit. . . . Future pros-
> pects for social change will be increasingly shaped not by low income
> influence but by the expansionist forces of public bureaucracies. . . . If
> the emerging . . . programs successfully impart competitive skills, the
> bureaucracies pursuing their own enhancement may thereby succeed in
> raising low income people into the middle class. In this way the clients of
> the bureaucracies can, one by one, join the middle-class political majority,
> and government involvement can indeed be said to have increased their
> political influence. . . .[27]

To which one must comment, with Lipset, that a country which
does not have rigid status groups, has never nurtured a working-
class party, and in which the impoverished continue to build their
personal perspectives on premises of social mobility cannot expect
an antipoverty war to have other consequences, even if some early
enthusiasts based themselves on the premise that the poor were a
homogeneous, unified rigid caste—and knew it.[28]
   Nor need one accept the premise that Community Action Programs will generate only therapeutic and educational changes and
have no institutional change results at all. Local action and protest
can and does change departmental and governmental administrative
procedures and policies and may affect state legislation. The Neighborhood Legal Services, financed under the Community Action Programs, may be even more potent, as long-ignored constitutional
rights of the disadvantaged are asserted and create spiraling effects
on governmental agencies. Similarly, Operation Headstart may suc-

cessfully generate a wave-effect which will alter public school programs. Clearly, one should not ignore the institutional innovative
and change potential of the Community Action Programs while ac-
knowledging that these gains will be modest and that the major
thrust is toward treatment-motivation-socialization-education-relo-
cation of the individual poor person. CAP cannot of itself eliminate
that poverty which requires new economic or political policies or
new forms of money transfer to the poor.

To some people, the limited institutional change potential of
the CAP should not be defined as a defect at all. They ask whether
the very premises involved in assigning special prerogatives to "the
poor" in the control of neighborhood programs are not questionable
since this was an effort to provide for "democratic control" by removing a program from the normal political process. They inquire:
Could the many devices for electing or designating representatives
of the poor actually succeed? Should one not have expected the less-
than-token turnouts for elections of "representatives" of "the
poor"? Furthermore, is an economic means test (i.e., only the poor
may vote) wise for local community participation? Is it not a bit of
neo-Marxist romanticism that would create a variation of Greek
democracy applying to the poor of the 1960's and expect special wisdom to emerge? Should elected officials actually be excluded while
people of questionable constituencies vote? In this view, planning
for local involvement in Community Action Programs calls for neigh-
borhood-based groups, not chosen by means test, plus considerable
organization of independent interest groups, whatever their incomes
(minority groups, civil rights, tenants, etc.). People who do not join
organizations of the poor do participate in considerable interest-
group activity. Our pattern of democracy by consent of the governed
through our general political machinery will continue and should
not be expected to be changed by the antipoverty war.

While expectation of general political impact is probably excessive, what may occur as a result of the participation of the poor on
boards and committees, even where such participation does not approximate control, may be a very significant more general democratization of voluntary social agency boards and public advisory
committees in the welfare field. Already, where local antipoverty
programs contract with local or city-wide programs for service,

some of the groups have insisted upon dealing only with agencies which in themselves are governed by reasonably representative community boards. The social welfare network will feel the impact of the CAP's even though the general political system may not. It may be expected that some services now available largely to the middle class may become accessible and suitable to the needs of the more disadvantaged citizen as a consequence of this process.

More may occur to confirm the expectations of the most expansive proponents of the effort. In one low-income community (in Columbus, Ohio) residents have been "given" a settlement house and its properties and, through a neighborhood "foundation," have hired staff and begun to run programs and contract for services.[29] Here "maximum feasible involvement" does mean providing local people with a stake in community property and services with a view to coping with the more general urban problem of alienation of individuals—particularly disadvantaged individuals—from the political process. There is no expectation that *poverty* can be conquered by success of such efforts even if many neighborhoods in many cities should copy it, but what might eventually develop would be a significant increase in participation in decision-making (which does not mean control) by members of deprived communities.

The Broader Social Context

It would be an error to characterize the entire antipoverty strategy through examination only of the Economic Opportunity Act in its various phases. True, the act itself draws upon a limited part of the total possible interventive repertoire. For the most part, as noted, the system is a "given"—casualties are to be treated, residual services developed, defects corrected. Some potential forces for change are generated. Yet a broader view of governmental social policy and economic intervention, as it affects poor people particularly or the disadvantaged among others, introduces a very different perspective.

Obviously, a whole series of acts, legal decisions, and governmental policies going back more than a decade and designed to open equal opportunity and citizenship to the Negro American are also playing a significant role in our attack on poverty. But this, too, is only part of the story. Broader economic and social forces continue to expand the American commitment to a welfare state serving all, and the "Great Society" is only its most recent euphemism. It is just as well that the major measures enacted are not covered by an anti-poverty umbrella. For as Richard Titmuss has observed in an unpublished lecture: "Separate services for second-class citizens invariably become second-class services. . . . Moreover, those who staff these services may come to believe that they themselves are second-class workers."

The full scope of what we in this country are actually undertaking by way of social policy and how it may relate to a comprehensive antipoverty effort may be summarized briefly. Each of the areas would require a volume for full presentation.

Demand management. We have already noted that despite hesitation in the ethic the United States increasingly moves toward a guarantee of health, education, and welfare minima. Ours, to use Wilensky's phrase, is a "reluctant" welfare state, but it does also increasingly intervene into the economy at the demand end.[30] It provides vehicles for government-industry agreements and facilitates considerable planning by private industry.[31] The not-for-profit sector accounts for one-quarter of our gross national product.[32]

Guided by the analyses of the Council of Economic Advisers, propelled by the success of the 1965 tax cut, encouraged by an unprecedented period of industrial expansion without recession, supported by a 1965 record in which United States growth excelled that of previously high-performing nations, the United States continues a variety of policies which stimulate and support aggregate demand. The President periodically dramatizes the federal government's role, whether it relates to influencing the balance of payments, guiding interest rates, or affecting prices. While voluntary compliance is sought, price and wage interventions increase. And the argument of success overcomes earlier hesitations. It was no longer headline news when the President noted in his January 1966 *Economic Report* that it is a main task of federal economic policy to ". . . use fiscal and monetary policies to help to match total demand to our growing productive potential, while helping to speed the growth of that potential through education, research and development, manpower policies and enlarged private and public investment. . . ."

Thus it appears likely that to the extent to which policies deriving from inexact knowledge and dependent on some uncontrollable factors can sustain growth, that portion of our poverty attributable to inadequate growth (and it is significant) will continue to decrease.[33] This will probably remain the case even when the production increase attributable to the Vietnam escalation is (hopefully) removed as a factor. However, as seen, economic growth will not end all poverty.

New social minima. Nor is the concept of socially guaranteed minima a static one. Automation creates pressure for a more highly educated labor force. The civil rights revolution demands more equitable access to jobs, housing, education, health services, and opportunities. New technology and knowledge generate their own pressure and demands.

In this context the Great Society seeks to strengthen the provision of basic minima; insure against previously ignored common risks (especially major illness in old age); strengthen public facilities and social utilities, transportation, public recreation areas, and child care facilities; and recapture urban amenity. The services are valuable *per se* but also represent that investment in human resources expected to do much to break the poverty cycle for many.[34] One responds quite differently to the Economic Opportunity Act as a strategy if it is seen as passed and then amended by a Congress which also gave us (to illustrate):

The Elementary and Secondary Education Act of 1964
The Appalachian Regional Development Act of 1965
The so-called Medicare Amendments to the Social Security Act, 1965
The Manpower Act of 1965
The Heart Disease, Cancer, and Stroke Amendments of 1965
The Older Americans Act of 1965
The Department of Housing and Urban Development
The Community Mental Health Amendments of 1965
The Higher Education Act of 1965
The Drug Abuse Control Amendments of 1965

The combination of programs in the fields of basic education, manpower development, elementary and secondary education, preschool education, counseling, retraining, placement, and work experience begins to address a large category of additional needs and problems shared by many Americans but also vitally affecting the poverty group. To a considerable extent, Economic Opportunity Act developments (especially under the Community Action Programs) overlap and are potentially competitive with some of the other efforts but have their justification and rationale in the need to reach citizens previously ignored or bypassed by inaccessible or inappropriate services. There remain major problems of coverage, quality, and sufficiency, but progress is made. One is struck by the desperate need for planning and coordination, although overlapping and competition also have some merit. Retraining, for example, should relate to job trends; training allowances should be comparable in several different programs, and so on.

Further, the debate between residual-deterrent-individual need philosophies on the one hand and institutional-social-provision-rights philosophies on the other has its counterpart and consequences in all of these program areas.

Area redevelopment. There also is a commitment to the concept of area redevelopment, although there are contradictory notions about its nature.[35] Thus far the least controversial steps (highway building) have been taken. We have yet to decide whether we will reinvest in the economies of areas which the market would bypass or help economically viable spots and permit them to absorb personnel from less successful hinterlands. Shall we, too, aid large-scale labor migration? At stake is a fundamental question of criteria for economic viability where retraining, credit, and "public goods" will not alone put an area in competitive status.

The subject is too large for adequate coverage here; but, in effect, the unresolved issues about area redevelopment are counterparts of all the strategy alternatives involved in the antipoverty war. Depressed area programs do not thus far appear as encouraging means to reduce poverty, according to Levitan.[36]

Tasks and Issues

If one is not outraged at the suggestion that Adam Smith's world will not return, if indeed it existed, and that the United States has in fact utilized to some degree all the welfare state strategies

listed earlier, it becomes possible to look at the antipoverty effort as
a phase in our total social welfare and social policy undertaking.
One can do this while agreeing that market mechanisms are probably the best way to make choices and to coordinate interests in
many areas and that diversity, diffusion of power, and strong voluntary components should be built into our programs so as to preserve key American values.

In this perspective, we note considerable commitment to some
methods for coping with poverty outside of the Economic Opportunity Act—and a failure thus far to utilize other available methods.
More specifically, the proponents of the "aggregate demand" approach to poverty's eradication find much being done of which they
approve. The government has acted successfully to support business
efforts and to encourage economic growth, the creation of jobs, and
a long period of prosperity. On the other hand, jobs are not being
created in numbers and locations which will absorb many of the
"hard core" poor. Nor is money being granted or services in kind
being made available to a sufficient degree to those among the poor
who will not automatically find their status improved as the economy flourishes and general unemployment declines. Each of these
matters deserves somewhat more attention.

Transfer payments. Methods will need to be developed to put
more money into the hands of some people who will not live on an
adequate standard no matter how low the unemployment rates. Almost all those now in receipt of public assistance are by definition
living in poverty, and they constitute 8 million of the 34.1 million so
defined. Many recipients of social insurance benefits also have below poverty incomes.[37] Approximately 4,400,000 (of whom
3,295,700 are children) are on Aid to Dependent Children. Another
2,140,000 receive Old Age Assistance, and 275,000 medical assistance for the aged. The general relief load (no federal aid) is approximately 650,000. The remainder receive Aid to the Permanently and
Totally Disabled (506,000) and Aid to the Blind (95,000). About 41
per cent of the 11 million retired Old Age, Survivors and Disability
Insurance beneficiaries in 1962, aged sixty-five and over, were
living at a poverty income of below $1,500 for individuals and
$1,800 for couples. Economists, social security experts, students of

taxation, and social workers may continue to debate the respective merits of federal minima to place public assistance grants above the poverty line as contrasted with children's allowances, negative income tax, or other approaches to income maintenance. Some favor general revenue cost-of-living supplements at least to retired Social Security beneficiaries, including automatic corrections as the price index rises. Evaluation of specific proposals is not here possible. It is clear, however, that the national effort will be deficient until the people represented by these totals are in receipt of additional funds through some system of transfers. Whatever device is invented will also need to consider the plight of the many poverty-bound large families with fully employed heads whose meager earnings do not support their many children. The pathway of a higher minimum wage leads only a limited distance because a point is rapidly reached at which it becomes profitable to replace men with machines.

The choice of new income-transfer devices will not be easy, however. On the one hand it is not socially useful to withhold the income minima, particularly from young children and the mothers who care for them. Inadequate socialization, poor nutrition and health measures, inadequate education are, in the long run, expensive for the community. Cybernation relieves us of the need for the labor of unskilled women and children. On the other hand, a Puritan work ethic demands a punitive, limited Aid to Dependent Children program which keeps people in poverty, perpetuates the cycle, and forces mothers to work (leaving many of their children ultimately to be taken care of by others in more costly foster homes or institutions).

Job creation. Students of manpower and labor-market trends also call attention to the need to assure specific *types* of jobs if economic growth is to help with most poverty. Some unskilled and semiskilled individuals will find their way quickly into the economy on the basis of retraining, but others will not unless steps are taken to assure the kinds of work for which they can be trained specifically and quickly—and which is available over a long period. More jobs are needed—in the right places and of the right kind—for a comprehensive poverty war. It is for this reason that proposals to rebuild our cities and public transportation and to add to our housing stock at an unprecedented rate need serious consideration. A massive ten-year program would give clear marching orders to all the retraining, counseling, and youth employment programs. The current requirements of the armed forces in Vietnam may defer the issue for a while. An effort to develop even more extensive foreign aid, particularly in the form of food, may affect the size of the effort. But a domestic rebuilding task aimed at the unemployed and generally unskilled segment of the youth labor force remains urgent. If, at the same time, one could upgrade the status and pay of the millions of service jobs in the market economy which are now often unfilled (cleaners, child care workers, repairmen, domestics) and follow the suggested strategies for using many forms of service and health aids in public service,[38] much could be accomplished.

From this point of view, the President's January 1966 messages on housing and city renewal, on food, and on medical aid to foreign countries are all part of a general social welfare strategy which addresses some of the gaps left by the Economic Opportunity Act. Although the latter act may take an essentially residual stance toward poverty, despite all the slogans to the contrary, the Great Society's full perspective is much broader.

While this type of condensed discussion of new forms of income transfer, of job creation by government program and incentive, of area development, and of new social resources may chill the spine of modern-day *laissez-faire*-ists, it is relatively tame talk in the context of current precedents for fiscal and monetary policy, wage and price intervention, and further plans to use tax programs to maintain economic growth and control inflation. Nor is it intrinsically more radical than a publicly financed highway program which supports an expanding automobile industry; atomic energy, power, and mineral policies which sustain private industry; federal distribution of TV and radio rights to benefit given corporations; or a federal pattern of aircraft research and development support and purchase via private industry.

Planning?

Yet specific directions are not inevitable; choices need to be made, difficult decisions taken. There is need therefore to point to additional dimensions of a much-needed debate and to inquire about forums and media.

The local social welfare executive or board member in the fields of health, education, public assistance, youth programs, poverty programs, and so on can provide a disconcerting series of case illustrations of federal interdepartmental, interbureau, and interprogram rivalry, competition, and overlapping as these programs come down to state and locality. The waste is considerable. Our welfare state has long experienced the need for the coordination which Myrdal predicts as inevitable, but much of the focus thus far has been on coordination in the locality. If press rumors are predictive, however, the search is now under way in Washington for a device or series of devices at the executive level. There is even talk of a domestic policy equivalent of the National Security Council.

Whether or not steps are already being taken, we shall find some such measures essential before long. Indeed, the poverty-war strategy discussion above in fact outlines the need for policy development and coordinated programing on the federal level in the light of choices to be made. In short, there is need for planning.

The pace at which this may occur and the forms to be evolved are dependent, however, on public understanding and discussion. It is not assumed to be politically wise today to talk of planning, a term which conjures up visions of monolithic, central control. Thus a variety of euphemisms may continue to substitute and to mask the need for public involvement in and political spotlighting of the process. For there are complex, substantive issues and areas in which public preference should become visible. There are many directions, goals, and approaches to planning, however necessary it may be.

To illustrate only briefly: Social welfare programs designed to assure growth of the economy and to guarantee public social resources, minimum service, and financial underpinnings may or may not be economically redistributive. It is not generally known, as Titmuss has shown in England and as several authors are beginning to show in the United States, that present programs of the welfare state generally benefit the "haves" more than they do the "have nots." Only a minority of programs actually redistribute income to the greatest advantage of the very poor.[39] Unless it truly wishes to end poverty and assure a social minimum at a decent level, a society may not need to increase the redistributional effect of programs. But do we wish to? Where and how is the debate to take place?

Similarly, Congress has learned how federal funds may be employed to instigate planning in cities, neighborhoods, states, regions, or functional fields. Recent legislation for community mental health, services to the aged, city rebuilding, urban transportation, relief, and area redevelopment are illustrative. Yet the very definition of planning units and channels of approval has tremendous meaning for future power and patterns of relationships of governments of towns, cities, suburban areas, states, and groups of states. The values and prices of possible outcomes need serious exploration and discussion. Our image of the function of local government needs considerable clarification.

These are merely illustrative issues. On the agenda of our society, at the very time that we are concerned with poverty, are questions of how to: (1) humanize the urban environment, (2) strengthen the family in new roles, (3) cope with the relationship of the individual and the primary group to a myriad of bureaucracies, (4) assure a constantly redefined health, education, social service minimum to all, (5) reform delivery of social service to maximize effectiveness and utilize scarce manpower resources efficiently.

In each of these areas there are problems of goal, knowledge, skill, and manpower—but significant efforts are under way.

Departmental planning on the federal level is now being exposed to the program-budgeting concepts introduced originally in the Department of Defense.[40] Serious efforts are being made to define program goals and objectives. Thus, the very process of planning allows increased possibility of making visible the issues relating to preference, problems of priority, perspectives, or policy. It is not yet clear, however, whether this is to be achieved through activities in the Executive Branch, through new capabilities in the Congress—or entirely by activity in the voluntary sector. Both modest and far-reaching proposals have begun to appear.[41] The need, however, is present. Planning may decentralize decision-making, increase participation, protect diverse interests—or do all the anti-democratic things long feared. The form and locale are crucial.

In this light the antipoverty war's slogan of "maximum feasible involvement" might well become a manifesto for the more general democratization of public and voluntary social welfare planning and service. If so, the ramifications will be considerable.

In short, the antipoverty war makes manifest the considerable expansion of the American welfare state. Our culture finds more comfortable the designation Great Society. Whatever the words, however, problems of innovation, change, planning, and coordination generate issues about values, preferences, and priorities. There is need for considerable national debate. Here the media of communications have a most strategic role.

---

1. Margaret S. Gordon (ed.), *Poverty in America*, San Francisco: Chandler Publishing Company, 1965; Louis A. Ferman, Joyce L. Kornbluh, and Alan Haber (eds.), *Poverty in America*, Ann Arbor: University of Michigan Press, 1965.

2. Mollie Orshansky, "Counting the Poor: Another Look at the Poverty Profile," *Social Security Bulletin*, January 1965, and "Who's Who Among the Poor: A Demographic View of Poverty," *Social Security Bulletin*, July 1965. (Since presentation of this paper, the following additional reports from the Social Security Administration's poverty analysis has been published by Mollie Orshansky: "Recounting the Poor—A Five Year Review," *Social Security Bulletin* (April 1966); "More About the Poor in 1964," *Social Security Bulletin*, (May 1966). Also see James N. Morgan *et al.*, *Income and Welfare in the United States*, New York: McGraw Hill Book Company, 1962; Oscar Ornati, "Poverty in America" in Ferman *et al.*, *op. cit.*, pp. 24–38; Robert Lampman, "Income Distribution and Poverty," in Gordon, *op. cit.*, pp. 102–114.

3. *Low Income Groups and Methods of Dealing with Their Problems*, Paris: Organization for Economic Cooperation and Development, 1966. Includes country reports: 1) *France* (Maurice Parodi); 2) *Italy* (Luigi Fery); 3) *Norway* (Vilhelm Aubert); 4) *United Kingdom* (Brian Abel-Smith); 5) *United States* (Oscar Ornati); 6) *Japan* (Koji Taira); and 7) "Inherited Poverty" by Lloyd Ohlin.

4. Machlip in Gordon, *op. cit.*, p. 447.

5. Ornati in OECD report (note 3); and Robert J. Lampman, "Ends and Means in the War Against Poverty" (publication pending).

6. Victor R. Fuchs, "Toward a Theory of Poverty," in Task Force on Economic Growth and Opportunity, *The Concept of Poverty*, Washington, D.C.: The Chamber of Commerce of the United States, 1965, p. 73.

7. See note 5.

8. Koji Taira (see note 3).

9. W. W. Rostow, *The Stages of Economic Growth*, London: Cambridge University Press, 1962, Ch. 6.

10. See note 2.

11. Orshansky, "Who's Who Among the Poor," p. 8.

12. Oscar Ornati, *Poverty Amid Affluence*, New York: Twentieth Century Fund, 1966.

13. See note 3.

14. *Ibid.*, Brian Abel-Smith, *United Kingdom*. Also see Brian Abel-Smith and Peter Townsend, *The Poor and the Poorest*, London: G. Bell and Sons, Ltd., 1965.

15. Sar A. Levitan, " The Poor in the Work Force," publication pending, *Task Force on Economic Growth and Opportunity*, Washington, D.C.: The Chamber of Commerce of the United States, 1966; Charles E. Silberman, "The Mixed-Up War on Poverty," *Fortune*, August 1965, p. 156.

16. S. M. Miller, "The American Lower Class: A Typological Approach," *Social Research*, Vol. 31 (1964), No. 1.

17. Lloyd Ohlin, "Inherited Poverty" (see note 3).

18. *Ibid.*

19. Alvin Schorr, *Slums and Social Insecurity*, Washington, D.C.: United States Government Printing Office, 1963.

20. Ohlin, *op. cit.*, p. 10.

21. Documented in Alfred J. Kahn, "New Policies and Service Models: The Next Phase," *American Journal of Orthopsychiatry*, Vol. 35, No. 4 (July 1965), pp. 652–662 and "The Societal Context of Social Work Practice," *Social Work*, Vol. 10, No. 4 (October 1965), pp. 145–155.

22. Jacobus tenBroek, *California's Dual System of Family Law*, reprinted from *Stanford Law Review*, Vol. 16, Nos. 2 and 4 (March-July 1964) and Vol. 17, No. 4 (April 1965); Edgar and Jean C. Cahn, "The War on Poverty: A Civilian Perspective," *Yale Law Journal*, Vol. 73, No. 8 (July 1964), pp. 1317–1352.

23. Harold L. Wilensky and Charles N. Lebeaux, *Industrial Society and Social Welfare*, New York: Russell Sage Foundation, 1958.

24. See note 21.

25. Office of Economic Opportunity, *The First Step on a Long Journey*, Congressional Presentation, April 1965, Washington, D.C.: United States Government Printing Office, 1965, Vol. 1, p. 48.

26. Richard A. Cloward, "The War on Poverty: Are the Poor Left Out?" *The Nation*, August 2, 1965, pp. 55, 56.

27. Richard A. Cloward and Frances Fox Piven, "The Professional Bureaucracies: Benefits Systems," in Murray Silberman (ed), *The Role of Government in Promoting Social Change*, New York: Columbia University School of Social Work, 1965.

28. Seymour Martin Lipset, *The First New Nation*, New York: Basic Books, Inc., 1963, p. 290.

29. Milton Kottler, Institute for Policy Studies, Washington, D.C., unpublished memoranda.

30. Eli Ginzberg, *The Pluralistic Economy*, New York: McGraw-Hill Book Co., 1965, and H. Wilensky introduction to paperback edition of *Industrial So-*

ciety and Social Welfare, New York: Free Press, 1965; *Economic Report of the President, together with the Annual Report of the Council of Economic Advisors,* Washington, D.C.: U.S. Government Printing Office, 1965; Joint Economic Committee, *Subsidy and Subsidy-Effect Programs of the United States Government,* Washington, D.C.: U.S. Government Printing Office, 1965; Joint Economic Committee, *Fiscal Policy Issues of the Coming Decade,* Washington, D.C.: U.S. Government Printing Office, 1965.

31. David T. Bazelon, *The Paper Economy,* New York: Vintage Books, 1965.

32. Ginzberg, *op. cit.*

33. Lampman, *op. cit.*

34. Michael S. March, "Poverty: How Much Will the War Cost?" *The Social Service Review,* Vol. 34, No. 2 (June 1965), pp. 141–156.

35. Sar A. Levitan, *Federal Aid to Depressed Areas,* Baltimore: The John Hopkins Press, 1964.

36. Sar A. Levitan, *Programs in Aid of the Poor,* Kalamazoo, Michigan: W. E. Upjohn Institute for Employment Research, 1965, p. 23.

37. *Ibid.*

38. Arthur Pearl and Frank Riessman, *New Careers for the Poor,* New York: The Free Press, 1965.

39. Robert Lampman, "The American System of Transfers: How Does It Benefit the Poor?" in Leonard Goodman (ed.), *Economic Progress and Social Welfare,* New York: Columbia University Press, 1966; Richard M. Titmuss, "The Role of Redistribution in Social Policy," *Social Security Bulletin* (June 1965); S. M. Miller and Martin Rein, "Economic Equality," *AFL-CIO Industrial Union Department Agenda,* September 1965.

40. Charles J. Hitch, *Decision Making for Defense,* Berkeley and Los Angeles: The University of California Press, 1965.

41. Harvey Wheeler, *The Restoration of Politics,* Santa Barbara, California: Center for the Study of Democratic Institutions, 1965.

7
Automation–Impact of Computers

Eli Ginzberg
COLUMBIA UNIVERSITY

Let us begin by recalling some connections between social science and journalism. Three or four years ago, a journalist by the name of Abe Raskin did a series in the *New York Times* on technology and unemployment. To the best of my knowledge, he did it before anybody in the academic community had become alert to the fact that the economy is not necessarily self-regulating with respect to technology and employment, as we had presumed it was. He also dealt with such complex subjects as private demand and public services and related matters. Therefore it does not seem that knowledge and insight are the special preserve of academics any more than felicitous prose is the exclusive province of newspaper and magazine writers.

I will ask five questions very rapidly. What do we know about this subject? How do we happen to know it? What do we know about what we don't know? What can we say about the linkages between automation, technology, or whatever word you prefer to use for technological change, and some related dimensions of our society? And what should we keep our eyes on? I gather a journalist has the necessity of being alert to emerging problems.

It has been stated here, and it's implicit in the whole discussion, that our society has been changing very rapidly. However, this is now my thirty-first year of teaching at Columbia, and there hasn't been a single technological change that has affected my life since the day I walked into that office, with one exception—the airplane. By and large, nothing else has changed. I had a typewriter in 1935, a telephone, an automobile. I write by longhand on yellow pads which were available then. The technological advance which I use is the ball pen. The change is that I don't get my fingers dirty any more. The only really significant factor has been airplanes—propeller airplanes and later jet airplanes.

I used this personal example to show how fast or slow we're going. The other day somebody said that I had a male bias, that if I thought about technological change in my wife's life, there would have been greater orders of change. Well, this may be worth speculating about.

The first point I want to make is that a lot of things that we believe to be changing are in fact changing, but they may not be changing at a *faster* rate than in the past. Moreover, the changes may or may not be connected with technology, or they may be only incidentally connected with technology. If we think about the United States during the last thirty or forty years, we will see that perhaps more things have changed because of two world wars than because of technology. This is at least a reasonable proposition. Perhaps there are more changes currently under way because we know how to manipulate economic policy a little better. Perhaps that itself is a more significant change than those engendered by technology. In other words, it may be that we ascribe too much to technology.

When I studied at Columbia during the Great Depression, there was a group of professors and outsiders known as the "technocrats." They had all kinds of theories about the crucial role of technology. But most of them were irrelevant or wrong. How many of you have seen a new report on *Technology and the American Economy*, which contains the key findings of a government commission that worked on the subject for fourteen months.[1] This report is well written and has a fair amount of substance. It was broadly disseminated, but it obviously hasn't been widely read and used.

Following are some historical facts of the recent past. In terms of the relationship between input and output, productivity used to increase at about 2 per cent a year. Since World War II it has increased at a rate of about 3 per cent a year. This is not a small increase; this represents a change of 50 per cent. Productivity then has been going up. Interestingly, it has been increasing most rapidly in agriculture. We always think of manufacturing as the backbone of American industry, where most of the progress is made, but actually more productivity increases have been made in agriculture. Excluding agriculture, the annual gain in productivity has been at a rate of only 2 to $2^1/_2$ per cent.

Another phenomenon that is included in the rates of change has to do with how many additional people we add to the labor force every year. At the beginning of the 1950's, we added about 1 per cent to the labor force per year, in the middle fifties we added $1^1/_2$ per cent, and now we add 2 per cent or just under 2 per cent a year. That is a 100 per cent increase in the growth of the labor force. This change has nothing to do with technology *per se;* the growth of the economy made it possible to create jobs for married women who want to work.

If we put the productivity and labor-force growth factors together, we come to an interesting social problem. Unless we can somehow keep the market functioning so that the total economy manages to grow at about 4 per cent a year, there will not be enough new jobs for the people who are being forced out of jobs because of the changing technology as well as for all the youngsters who are coming into the labor force. Our economy must grow at about 4 per cent a year to stay in balance. However, it has never grown at that rate for any prolonged period of time. Therefore, before we decide that the American economy is in fine shape, our history will remind us that we've never succeeded in maintaining a 4 per cent growth rate for any number of years. And that is the approximate rate we need to sustain if unemployment is not to increase. During the last twelve-year period, the growth in the economy was strong enough to prevent unemployment from increasing in just half of these years. During the other half of the period it didn't grow fast enough, and we had increases in unemployment. Now there are all kinds of theories about how well we've been doing in the last five years. I have some reservation as to the source of our progress. We're in the middle of a credit inflation, and I don't believe that we've solved all of our growth problems.

We can distribute the gains from productivity in one of three ways. We can take it out in terms of more goods for the consumer, more goods for the public at large—more defense and/or more road systems—or we can take it out in more leisure. Since the end of World War II the American public has taken the gain in more leisure only up to 7 per cent. We've decreased the hours of work per year very little. I expect that soon the average work week will move again —down. It moves in spurts, and it's hard to understand. It depends heavily on trade union priorities.

These are a few of the facts. Now, how do we know about them? We know some of them from history. I'm an old-fashioned economist, and I still think history can tell us perhaps more than most other sources. It is probably true that the length of time from scientific discovery and technological breakthrough to merchandising a product has been substantially reduced. That is probably true, although the evidence is not unequivocal. I do some consulting for Dupont occasionally, and I have learned from them that it still takes ten to fifteen years to move from a laboratory breakthrough to the market. It's very complicated to introduce a new product.

A next source is our statistics, but they are imperfect, and in one respect they are getting worse all the time. The statistics we do have relate primarily to a sector of our economy which is diminishing in importance—manufacturing and goods output, which can be most easily measured. It is difficult to measure the service sector, and that is increasing in importance. One cannot compare the growth of the United States and Soviet Russia, because so much more of our output is in the form of services. Just think about an appendectomy twenty years ago and an appendectomy today, in terms of length of time in the hospital, possibility of infection, etc. These critical changes do not show up in the data at all. The statistics of economic change leave much to be desired. In addition, we need some theory in order to use the data.

Now, about problems that we don't really understand. We will spend this year about 21 billions of dollars for what is called "R & D." One might conclude that these tremendous expenditures for research and development foreshadow a great advance in science and technology and in economic growth. But that is questionable. If we consider that part of technology that affects the economy—reflected in patents, for instance—we find that the number of patents granted in 1900 when we didn't spend a dollar on "R & D" was

about the same as the number granted today. The relationship between "R & D"expenditures and economic progress is indirect.

Secondly, it has become fashionable to talk about expenditures
for education and health as investments in human resources. Now
there is certainly some relationship between investment in human
resources and the growth of the economy, but, as I ask my students,
"Why do you need a master's degree to sell soap for Procter and
Gamble?" There is no proof that a young man who has graduated
from high school couldn't sell soap as well as one with an M.A. In
fact, he might do better, because he'd be more interested in his job.
Therefore, to count all the additional investment from high school
to graduate school as a contribution to the growth of the economy
is a misreading of the facts.

We like to think that democracy contributes to our substantial
economic growth. But let us think about Japan and Germany—any
Germany, including the present Bonn government, which incidentally is always misinterpreted as the great model of a free enterprise
economy. I can tell you in passing that the highest percentage of
governmental expenditures in any national economy outside the
Communist bloc is made by Germany. If democracy is related to
economic progress, so are other forms of government.

Now to linkages. Technology does change the structure of jobs.
We know that the number of blue collar jobs is not growing very
much and that the white collar job area is growing a lot. Now I want
to link this to the Negro. Negroes are less educated, less skilled,
and if as a result they can't fit into the jobs that are opening up,
the race problem will not be unresolved. The Technology Commission estimated that if the Negroes do not find jobs faster than they
have in the past, the Negro rate of unemployment will be five times
greater than the rate for the white population in 1975, instead of
double as at present. This gap reflects the fact that opportunities in
the job market depend more and more on a man's educational background. Whether a man really needs the education asked for is another matter.

Another linkage relates to the interrelations among jobs, people, and transportation. Let's examine Watts, in Los Angeles, for a
moment. I am no expert on Watts. I know people are stranded in
Watts, unable to get to where the jobs are. They're not stranded

solely because they are Negroes; they are stranded because there is
no public transportation. We need a press with people who can see
such linkages. The Watts story cannot be written too simply. One
of the missing links in Watts, and this is also true to some extent in
Chicago, is the separation between people and jobs because of inadequate transportation.

The title of this paper includes computers as well as automation. Our research group is doing a study on electronic data processing in New York City. We are looking at electronic data processing
in depth in order to get some indication of the impact of a dynamic
new industry on the future of New York City. A good story would
be about the feasibility of some of these processing industries. In
the old days one couldn't pick up a steel mill and relocate it away
from Pittsburgh. EDP may, however, be much more mobile.

To shift for a moment to another area, since we are all semi-
academics, I would like to raise the question of printing, especially
in relation to education. I sometimes wonder whether the stocks of
book publishing companies are as good as they look when I find my
colleagues are no longer telling their students to buy a $12 book;
instead they reproduce a chapter of the book and distribute it free
or at cost. This seems to be the beginning of a second revolution—
the first one, of course, was the paperback.

A few more suggestions and I'm finished. NASA spends about
$5 billion a year, and many of us think that this will have a wonder-
ful spill-over for the economy. Why don't one of you in the communications industry look into this and determine what the economy is actually receiving from the space program?

Secondly, we all recognize that we have major problems in
housing and in transportation. Since we have scientific know-how
and a powerful technology, what are the real blocks? What do we
need in order to build a less expensive house or to refurbish our
railroad system? Along a similar axis, we know that the growing
sector of the economy is the services. The *Technology Report* speculates that medical practice will be revolutionized by the computer.
It's worthwhile to think about this. The Ford Foundation has put a
great deal of money into educational television in the Midwest; I
haven't seen any good studies on the results. These are studies that
journalists ought to do. I would much prefer to read a good journal-

istic account than an overelaborate, evaluative study by a fancy statistician.

I will conclude with these comments. The most important concept which one can learn from the social sciences—I don't like the
word "behavioral" so I haven't used it—is *how* to think about a
problem, not *what* to think. What position does one take toward the
problem area? How do you get a sense of the important linkages?
Let me illustrate: I think the Negro will have better job opportunities in the event of an acceleration of the war in Vietnam than if we
expand the Great Society programs. According to my understanding of the labor market, the kinds of jobs that would be created by
an acceleration of the war in Vietnam are the kinds of jobs Negroes
can get into more easily. They are production jobs, blue collar jobs.
This is exactly what happened in the second half of last year. On the
other hand, more poverty programs mean more jobs for social
workers and bureaucrats. That's what I mean by a study of linkages.

Obviously, the communication arts must have an effective relationship with the social sciences. I don't think the pursuit of social
sciences can be independent of the nature of the society; the pursuit
of truth must be connected with society. And the communication
arts are also connected with democracy. Now I think a certain
amount of modesty is called for on each side. I think we are living
in a pseudoscientific age. I think that the social sciences have gone
"number wild," or call it what you will.

I would like to end with one observation that cannot be proved,
but I consider it suggestive. We are very smug in this country about
our technology and our economic progress. I have been doing some
work in Ethiopia, where the per capita income is less than $50 per
year, per head. And I see a likelihood that we will use our trillion-
dollar national income—which we'll reach before too long—to buy
back all the things we used to get for nothing: clean air, clean water,
and space!

---

1. National Commission on Technology, Automation, and Economic Progress, *Technology and the American Economy*, Washington, D.C.: United States
Government Printing Office, 1966.

8
Crime and Violence*

Stanton Wheeler

RUSSELL SAGE FOUNDATION

It is manifestly impossible, in the brief space of a single paper to provide a thorough review of the major social science concepts and findings concerning crime. I have therefore restricted my comments to a few selected topics, each of which will necessarily be treated in less than complete fashion.

Characteristics of Crime in the United States
The most salient features of crime in the United States would appear to include at least the following:

1. Crime rates are high, and may be getting higher. To say that a rate of crime is high is to suggest a criterion that distinguishes a high from a low rate. Here we mean simply that crime rates in

---

* Much of the material for this paper is drawn from Stanton Wheeler, "Delinquency and Crime," in Howard S. Becker (ed.), *Social Problems: A Modern Approach*, John Wiley & Sons, Inc., 1966, and from "Criminal Statistics: A Reformulation of the Problem," in the *Journal of Criminal Law, Criminology, and Police Science*, Vol. 58 (1967), No. 3. This article is largely restricted to what have been thought of as the "traditional crime problems" and does not bear directly on either the problems of narcotics and drug use nor on those of riots and civil disobedience. Also, much has happened to the field of crime research and social policy since the time of the conference for which this paper was prepared, especially the work reported in the volumes published by the President's Commission on Crime and the Administration of Justice. Recent judicial decisions promise to change the character of our processing of offenders in important ways.

the United States are apparently among the highest in industrialized societies. Because of the lack of strict comparability of crime statistics from one political system to another, this judgment rests largely on informal observations of persons familiar with crime problems in a range of countries. Particularly with regard to violent crimes, there is relatively little doubt among such persons that the problem of crime in the United States is greater than in most other areas.

2. The vast majority of offenses are property crimes. This judgment is especially subject to the limitations of official statistics, because offenses against the person, notably those involving mutual consent, such as many types of sex offenses, are unlikely to be reported to the police. Perhaps most important, however, the work of the police, the courts, and the prisons is primarily with property offenders, rather than offenders against the person. Of the total of 2,259,081 offenses treated as most serious in the Uniform Crime Reports, 77 per cent involved the property crimes of burglary, larceny of $50 or over, or auto theft, and of the remaining 32 per cent, about one-third involved crimes of violence against the person, apparently committed for *reasons* of gaining property—that is, robberies.

3. Despite a preponderance of property crimes among the more serious offenses, the amount of personal violence is high— probably higher than in most Western nations, a view which necessarily rests on subjective comparison as well as evidence. Specifically, our homicide rates are much higher than those of European countries, as are our rates of assault.

4. A characteristic feature of American criminality is the presence of organized crime—the development of large-scale organizations for criminal activities. Traditionally, what has been organized is the control and distribution of illicit goods and services—alcohol during prohibition, narcotics, prostitution, and gambling. In addition, there are the organized efforts to control various legitimate business activities, such as labor unions, vending machine operations, and the like. Although the total number of major crimes charged to "organized crime" is probably small, its cost and its pattern within our central urban areas provide a distinctive element of American society.

5. The United States has much youth-gang crime. Here again, it is the patterning, rather than the total numbers, of such crimes that is important. Gang violence in our major urban centers has been a prevalent part of the American urban scene. It is found especially in our largest cities such as New York and Chicago, but it is far from unknown in other areas as well. In recent years similar patterns appear to be developing in Western European lands, as represented, for example, by the Mods and Rockers in England, the *raggeri* in Sweden, and similar youth groups elsewhere.

6. An additional feature is the presence of what the sociologist Edwin H. Sutherland referred to as white collar crime—crimes committed by businessmen in the pursuit of their business. The electrical conspiracy cases and the salad oil swindle are merely two examples of what is felt to be a widespread problem of crime in relation to business—a problem made less visible by the fact that most cases of white collar crime are not processed through the criminal courts.

These features—the high proportion of property crime, and the amount of violence, organized crime, and youthful gang activity—are salient characteristics of crime in the United States. A parallel series of characteristics emerges when we examine those charged with commission of crimes.

1. The rates are many times higher for males than for females. The 1963 FBI data suggest an overall arrest ratio of eight males for each female. The ratio of male to female crime is greater for property offenses than for personal offenses, and the ratio tends to decline under conditions when crime rates are at their highest. That is, the ratio of male to female crime tends to decline in our urban centers among young people, and among other segments of the population that tend to have higher crime rates.

2. Official crime rates tend to be highest among those in the lowest socioeconomic groups. Whenever studies have been conducted that relate crime to one's location in the socioeconomic order, those at the bottom tend to have the highest rates. The extent to which this is true varies under different conditions, but the

general point has been made in many studies. The apparent re-lation of socioeconomic status to crime probably indicates both some true difference in the amount of serious crime committed by lower- and middle-class persons, and an impact of police and judicial procedures that is likely to lead to higher rates of arrest, court action, and conviction among those socially and financially less capable of fighting for their release.

However, not all the seemingly discriminatory action is chargeable to negative bias or the lack of funds. Many court of-ficials feel that, especially among delinquents, removal from poor environments into institutions may be more beneficial than leaving them in unfavorable environmental settings. Such action is taken in the name of humanity and therapy, but its consequence is the application of what society regards as a more severe reaction. Again, an important feature of the rela-tionship between crime and socioeconomic status is that "white collar crime," for reasons indicated above, is not likely to be included in these statistics.

3. Crime rates tend to be highest during middle and late adoles-cence, declining rapidly with the onset of adulthood. Here again, it is difficult to get adequate measurement, because ad-olescents are frequently handled by special administrative pro-cedures. They are less likely to be fingerprinted, and less likely to have official records with the FBI. But such evidence as is available suggests strongly that crime is primarily a young man's activity.

4. Crime rates tend to be highest in the central areas of our major cities, with the rates being much lower in small towns and rural areas. This differential is especially true for property crimes, and much less so for offenses against the person, where the differential between rural and urban rates is far less extreme.

5. Crime rates tend to be higher than average among certain mi-nority groups, and lower than average among others. Most forms of crime tend to have relatively high rates among Ne-groes, Puerto Ricans, and Mexican-Americans living in our large urban areas; the rates tend to be lower than average for populations of Japanese and Chinese ancestry. A large portion

of the differential rates for the minority group members appears to be related to the frequent concomitants of minority group status, especially those already enumerated above—living in the central sectors of cities and low socioeconomic status. Additional features that may partly account for the differentials between the Oriental and Negro rates relate to typical family structures, which tend to be solid and strong among Orientals and more frequently weak or broken in the Negro population. In those few attempts that have been made to compare rates among different racial groups, holding constant such features as socioeconomic status, there still appears to be some differential in the rates by race, although it is difficult to find comparable units for comparison because of the association between race and poor socioeconomic conditions.

Efforts at Interpretation and Explanation

This brief list of characteristic features in American crime invites the question: Why? What is there about the character of American society that gives it these specific properties? A convincing and thorough answer to this question is impossible at this time, since so little is objectively known about how we compare with other countries, and since in any case it is so difficult to attribute *causal* significance to one or another of the ways in which we differ. It can be shown, for example, that the homicide rate in Norway is much lower than in the United States. But in attempting to tell why Americans kill each other at a higher rate than Norwegians do, we might list a combination of *any* of the vast number of other ways Norway differs from the United States: growth rate, size, nature of the political system, rate of industrialization, racial composition, rate of urbanization, average level of income, range in level of income, differences in patterns of child-rearing. Or among characteristics that are conceptually closer to crime, there are the differences in police systems, in public attitudes toward law and its enforcement, in the severity of punishment for offenders, in the rate of their detection, and so on.

Occasionally there are techniques for statistically controlling some of these forms of variation, thus removing their influence, so that we can see whether the effect still remains. In this instance, for example, we might be able to compare homicide rates among rural and urban people in both Norway and the United States, to see if the overall difference is because of the difference in rate of urbanization. Typically, however, such comparisons are difficult because the necessary data are lacking. It is thus nearly impossible at present to explain the characteristic features of American crime in an intellectually compelling and satisfying way. But this does not prevent us from using what knowledge can be gathered to attempt to piece together a plausible account of the characteristic differences. It should serve to forewarn us, however, of the possibility of error and of the great need for more systematic comparative studies that make possible a clearer assessment of the conditions related to crime in different societies, and the explanation of changes in volume of crime over time and place.

In presenting and assessing these accounts, we should remember that some are addressed to the *general character* of crime in America—its various types and amounts. Others are addressed more to an explanation of the *distribution* of crime among various segments of the population. (These differences correspond roughly to the different sets of facts just noted.) The theories also differ in generality; some point to features common to modern industrial societies and are useful in explaining why crime patterns may be different in such societies from the patterns found in the preindustrial or developing nations; others point more directly to factors that distinguish the United States from other industrial nations.

Finally, the arguments reviewed here are designed to explain differences in the rate or quality of crime, not to describe in detail the process by which a given person becomes criminal. Even for social categories where the rates are highest, some individuals do not commit offenses. It requires a more detailed review of their personal and family backgrounds to explain why, within the same broad category, some persons do and others do not become criminal.

The Disruption of Social Relationships. Some efforts that account for variations in crime rates focus on disrupted social bonds and the consequent weakening of motives for conformity to conventional standards. The central notion is that personal stability and

willingness to abide by conventional norms depend on the stability
of social patterns and relationships. Individuals bound up closely
with persons from groups that they know and admire would be unlikely to violate the norms of such groups. And for most groups,
most of the time, the norms include conformity to the law. Proponents of this view hold that any condition that leads to a weakening
of social bonds, or to the development of conflict and dissension in
place of cultural uniformity and homogeneity, may so weaken motives for conformity that individuals would be willing to commit
criminal acts.

Such conditions are typically found in modern industrial societies, where rates of social change are rapid, producing a breakup in
the continuity of training and socialization, and therefore a potential
weakening of ties across age-graded positions in the life cycle.

There is also likely to be rapid change in the position of given
individuals in the social order. High rates of social mobility, either
upward or downward, produce disrupted social relationships and a
weakening of solidary bonds.

The Nature of Role and Status Definitions. Other ideas focus
on the major status and role structures of society. The definitions
of appropriate behavior for males versus females, adolescents versus
adults, lower-class youths versus middle-class youths may predis-
pose, if not require, characteristic forms of criminal behavior. One
of the leading reasons for the predominance of male over female
crime is that males are expected to provide material goods and services. They are also expected to play more aggressive and instrumental roles, while females are expected to be more passive and expressive. The combination of these role definitions provides a basis for
expecting high rates of male crime relative to female crime, especially since the bulk of all crimes is property offense.

Another set of role and status definitions that may influence
rates of crime are those associated with different positions in the social stratification system. Since today many of those Americans who
compose the lower levels in the stratification system are members
of ethnic and cultural minorities, these patterns of role definitions
are in some respects tied in with ethnic status. Some investigators,
like the anthropologist Walter Miller, feel that there is a core set

of values and problems in lower-class culture that distinguishes it from other levels in the system and raises the probability that anyone raised in that culture will engage in violations of the law. On the basis of long-term experience in the study of lower-class streetcorner groups, Miller has arrived at a set of what he calls "focal concerns" of lower-class culture that differentiate it clearly from other positions in the social order. These include:

Trouble: various forms of unwelcome or complicating involvement with society's agents, such as police and welfare investigators
Toughness: including not only skill in physical combat but a surrounding set of values that emphasizes the ability to "take it," lacking sentimentality, and a contempt for anything smacking of femininity
Smartness: being able to outwit, dupe, and in general, outsmart others
Excitement: a value placed upon thrills, taking chances, and flirting with danger
Fate: a value that assumes that most of the important events in one's life are beyond one's control and governed by chance, destiny, or circumstance
Autonomy: on the level of expressed values, though not necessarily in actual behavior, an emphasis on the importance of not submitting to others' demands, a resentment of external controls or restrictions—especially coercive authority.

Miller's point is that an orientation toward these sets of concerns necessarily will involve some in unlawful activity such as fighting and disturbing the peace, and that it creates situations in which unlawful activity is likely to emerge. The craving for excitement leads to auto theft, or the stress on toughness leads to the return of verbal insult with physical attack. It is not that lower-class cultural values *demand* violation of the law, but rather that they help create circumstances where violation is more likely.

Culturally defined expressions of appropriate behavior also relate to crime through what some have called the "subculture of violence." It appears that Negro communities and southern white communities are more likely to condone the use of aggression as a response to problems. Rates of homicide are generally higher in the South than in the North, even when racial differences in homicide rates are removed. Many homicides result from initially innocuous arguments among intoxicated persons. No clear-cut set of social controls keeps a verbal dispute from becoming physical, a physical dispute from becoming a fight with deadly weapons, and so on. Indeed, according to a study of some five hundred homicides in Philadelphia over a five-year period, 26 per cent were "victim precipitated" in that the person who was killed *began* the dispute that led to his death.

The Struggle for Success and the Response to Failure. One of the most influential sets of ideas about crime causation has been developed by a long list of scholars, stemming primarily from the French sociologist Emile Durkheim, with a major restatement by the American sociologist Robert K. Merton with additional contributions by others.

The central notion involves a distinction between cultural goals and the institutionalized and legitimate means by which they may be achieved. The goal is what is worth striving for—the item or condition of value toward which we direct our activity. The legitimate means are the various procedures by which we can seek to achieve the goal without violating social or legal norms.

People within a society differ in their proximity to the legitimate means for achieving the goals. Some are in positions that provide easy access to the goals through legal means for achieving them; others are in positions where access to such means is difficult. The central concept here is one of *differential* opportunity or access: crime rates will differ according to the extent of "disjuncture" between the goals persons internalize and their socially structured opportunities for achieving them. In American society, where the goal of material success seems dominant and where the legitimate means to such success typically call for high levels of education and professional training, one would expect high crime rates among those least likely to have such skills.

This is not a general prediction that, anywhere and everywhere, persons of lower socioeconomic standing will have higher rates of crime. It is where they stand *relative to the goals which they seek* that we use to predict their rate of crime or deviant behavior, not where they stand in any absolute sense.

An Historical Tradition of Lawlessness. A final set of ideas about crime in America uses an historical mode of explanation to account for the seemingly high rate of crime and violence. A combination of historical factors has given rise to conditions where the restraints on crime are apparently not as great here as in some other countries. Our Puritan heritage has meant that many human vices were strongly condemned, and an emphasis on legal control has meant that laws have been passed to prevent them. Thus gambling, bookmaking, the use of alcohol, premarital and extramarital sexual relations, and other forms of behavior are criminal in many, if not all, jurisdictions of the United States. One pressure toward higher crime rates has come from the simple fact of passing numerous laws in an attempt at legal control of personal conduct.

At the same time, the settling of a vast country required strength, aggressiveness, and manliness. The most successful man was likely to be the most aggressive and powerful, rather than he who lived closest to the letter of the law. Moreover, many of those who settled the country did so partly to escape past histories of failure or deviance. Some of the early settlers of our country arrived here after being banished from England for criminal offenses. In short, the condition seemingly necessary for successful expansion and settlement of the country, coupled with the personal backgrounds of many of the early settlers, was hardly supportive of a passive, mild, and peaceful way of life.

Our methods for responding to criminal behavior were equally aggressive and violent. In the absence of settled legal and protective institutions, local groups often took the law into their own hands, and lynch law emerged as a form of violence supported by many elements in the social order, including law-breakers and law-enforcers. Such activities are by no means limited only to our historical past, as is obvious from recent events in connection with the civil rights movement.

With the settling of the West, many of the central problems of crime reappeared in our growing cities. Here, the combined forces of ethnic immigration and corruption in politics led to high rates of organized crime in urban machine politics. And again, lest one imagine that such problems died in the 1920's and 1930's with the Capone era, we should remember that Boston alone is reported to have had more than twenty gangland killings in the last two years.

Currently, a great deal of attention is given to violent youth crime. It is receiving the attention previously devoted to the gunmen of the West and the corruption in the syndicates of our urban areas. This recent attention is in no sense the first time public concern has been expressed about youth crime. For example, here is an account of youth gangs in nineteenth-century New York City:

The gang fights of those days were fearsome. On the Fourth of July in 1857, the Dead Rabbits from the Five Points district [now being torn down for an urban renewal project] clashed with the Bowery Boys in Bayard Street. Sticks, stones and knives were freely used. Men, women and children were wounded. A small body of policemen, sent to quell the disturbance, was repulsed after several of these were wounded. Finally, the Seventh Regiment was summoned from Boston, and the city militia called out. By the time the riot was put down, late in the evening, six had been killed and over a hundred wounded.

The amount of violence may also vary by region of the country. There is good evidence, as noted earlier, that the violent tradition is more widespread in our southern regions than in other areas. Not only are the actual rates of violent behavior such as homicide higher in such areas, even when we control for the racial balance, but values supporting the use of weapons and guns appear to be stronger. A recent public opinion poll showed that 53 per cent of Southerners believed it should be legal to have loaded weapons in homes, compared with smaller percentages in other regions. There is even one study suggesting that those who migrate from the South to the North or West show the effect of their southern heritage in that they have higher rates of homicide in the northern communities than do those who have always lived in the North. These observations have the character of variations on a theme and should not obscure the fact that violent traditions are part of our total cultural heritage.

Crime Prevention and Social Policy

Most of us are interested in ideas about crime causation from the perspective of social policy. We would like to know what can be done about the problem, for crime seems so clearly damaging to the health of the society. Even the brief review above should serve to forewarn us, however, of the difficulties facing programs of crime prevention and control. For to the extent that crime and violence are part of our cultural heritage, they may be responsible to features of our society that we applaud. Conceivably there is an irreducible minimum of crime generated by a highly mobile, economically aggressive society, and we may have to accept that minimum as part of the cost for the things we value, just as we accept a certain portion of automobile accidents as a normal cost of a modern society operating, quite literally, at high speed. But even with this caution, it seems clear that we have hardly begun to experiment with alternative methods of crime prevention and control, and that we are still, therefore, in deep ignorance regarding our capacity to affect the crime problem without transforming the nature of the society.

Our ideas about prevention come fairly clearly out of the variety of social science perspectives on the causation of deviant behavior, and here the interesting fact is that crime and delinquency have been battlegrounds for competing theories, most of which have been derived from the study of some other form of behavior. It was a short movement, for example, from the application of mental health concepts to neurotics and psychotics to their application to delinquents and criminals, on the assumption that criminal behavior is pathological, or at least that the criminal is responding to the same general forces of family instability that are found among the clients in mental health and child guidance clinics.

Indeed, it is within this general framework that most of our preventive and corrective efforts have been framed. We make an effort at early identification of the problem child by noting defects in his parents, or we reduce the case load of probation officers on the assumption that they will have more time for counseling the deviant and that he will respond to such counseling by ceasing to commit crimes. Most of the experiments in crime prevention, then, have taken the form of attempting to modify the individual who either has been or is deemed likely to become a criminal. Without reviewing the evidence in detail here, it is sufficient to say that such programs have not accomplished their task. Whenever experimental evidence has been collected on their effectiveness, it has shown no impact of the program. It is only fair to point out that there have been few such tests, and that many of the programs were never fully implemented.

An alternative set of programs has emerged in recent years, under the renewed federal interest in delinquency and youth crime. One of the most influential volumes in the field of delinquency was *Delinquency and Opportunity*, by Richard Cloward and Lloyd E. Ohlin. That volume applied the general theme of anomie theory to delinquency, and became a basis for developing preventive programs centering around the provision of opportunities to learn legitimate ways of earning a living, to improve educational skills, and the like. These programs find the problem of delinquency in the structure of the broader community, particularly its provision of opportunity for social ascent, and not in the personal problems or family backgrounds of the delinquent. It is not surprising to find, therefore, that several of the programs now supported by the Office of Economic Opportunity were begun under the President's Commission on Juvenile Delinquency and Youth Crime. These programs remain to be carefully evaluated.

A third set of programs can be derived from a more situational view of delinquency and crime causation. The preventive programs outlined above rest on the assumption that delinquency and crime have deep roots. In the mental health tradition, these roots lie within the individual, and in the sociogenic tradition they lie within the structure of the broader community. In either case, delinquency and crime are seen as severe responses to severe problems. But criminal acts take place in social situations, and if the motives do not always run deep, it is possible that various programs of environmental control will have some impact. This of course is the common-sense logic underlying concern for the ease with which deadly weapons can be purchased, for the impact of the distribution of police in a city on its crime pattern, and for the sale of burglar-proof locks.

If motivations to criminal activity run deep enough, these concerns will be of little avail, for surely persons will roam far and wide in search of opportunities to commit their offenses. But if such motives are not terribly deep, it seems feasible that programs of environmental control might work. The rate of auto theft ought to fall with an increase in the proportion of automobiles that are locked, the rate of rape to fall with a decline in the number of unlighted streets and passageways, and so forth. Undoubtedly there are severe limits to such modes of environmental control, and surely many offenders would not be stopped by them. But if even 10 per cent of our crimes could be prevented in this way, the saving might well be worth the cost of the preventive efforts.

Perhaps the chief point to be stressed is the inadequacy of current data for the formulation of rational public policy. Most of the preventive programs have been launched hurriedly, often under political pressure, with little attention to the problems of implementation on the one hand, or evaluation on the other. Thus it is literally the case that we do not know what works and what doesn't. Part of this is inevitable. Communities cannot stand still while theories of prevention are being implemented, nor can a truly cumulative body of knowledge develop when agencies, programs, and personnel change rapidly. It still seems, however, that a stronger commitment can be made to rational program evaluation, so that we can substitute reliable knowledge for the guesses, no matter how educated, of agency administrators or professional social scientists.

The Administration of Justice: Issues and Problems

By the administration of justice I mean all those processes that intervene between an initial criminal act and its final disposition by the courts. Historically, the prime purpose and function of criminal law and its administration were to distinguish the innocent from the guilty and to impose penal sanctions on the latter. The purpose of imposing the penal sanction was both to punish the wicked and to deter those who might but for the fear of punishment engage in the forbidden activities. This is an oversimplification, of course, and there are many refinements of conception underlying the application of criminal sanctions and justifying alternative rules for insuring safeguards to the innocent. But the nub of the problem is clear.

Much remains of this line of reasoning, but much has been added to it over the years. Although the changes are intertwined and difficult to disentangle, there are at least three important types of changes in our conception of and attitude toward the administration of criminal justice. First, there has been a growing spirit of *humanitarianism.* When criminals could be viewed as part of the lower elements, different in kind from conventional members of society, and especially from those who man its administrative tribunals, it was possible to treat the criminal as a thing rather than as a person, and consequently to justify harsh actions against him. As one illustration, it was only 180 years ago that there were over two hundred capital offenses in English law. The last few decades have witnessed a great reduction in both the number of capital crimes and the number of persons actually receiving capital punishment.

Second, scientific study has been added to moral judgment as a basis for decision-making in the field of criminal justice. This change is perhaps best symbolized by noting the frequency with which we now ask "Why did he do it?" and "Will he do it again?" No longer is it enough to know that what the person did was morally wrong. We assume that what he did had its causes, that they were determinable, and that knowledge of them will lead us to greater understanding and greater wisdom in our actions.

Third, and clearly interrelated with the other two, is the growth in what one author calls "the rehabilitative ideal." Above all, we have come to think of the purpose of our actions regarding the offender as including therapy or rehabilitation. Sometimes this reaction is seen as the opposite of punishment: "Our purpose is not to punish the offender but to reform him." While it is not necessary to see these two as opposed (and indeed one of the early Italian penal reformers, Garofalo, saw the possible therapeutic functions of punishment), it is a relatively new idea to consider as one primary goal of the system of criminal justice the therapeutic effect of that system on the person who is processed through it—on his well-being, his personality, and more generally his future life.

This shift in social philosophy has been matched by changes in the arrangements by which we process offenders. There has been the growth of administrative discretion through the development of special sentencing and parole authorities. There has been rapid development of alternatives to imprisonment, in the form of probation, parole, minimum custody arrangements, and furloughs. The changing character of rules and evidence regarding criminal responsibility and the development of special legislation for sex offenders and certain other kinds of offenders give further evidence of an attempt to

incorporate elements of the new philosophy. Finally, there has been
the development of the Juvenile Court and youth institutions as a
way of incorporating part of the rehabilitative ideal.

What actual consequences, for offenders and for society, flow
from all these changes? It is one thing to establish a changed philosophy and incorporate it into actual social arrangements. It is quite
another to come to a balanced assessment of the consequences of
the change, both for the community at large and for those individuals directly exposed to its operations.

There is no question but that the trend has been toward a reduction in the more extreme forms of direct brutality and physical
punishment. The rate of executions in the United States has declined, and the prisons in which we hold persons who might previously have been put to death also show signs of a more humanitarian regime. Less often than in the past do we build them in dark
and forbidding styles, nor do we emphasize quite as heavily the
clearly incapacitating features of the prison such as high walls,
fences, and guards. In the more progressive states, a large portion of
inmates are likely to serve out much of their sentence in honor
camps or farms, where they live in dormitories, rather than serving
in old bastilles, living in cell blocks. These and other changes too
numerous to mention do indeed give expression to the modern rehabilitative ideal.

These same changes, however, have had other consequences
that are not so clearly in line with the original objectives. The emphasis upon scientific study of the criminal and on the character of
the offender rather than his offense has led to a withering of concern for some of the fundamental elements of civil and political
liberty in connection with criminal actions. One study suggests
that use of the indeterminate sentence, for example, has apparently
led to sentences at least as long as those prevailing under the older,
seemingly more punitive doctrines. It is clear that once concern is
transferred from the nature of the offense to the probability that
an offender will repeat it, there may be a basis for keeping a person
in prison for a long time even though he may have been convicted of
a minor crime.

These problems appear in direct form in juvenile court proceedings. If we can effectively argue that we are acting on behalf of

the child rather than on behalf of the community and that what we are providing is therapy rather than punishment, it is but a short step to arguing that we should feel free to keep the individual in an institution for a long time if his needs seem to warrant it, since what we are doing is beneficial to him and is not determined by a punitive ideology. Indeed, one study suggests that those juvenile court judges most sympathetic to a therapeutic interpretation of their function are somewhat more likely to send youths to institutions. Here it is extremely important both for decision-makers and those exposed to their decisions to distinguish between the intentions that motivate actions, the actions themselves, and their social consequences. If one person is "treated" by a year's confinement behind walls and bars, while another is "punished" by six months behind similar walls and bars, we might well ask which is the more benign, humanitarian, therapeutic setting. And it is important to look closely at what goes on behind the walls and bars and not simply at the vocabulary used to discuss it. A program of rehabilitation may mean spending one hour, out of the approximately 120 waking hours a week, talking to a guidance counselor. Or vocational rehabilitation may mean being one of forty inmates assigned to a shop designed for ten, working with equipment that is no longer used in private industry.

The point of all this is merely to accentuate the fact that intentions are not enough, and that the consequences of alternative programs and courses of action cannot necessarily be known in advance. There is no simple movement from ideology to action in this field, and many programs appear to have consequences other than those originally intended.

Crime and the Mass Media

It certainly comes as no surprise to participants in this conference to find that what people read in the papers influences their views about crime and law enforcement. Indeed, one of the early social science studies in this area showed how citizen estimates of the amount and type of crime in their community were more closely related to newspaper reports than to the actual amount of crime as registered on the police blotter. Thus it goes almost without saying that there is a responsibility for clear and adequate communication of facts about crime, and also a responsibility to place those facts in meaningful context. Beyond this there are three specific problems that often occur to me as I read coverage of crime news, and I would simply like to pass them on in hopes they might be worthy of discussion.

The development of consumer-oriented crime statistics. As part of its responsibility for reporting, the mass media need information on crime rates that is expressed in ways that have real meaning for the public. The police system itself exists for the protection of the community, but so far we have done extremely little to provide data that is directly relevant to community members. This becomes apparent by examining the denominators that typically are used in construction of crime rates. If one is diligent, one can find arrest rates for Negroes, for Puerto Ricans, for whites. Or one can find age-specific rates of offense. In a handful of cases, one can find cohort analysis tables indicating what the probability is that a person will ever be arrested between, say, ages seven to eighteen.

All of these figures have a curious cast. They tell us much more about who commits the offense than about the person against whom it is committed. Yet if we think now as citizens, and not as persons interested solely in offenders or policing, it seems that we might ask rather different questions. Personally, it concerns me more whether my wife or children are assaulted at all, than it does whether they are assaulted by a Caucasian, a Puerto Rican, or a Negro. Yet I can find figures on the latter topic but not on the former. Similarly, one may wonder what New York City residents would make of the fact that the reportedly rising crime rate in the city could be explained as a function of the increased number of persons of juvenile age, which is of course the age at which most crimes are committed (so far as we can tell from official statistics). Certainly it is important theoretically to understand that the rising rate does not appear to be a response to new forces and fears in mass society, but rather can be explained fairly directly as a function of the age structure of the population. But for the typical resident, the important question would seem to be whether or not the rate has gone up for victims in his category.

This is simply to suggest that a useful way of reporting crime data would be to use as a denominator not some characteristic that might describe offenders, but one that will describe their victims. Apartment dwellers might well want to know what the probability is that their apartments will be burgled within the next five years. Others might want to know what the probability is that they will be robbed. In principle, it should not be difficult to prepare such statistics. We take the number of offenses appearing in a particular area against a particular type of victim, and express it as a proportion of all persons who have the social characteristics that the victim happens to hold. In this way we have victim-specific rather than offender-specific crime rates—in effect, a box score which the citizen can use to keep tabs on differing areas in his community and, hopefully, on differing communities. It would become abundantly clear, for example, which areas of the city are most dangerous at night, and for what categories of persons they are most dangerous. Such consumer-oriented statistics would seem to be more important as a public service than are offender-oriented statistics such as those we now produce.

The issues are clearly more complicated than suggested here. One problem is the necessity of correcting for the daytime and nighttime populations of the areas. And in order to get detailed victim-specific rates, we would have to learn more than we normally do about the nature of the victim. In the latest *Uniform Crime Report* available to me, only one out of some 49 tables tells us anything about the victim. This one has to do with the victims of homicides, and classifies the victims according to their age, sex, and race. At least, I would argue, it is an effort in a much-needed direction. It seems reasonable that the mass media, serving the critical function of reporting events to the public, are in a strong position to urge reform in the kinds of data routinely recorded and collected.

The issue behind the story. With the currently great concern for the balance between community protection and the civil rights of citizens, there is a special need for public understanding of the reasons that lie behind the actions of official agencies, including the courts. One of the fascinating features of crime reporting, of course, is that the details are typically so stark and the actions taken so clear; a seemingly guilty offender is released because the evidence was improperly gathered, or because he was not properly advised of his civil rights. There is the victim, beaten and bloody, while the apparent offender is free to walk the streets. Yet one seldom finds stories that convey the full rationale that underlies such actions: what interests the courts attempt to protect by such decisions, what values are at stake. As problems of the police, the courts, and the community come to public attention, it seems essential that the full range of issues and views be presented so that public understanding is increased. This in no way precludes criticism of official agencies or policies, but would serve to provide the public with a broader understanding of the issues.

The problem of the case and the rate. When criminal events are reported in the mass media, it is of course natural to focus on the immediate case. That is where the drama lies, where the action is, and what the public wants to know about. But in the nature of the case these materials provide a poor basis for the development of a full and rounded understanding of crime. The formation of sound social policy typically depends on knowledge of changes in the rate and distribution of the relevant events, but policies more frequently are formed in reaction to certain extreme cases. Years ago the late Edwin Sutherland showed, for example, how new laws regarding sex offenders were a response to an occasional dramatic sex crime, and were not based on a more complete analysis of the problem.

Now these are issues addressed by public officials—in this example state legislators—but one supposes that they are responsive to community sentiments and fears, which in turn are shaped in part by the mass media. It should be possible to develop creative ways of reporting that would show how and where a particular criminal act fits into the broader picture of the nature and distribution of crimes. To do so would be to encourage a more responsible public opinion.

It is perhaps fitting to close this paper by putting the problem of violence in American life in similar perspective. According to 1960 data, white males were about four to five times as likely to lose their lives by suicide as they were by homicide, and their death rate for traffic accidents was approximately fifteen times that of the rate for homicide. This in no way excuses homicides, nor does it remove the problem of personal violence from American life. It does suggest, however, that we might promote a better balance between fears on the one hand and objective consequences on the other.

Session Three:

JOURNALISTS AND BEHAVIORAL SCIENTISTS

9

Social Sciences in the Mass Media

Leo Bogart
BUREAU OF ADVERTISING
OF THE AMERICAN NEWSPAPER
PUBLISHERS ASSOCIATION, INC.

Whether we think abstractly of the social sciences and the mass media, or somewhat more realistically of social scientists and mass media practitioners, we are dealing with two very large and diverse entities, each encompassing an enormous range of distinct subspecies. The social sciences, after all, range from the steaming borderlines of physiological psychology to the icy regions of econometrics; the mass media cover all the ground between Cinemascope spectaculars to the news ticker disgorging baseball scores and stock quotations. When we delimit either area, say, to the so-called behavioral sciences of sociology, social anthropology, and social psychology on the one hand and to the so-called news media on the other, we in each case arbitrarily sever innumerable necessary and natural connections and sources of nourishment.

There are three problem areas in the relationship of social scientists and media practitioners. One is the amount of coverage media give to the doings and sayings of social scientists, which at least some of them regard as inadequate. Second is the overlapping of subject matter and substantive interests between social scientists and newsmen, which is likely to continue as long as the two fields coexist. The third relates to the standards of sophistication which journalists apply in their use of statistics, which are the stock in trade of social scientists.

The Scientific Tradition

In the broadest terms, the social sciences may be thought of as sciences, reflecting certain disciplines of method and a tradition of

153

integrity and dedication to the quest for knowledge. The mass media may be seen as agencies for widespread diffusion of ideas and information which largely serve to reinforce the social norms. The roots of conflict are very much inherent in the existence of two such disparate forces, one radical by nature, the other conservative.

The tradition of the pure scientist, the man with a white coat in the laboratory, is one of personal devotion to his calling in disregard of the opinions of the multitude. Yet the scientist as an individual, with material needs and human demands, has never operated in isolation from social pressures and powers. He can remain in his ivory tower only as long as pope and emperor tolerate or encourage him.

In reality, the man in the white coat, immune to worldly motives and disinterested in the worldly consequences of his discoveries, exists only as an abstraction, a late Victorian ideal type. This abstraction, still held up as a model for first-year graduate students to emulate, has faded into even more obscure unreality with the increasing complications of scientific research and the widening ramifications of scientific theory. Most scientists today are team operators, working in institutional settings with substantial budgets. And the atomic bomb has destroyed forever the ideal of the scientist as disengaged and unconcerned with the social uses of his discoveries.

These developments have had profound consequences for the relationship between the sciences (in general) and the mass media (in general). In an economic order dependent on continuous technological innovation, what scientists do becomes important as a source of public news but also as a source of public fantasy. Particularly in a postwar world disillusioned with Marxist romanticism, there is great potential appeal in the thought of flying to the moon. The scientist has become again an explorer in the Jules Verne sense. He retains the faint halo of madness which surrounded the ancient alchemist, bent on solving impossible tasks, surrounded by mysterious paraphernalia. Magic has always evoked distrust as well as awe.

There are two reasons for scientists to feel dissatisfied with the media. One is a sense that their activities and discoveries are neglected in the information sector, that the *real* importance (as news) of what they do is often not recognized. The other is the widespread caricature of the scientist in the entertainment sector. This reflects

his convenience as a symbol of offbeat nonconformity. He is a distinctive figure in a society where social types have faded into each
other in a loosening class structure, and in which pressure groups
are ready to rise in revolt if Peruvians, Tibetans, plumbers, Sunday
School teachers, or Legionnaires are treated by the mass media with
anything less than fitting dignity.

Dr. Strangelove is the lovable prototype of the perennial mad
scientist who has been part of our culture since the early days of the
comic strip and the horror movie. In more benign manifestations he
takes the form of the professorial dimwit or crank, or of the sinister
psychoanalyst. This kind of figure, however prevalent he may be in
the popular culture, is distinctly absent from the information (as
opposed to the entertainment) sector of the media, but the entertainment sector occupies a far greater share of the total mass media
experience, as defined by audience exposure.

In the treatment of science as a subject, individual media, and
media vehicles, differ very widely. The main form this treatment
takes is didactic, reviewing in the most simple, clear, and entertain-
ing manner possible, information which is common knowledge and
generally old hat to scientists in the specialty being covered.

Science is staple fare for the magazines, especially *Life*, which
has made it a magnificent and significant part of its editorial formula
since its inception. On television and in film, the scientific documentary is largely confined to the educational area, greatly restricted
as a percentage of total output, and even more restricted in audience. Most of the press and broadcast treatment of science news
comes straight from the wires of the press services. For the most
part it reflects spot reporting of breakthroughs and discoveries, usually in technological applications rather than in pure theory.

The prevailing attitude toward science on the part of the media
seems to be that it is an extremely difficult subject to make interesting to the mass public, despite its obvious importance. Palatability to
the average person is the standard by which potential content is generally judged, since all but specialized media strive constantly to
expand their audiences as much as they possibly can. When people
are offered the choice between entertainment and information, most
inevitably choose the former. Since most people do not retain daily

reported factual information (e.g., the name of the Senate majority leader), they are all the less likely to retain what are essentially abstract concepts.

The handling of scientific subjects may also be handicapped by a distorted notion of what public attitudes and expectations really are. Percy Tannenbaum has compared information and attitudes on mental illness for a sample of experts and a sample of the public.[1] He found quite a different picture in a content analysis of mass media (mostly magazine and TV) portrayals of mental illness. When he interviewed producers and writers of TV shows dealing with mental illness, he found their personal views on the subject to resemble those of the experts and of the general public. But when he inquired how they thought the mass audience typically would respond, he found assumptions which differed from the reality but jibed with the distorted portrayal in the media content. Tannenbaum concluded, "Giving the audience what it wants may or may not constitute a legitimate and equitable basis for regulating our cultural industries but the fact remains that if you are to operate by such a principle you should at least know what the public *does* want. In the mental health area, at least, the mass media gatekeeper may be badly mistaken."

Tannenbaum goes on to observe that people reading science news do not bring the same expectations to it that they do to general news content. "Because the specific science audience has not been differentiated from the gross audience, the same criteria have been used in selecting and handling science news and general news. While the 'exciting' may be an appropriate criterion for the selection of news stories about accidents, crime and economics (there is even some doubt about this), it is not a good basis for selecting science news."

The complexity of modern science, the vast flow of scholarly literature, the innumerable associations and meetings, the great number of significant personalities, the diverse sets of specialized vocabularies, terms and concepts—all these create a formidable obstacle to good coverage of the subject by the mass media.

Treatment of scientific developments as straight news is hindered because their timing and character are rarely newsy and because the media employ very few specialists qualified to appreciate and explain the importance of what scientists are saying at the moment they say it.

A science writer or editor must necessarily be a generalist, with the proper editorial judgment and writing skill. His knowledge of the sciences is likely to have been acquired on his assignment. He cannot possibly be technically proficient in all the fields he has to cover. It is simply impossible financially for even the biggest news-gathering organizations to retain the number of specialists required to provide full-scale professional treatment of all the major areas of science. The Science Writers Association, which includes free-lancers, book authors, and journalism teachers, as well as working journalists, has a total national membership of about 350. The Associated Press employs only two writers on its New York science desk, the United Press International one.

In the news media, priority always must go to *spot* news, to the things that are happening at the moment. Scientific news is rarely of this character, for it generally reflects the public utterance of results or inferences painstakingly arrived at and painfully considered before they are made public. Whatever importance a scientific paper or report may have, its timing is generally arbitrary, and no immediate consequences are contingent upon its release. It may be news because of *what* it is but rarely because of *when*.

In the news media, priority also goes to *hard* news, information which is confirmed and clear-cut. News editors are leary of rumors and speculations by people other than the commentators on their own staffs. This goes counter to the essential nature of science, in which conclusions must always be stated tentatively, in which theories are stated subject to confirmation by evidence, and in which evidence invokes a reexamination of past theory.

This interminable dialectic makes most scientific expressions cautious, hedged in by qualifying clauses, inevitably succeeding each discovery with new questions directed at a higher level of inquiry. To the layman, this aspect of the scientific attitude may appear ruminative, indecisive, not really important because it is not firm and definite.

Differences of Perspective

Everything said so far also applies to the behavioral sciences, which bear an additional burden insofar as the mass media are concerned. Their subject matter is one in which every man considers himself an expert: people and their motives; the groups and institutions in which they participate and which shape their lives. This is precisely the area which represents the central concern of the mass media, entertainment *and* informational. In fact, all creative literature can also be encompassed under this heading.

The behavioral sciences, the mass media, the modern novel were all spawned in the eighteenth century's age of enlightenment; all reflect the same dispassionate, questioning examination of the social order, the same preoccupation with the roots of the individual's humanity. Over the past two centuries all three have claimed jurisdiction over the same realm. The media practitioner's attitude toward behavioral science reflects not only his problems in dealing with science generically, but a more specific distrust of intruders into his own private domain of reporting what is of "human interest."

At many points the novelist, the playwright, the maker of dramatic films may stand closer in perspective to the social scientist than the straight reporter or documentarist. A film like *How Green Was My Valley* or *David and Lisa* may communicate social insights far more convincingly than any straightforward reportage on industrialization or schizophrenia.

Like the social scientist, the novelist or playwright is concerned with particular events insofar as they reveal essential truths about human beings and their relationships. The individual case may be far out. It may be highly idiosyncratic. Yet a work of fiction has merit only to the extent that it tells the reader or onlooker something important about his own human experience. Few novelists since Balzac have sought to emulate his self-conscious kind of clinical detachment from his characters. Yet the novelist, however personal or autobiographical his work may be, must be judged by his ability to penetrate into what is essential rather than merely interesting.

But this is also the historian's mission. Of all the fields of social science, history is hardest to distinguish from journalism. Historians and journalists are perhaps no different in their dedication to objectivity as an ideal. In both fields there is a distinction between the European tradition of marshaling evidence in support of a thesis and the empirical American tradition of "objectivity," of giving all possible interpretations.

The historian has more time than the working journalist to gather relevant material from more sources. He differs also in the time perspective he applies to the subject, and in the richness of precedents and parallels against which he can trace his chronicle. The insights he borrows from other social sciences help him understand the inner workings of institutions and social movements. But arbitrary classifications obscure reality. Where do we draw the lines between Max Weber the sociologist, Max Weber the historian, and Max Weber the political scientist?

Mass media create interest by focusing on individuals; the social sciences deal with individuals only as cases. Literature and drama communicate general truths about mankind through specific situations and heroes who arouse our sympathies and interests. One of the few atrocity stories reported in detail in the American press during World War II dealt with a group of Jewish girls who committed group suicide when they were placed in a Nazi brothel. This story was published because it dealt with individuals, at the same time that reports of mass murder in the tens of thousands were buried on the back pages, either because they were just statistics or because they were not "hard evidence."[2]

I think the distinction between the particular and the general is responsible for much of the neglect of social research by the mass media. The social sciences deal with large aggregates of people. They reduce social phenomena to statistics, which the editor or producer is apt to consider both a bore and something beyond his audience's depth. What the social scientist may regard as a generalization is to the mass media specialist an abstraction, and one which lacks the human interest which is the basic ingredient of his product.

Years ago, Gordon Allport distinguished between the "idiographic" and the "nomothetic" traditions in social science. The idiographic tradition is descriptive. It takes a particular example and tells us what's going on here. The nomothetic is necessarily comparative. It aims at laws or generalizations; it seeks to state theories and principles based on the comparison of many individual cases in which regularities can be observed. These two traditions are interwoven. The social scientist applies to his description of the individual case a knowledge of the relevant principles based on the past experience which leads to a general theory. Conversely, general theories are tested with each new case, so that the collection of cases is essential to the evolution and refinement of theory.

The journalist works wholly in the idiographic tradition. He takes each case as it comes and brings to it his best powers of description and interpretation. Since he commonly lacks both an interest in generalization and training in the technique of systematic comparison, his description of the individual case is not normally infused with the same insights or implications that it would have from the perspective of the social scientist who sees it as part of a recurring pattern.

I do not mean to suggest that the journalist's role is not analytical. But his capacities for analysis are bound to be limited by the absence of a theoretical structure which leads to a certain kind of question. (A good illustration of this was brought out in the course of the Arden House Conference. A news executive from one of the television networks reported on a project he had initiated on the occasion of the power blackout in New York City in November 1965. A group of people had been trapped in an elevator overnight. The idea was to interview them the following day in order to make a documentary feature. The reporters and camera crews went out, but they found that they simply didn't know what questions to ask. They asked questions like "How did you feel?" and "Didn't you get tired?" It did not occur to them to ask about how the individual members of the group related to each other, how they coped with the emergency, what tensions developed between what people, who took a position of leadership, and all the other questions which might occur to a social psychologist. Why hadn't the producer of the show asked for help from a very distinguished social psychologist employed by his own network in a nonprograming capacity? It just hadn't occurred to him! The expert was in another building, and he was typed as a specialist with entirely different professional functions.)

Who Is the Authority?

A willingness to use behavioral scientists as trained observers and to report what they do and say as news depends very much on the level of authority attributed to them. Thus substance and professional image are interrelated. *What* the social scientist says will be reported seriously to the degree that *he* is thought to be important.

Like his confreres in the natural sciences, the social scientist is concerned with the media portrait of himself, with the public relations of his discipline. Like them he is interested in the way the media report as *news* the professional activities and research reports in his field. He is concerned, like the natural scientists, both with the *accuracy* of reporting and with the *play* given to the things he considers important.

But the social scientist also confronts the mass media in another dimension. He must react to some significant part of mass media information content with the feeling that *he* is a trained expert on the subjects being treated. As an expert, he cannot help but be dissatisfied most of the time with the job nonexperts do.

Unlike many fields of endeavor with which the larger society is in direct daily contact, the mass media are the principal means by which the public at large gets its impression of social scientists and what they do. The prevailing climate of acceptance, prestige, tolerance, and understanding of the social sciences is for better or worse profoundly affected by the way they are handled in the mass media. This in turn is reflected in the degree of influence exercised by social scientists over decision-making in government and business.

The social scientist is perennially piqued by the intrusion of what he considers "amateurs" onto his professional terrain. He is pained by the popularizing and simplification of subjects to whose study, in all their complexity, he is dedicated. In the academic community, specialized preserves are jealously guarded from other departments and rival colleagues. How much more important to defend them from the laity! Newsmen may represent the one occupational group from which social scientists may expect not only no deference, but *consistently* irreverent treatment. Such irreverence is, after all, what newsmen are trained to show in their inquiries. This hits the peculiar sensibility of social scientists because of their own historical uncertainty as to whether what they do is science merely because they may use the methods of science.

Must we draw a sharp line of distinction between a reporter like Theodore White when he covers the news on a daily basis and when he covers it retrospectively as history in *The Making of a President*? Is *The Making of a President* to be considered less creditable history than *A Thousand Days* because Schlesinger is a professor and White is not?

It goes without saying that some of the most effective social analysis being written today comes from people without academic position or a university teaching background. Jane Jacobs is a mightier figure in the field of urban sociology than many urban sociologists with official standing in the fraternity.

Academic credentials are irrelevant in the case of well-read professional writers who go out and do field work as William H. Whyte did in his *Organization Man*, or as Joseph Lyford has more recently done in his study of Manhattan's West Side.[3]

Not only the field of history, but all the social sciences have perennially shared with journalism and borrowed from it. This was true of the theoretician Karl Marx and of the muckrakers whose interest in social reform and social work began the tradition of empirical social surveys in the United States. When Jacob Riis shocked the burghers of New York with his accounts of *How the Other Half Lives*, he was fulfilling the journalist's role of dramatizing the commonplace, but he was also in the headwaters of what became a main stream of sociology.

In this tradition Robert Park the journalist became Robert Park the sociologist, sending his students forth to study the gang, the ghetto, the gold coast, and slum. Park is perhaps the most notable case of a reporter who went on to get a social science Ph.D., but there have been a number of others.

There are remarkably few cases of reverse migration, although David Riesman has been on the cover of *Time*, and distinguished social scientists occasionally write an article for the Sunday supplements. A psychologist, Albert Wiggam, wrote a cartoon feature, "Explore Your Mind," which generally appeared on the funny pages. A nonmember of the American Psychological Association went from successful appearances as a contestant on "The $64,000 Question" to a TV program of her own. In the same spirit of dedication, Dr. Rose Franzblau has applied psychology to relieve the emotional suffering of New York *Post* readers. The TV program "Feedback," originated by the late Gary Steiner in Chicago, invites the audience to participate in an opinion survey in the form of a game. Max Lerner and, briefly, Arthur Schlesinger, Jr., became political columnists.

But Lerner, Leo Rosten of *Look,* and Harry Schwartz of the *New York Times* represent the very rare cases of social scientists who make their living on the editorial side of the mass media.[4]

Areas of Contact

It is harder and harder for a generalist to be competent in all the subspecialties of social science. And it is inconceivable that any media organization might be able to employ people who are at home in all of these professional fields and who at the same time have editorial skills and the common touch. Reporters are commonly required to cover anything from a fire to a civic meeting. It is asking a lot to expect them to be trained in the social sciences too.

To an extraordinary degree decision-making in American mass media is centralized in the Radio City area. Here the control is exercised over the content of the big magazines and of the news that is sent over the national wire services and the network news services. But the final shape of the news is controlled at the local level. It does no good for a story to go out over the wire services if it is not picked up and played prominently by local newspapers or broadcasting stations.

At the local level, the gatekeepers who decide what news to admit are not likely to be qualified in the social sciences. The essence of any news operation is speed, which means that the newsman's judgments must be made instinctively, fast, and normally without consulting the previous literature on the subject. Moreover, there is almost never just one gatekeeper, any more than there is just one source of raw copy—so the possibilities of uninformed treatment are high even when specialists are around.

And at the local level the newsman's contacts with the social sciences are typified by the professor of sociology or psychology at the local teachers college, junior college, or agricultural college, who may be hard to accept as an authoritative figure.

To the extent that the mass media practitioner is at all knowledgeable about social scientists, his criticism boils down to complaints about the big words that they use, the pretentiousness with which they apply jargon to everyday common-sense ideas and phenomena, and the trivia with which they characteristically occupy themselves in their academic research projects.

The May 1966 issue of the *American Sociologist* carried an interesting report on press coverage of the 1965 sociology meetings in Chicago, by Charles E. Higbie and Phillip E. Hammond. They point out that reporters are handicapped in covering a conference because they are working against a time deadline. The implication is that a reporter ought to cover all the hundreds of papers delivered at the convention on the very day they are read!

Higbie and Hammond observe that the reporters did not spend much time

. . . deploring the lack of involvement of the convention sociologists with their times: in fact they seemed to expect this of professors. Instead the newsmen quite cheerfully tried to make the application from the material to current events in their own pragmatic ways. . . . When sociologists did not mention such applications themselves they were invited and in fact directly asked to do so by reporters. In other words the sociologists seemed to feel that somebody should be making direct application to ongoing problems of the many thoughts, theories and data about society but seemed quite surprised and in some cases displeased if the reporters did so when they themselves did not. On the other hand reporters cheerfully accepted noninvolvement on the part of sociologists, but then seemed very surprised when sociologists resented the reporters' attempts to ask questions that would result in sociological material being introduced on the scales of judgment about headline news.

The authors offer some excellent specific suggestions for the handling of convention reports, but they do not question the notion that the primary concern of the mass media with the social sciences must be in spot news reporting of papers at scholarly meetings.

By and large, the mass media have had a most creditable record in illuminating social problems. They have been highly instrumental in changing the public reaction to psychological disorder from ridicule or aversion into acceptance as a curable form of illness. They have been extremely influential in creating widespread awareness of the racial revolution in the United States, especially in destroying the white majority's myth that Negroes *wanted* segregation. The media have focused attention on such problems as urban decay and poverty, both urban and rural.

First, the picture magazines and then, more powerfully, television have given a sense of vivid immediacy to the drama of human beings in crisis, wherever they may be. The faces and voices of people troubled by disaster or civic disorder in remote places are brought to the mass audience intimately, as those of fellow members of the same community, and thus what might have been purely local events a generation ago are transformed into a national experience.

The day-to-day record of news events is quite different from the background story or interpretative article into which social science insights may be infused. In live news coverage of big events by television, the audience often has an illusion of seeing events as they really happen, even though these are actually transmuted by the cameraman or the director. But it is only the occasional big story (a political convention or space launching) that gets this kind of coverage. With electronic media supplying the fast headline summaries of the news, the press must be encyclopedic in covering a tremendous amount and variety of information each day. At the same time, it carries a far greater load of background analysis. This makes it more vulnerable to criticism by social scientists.

It might be well to state explicitly the ways in which the content of the various media falls within the social scientist's sphere of interest.

A large percentage of straight news, as handled by newspapers, the wire services, and radio and television newscasts, bears on areas like social movements, propaganda, and a host of other subjects to which one or another specialty of the social sciences devotes systematic attention.

The area of mutual interest extends beyond the mere reporting of events to the area of interpretation. In the case of newspapers and magazines, this takes the form of feature articles, picture stories, by-line columns, interpretive news stories, and the like. In radio and television, it finds its way into the utterances of news commentators.

Since the tendency has been more and more for social research to become a collective project requiring large resources and large budgets, it is only inevitable that the federal government has become a major source of support. The combination of bigness and government support often adds up to an inherent newsworthiness, particularly if a research project becomes a subject of political controversy, as in the case of Project Camelot.

The handling of the Moynihan Report on the Negro illustrates how much the treatment of ideas from social science depends on timing and on the personality to whom they are attributed. Moynihan's basic conclusions regarding the instability of Negro family structure have long been common knowledge among social scientists. Why did this become news when Moynihan said it and not when Myrdal and Rose said the same thing twenty years earlier? The report was highly topical in the current climate of racial upheaval and Moynihan was himself a political figure. Moreover, the illusion was created that the administration was sitting on the report because of its controversial aspects. From the standpoint of news interest and play, the substance of the report was subordinated to the conflict of personalities and groups over its merits and the wisdom of releasing it.

Print media content of interest to social scientists goes beyond the realm of current events or topical news for the day or week of publication. The women's magazines have long dealt at length with such subjects as marital counseling, child rearing, mental health, job satisfaction, the problems of working women, family guidance, and other matters of concern to the sociologist and social psychologist. The big picture magazines have made a staple of photographic

documentary stories on social and political problems. But less than
1 per cent of the content of *Life, Look*, the *Post, McCall's*, the
Journal, and *Good Housekeeping* falls within the span of "sociology," as defined very, very broadly in the continuing content analyses made by the Lloyd Hall organization.

The radio, television, and film documentary form is one which
extends the interpretive treatment in print to the live recording of
scenes and voices. From its earliest beginnings the documentary
veered away from straight news reporting, not in the direction of
scholarly analysis but by dramatizing its subject matter. This is
done both to permit the documentarist to penetrate to what he perceives as the heart of the matter and also to make his product fit
into an entertainment context.

By his timing, by the juxtaposition of sequences, by montage,
by the splicing of tape, the use of close-ups, the selection of protagonists to represent points of view, the director of the documentary distinguishes good guys and bad guys, and introduces dramatic
tension into what might seem dull if it were reported straight. The
classical example of this is Edward R. Murrow's famous documentary on Senator McCarthy. Kurt and Gladys Lang, in their brilliant
description of "MacArthur Day in Chicago," contrast the dull reality of this event with the highly charged representation of it which
emerged on TV.[5]

As William Bluem points out in his fine book on the television
documentary,[6] the documentarist must often reenact reality to
sharpen an effect or to express an essential truth. In the radio documentary, he used paid actors to simulate the voices of real people.
In the television documentary, the real personalities may be used,
but as "performers," after the event.

Radio and television add an additional dimension in their use
of the symposium, discussion, or interview program as a device for
getting authorities to apply their special knowledge to a subject on
a spur-of-the-moment basis. (In many cases, such programs, like
the late night interviews made by reformed disc jockeys, use experts
only for their entertainment value, and juxtapose them with colorful
eccentrics and retired burlesque queens.)

Discussion programs or interviews featuring social scientists are common fare in educational broadcasting, where they are used as a pedagogical device, a pseudolecture in the form of a dialogue. On network television, such programs have the unique capacity to make news when important people participate in them, but social scientists are not commonly among them.

On Misusing Surveys

Up to this point, I have tried to suggest that the problems of the social sciences with the mass media are to a large degree those of the sciences generally, but that the social sciences also face special difficulties because their subject matter appears to fall within the area of common sense, and is in practice hard to differentiate clearly from the sphere of the working journalist. To the extent that the social scientist relies on personal observation and insight, it is also hard to differentiate his methodology from the practices of the intelligent reporter.

Social scientists vary greatly in professional competence. They differ in their professional opinions and even more when they sound off on nonprofessional matters. How can a layman judge when the social scientist speaks *ex cathedra* from evidence, when he speaks interpretively from experience or judgment, and when he speaks merely through his hat? If social scientists themselves have no universally acceptable criteria for differentiating truth from mere opinion, it seems futile to try to fix boundary lines between social science and journalism.

The area of greatest conflict between social scientists and the mass media arises precisely at the point where the journalist departs from his personal observation and reportage and tries to be systematic in putting his evidence together. In doing so he is likely to use terms which the professional social scientist considers his own preserve (like "survey," "poll," "sample," and "public opinion"), but he often uses them in a nonprofessional way. (The journalist uses these terms in a long tradition; "survey" and "public opinion" were part of his lexicon long before professional pollsters arrived on the scene.)

The critical point in the relation of journalists and behavioral scientists is the point where evidence is quantified. The social scientist is pained when the journalist makes inferences and interpretations from inadequate and biased samples, and from improperly conducted interviews. But there are also problems on the other side. The media practitioner's hostility or skepticism about the social sciences often arises because he identifies them with the survey method. This has three strikes against it, in his view.

1. Surveys are identified with the business office, the hereditary enemy.
2. Surveys are identified with political polling.
3. Surveys are identified with the art of asking questions, which is every reporter's stock in trade.

Let me take up these three points in turn. The principal use of social sciences by the mass media is on the business side, to assist in developing the audience figures that are essential to the promotion and sale of advertising. Enormous sums of money are expended on this, and a great many research technicians are employed by media or by organizations which sell their services to media for this purpose.

People on the editorial side of publications and the production side of broadcasting are engaged in constant warfare with those who supply the statistics by which their own efforts are judged.

Editors commonly resist being "starched." They don't want people from the business office telling them what to put in or leave out, even on the grounds that it's going to build circulation.

In broadcasting, those in program production commonly live in hate and terror of the ratings which determine the life or death of programs.

The media practitioner refuses to believe that his seasoned qualitative judgment of audience interest, involvement, and participation can be outweighed by a set of mere statistics, whose validity he is constantly encouraged to question.

The inherent conflict of professionalism and the business attitude was dramatized by the rift, early in 1966, between Fred Friendly of CBS News and John Schneider, the TV network's new president, over the televising of the congressional hearings on Vietnam. When the network dropped a rebroadcast of "The Lucy Show" to put on the hearings, its share of audience dropped substantially. When "The Lucy Show" returned, the ratings went back up.

That bad programs drive out the good seems to be an inexorable law of broadcast management. In the life of the average viewer an hour spent watching a rerun of "Lucy" may be indistinguishable from countless similar hours, and an hour spent watching Ambassador Kennan may be a unique experience, but a specialist in broadcast ratings would not ordinarily feel it necessary to point out this distinction to a sponsor, or to a network president. Yet it is the ratings specialist who represents "research," and by inference, the social sciences, to the broadcasting industry.

In the occasional fiction which deals with the advertising or broadcasting worlds, the research specialist is commonly shown as a statistician, calculator or slide rule at hand, cold, mechanical, smug, uninterested in the more subtle meanings that lie behind his numbers.

After his Flying Survey Squad took samplings from the bedrock opinion in a half-dozen representative states, and from the many strata representing income, race, religion, geography, sex and indefinitely so on, Schmucker put the samplings into a battery of electronic calculating machines which sorted, counted and analyzed the stuff. Then Schmucker knew. He *knew*.[7]

The point, of course, is that Schmucker doesn't *really* know in the sense that the free creative spirit does.

The same feeling that the social scientist is a pseudoscientist arises in regard to political polls, which many newsmen seem to regard with a strange mixture of fascination and loathing. The newsman considers political analysis to be his own particular specialty and doesn't like anyone muscling in on his territory.

Preelection polls are often considered presumptuous, predicting events that have not yet occurred and which it is the journalist's function to report when they *do* occur. This underlies the glee of the editorialist at the polls' occasional failures, which are then rationalized into the objection that they are inaccurate as well as presumptuous. This position is all the easier to maintain when the newsman is himself ignorant of the criteria by which valid polls can be distinguished from phony ones. Newspapers and magazines have for many years used syndicated columns by professional pollsters like Roper, Gallup, and Harris, or such regional organizations as the California, Texas, Iowa, and Minnesota polls. But polls that are run by journalists themselves, without professional help, are sometimes notoriously amateurish and unreliable.

To many newsmen, taking a survey means going around asking people questions. This they regard as the essence of any good reporter's skill. A reporter covering a story talks to people who seem to be informed or who witnessed an event. From an October 5, 1966, report in the *New York Times*[8] dealing with the gubernatorial race in Pennsylvania comes the following paragraph:

Random interviews with 20 persons on the street here disclosed that, in this small sampling, more than half thought Mr. Shapp's Jewishness was a factor in the strong "anti" feeling among the voters disclosed by polls. Asked if they would vote for Mr. Shapp, one man replied "Do I look Jewish?" and another said "How much will he pay me?"

Reporters eliciting opinions generally are unsystematic, both with respect to whom they talk to and to the questions they ask. Yet the words "poll" and "survey" are commonly applied to this practice.

On February 3, 1966, the *New York Times* devoted a front-page story continued over an entire inside page headed, "Wide Support Found in Nation for Renewed Vietnam Bombing." The authority for this was a "spot check" in which ten staff correspondents interviewed state and local officials, professionals and businessmen, editors, students, and others on opinion in their communities. "The results reflect a broad trend although they do not purport to be scientific," the article says, leaving the reader to wonder how a broad trend can be detected by unscientific means.

It goes on with generalizations like these: "Opinion across the nation appears to be in general agreement with the exception of the South." At another point the statement occurs, "The *prevailing national mood* [sic!] was summed up by a Methodist minister in Madison, Wisconsin, the Reverend J. Elsworth Kalas. 'I think the people as a whole support the resumption of bombing but with a troubled conscience.' " (The use of a single quotation to represent a mass position is not infrequently used by professional pollsters who want to enliven their statistical reports.)

The social scientist who cringes at this kind of haphazard treatment of life and death matters is certainly no happier with the trend studies of President Johnson's political popularity or the hawk-dove division on Vietnam.

An article carried by the *New York Times* on July 30, 1965, starts out with the lead "A nationwide public opinion poll taken hourly on Wednesday after President Johnson's news conference on Vietnam showed a shift from overwhelming endorsement of the President's actions to an endorsement tempered by a heavy 'I don't know' trend." According to Albert Sindlinger, who was commissioned to do the study, the 993 persons interviewed were "as reliable and representative as any sample can be."

Here is how the essential findings were given: "The first hour's results showed 54.23% of those interviewed in agreement with the President's actions, 23.55% in disagreement, 22.22% in the don't know category. In the sixth and final hour those in agreement had dropped to 46.97% and the disagreement group had dropped to 9.77%, but the don't know group had climbed to 43.26%." Each hourly sample consisted of about 160 people on the average, of whom somewhat over 100 knew about the press conference. The proportions of men and women interviewed changed substantially over the interview period. In short, a trained survey analyst might make a very different story out of this than the one which appeared, complete with two figures beyond the decimal point.

To the social scientist, opinions on matters as complex as Vietnam cannot be intelligently discussed in terms of "for" or "against." But who is to provide this kind of sensitive interpretation? News media pride themselves on their experienced political reporters who are experts at analyzing and interpreting the public temper. Is a seasoned Washington correspondent less well qualified than an academic political scientist to gauge the mood of the American people? The answer must be specific. Which Washington correspondent? Which political scientist?

Mass media attention to opinion surveys is often coupled with a total absence of professional judgment as to their significance or adequacy. Bad surveys and good surveys are given equal space as though they were to be equated in the reader's judgment, and their failure to agree may be cited as evidence of polls' inherent limitations.

Every day the journalist encounters the question of what is the truth. On the same day, a front-page story in the *New York Times* read, "300 Vietnam GI's Saved After 24-Hour Mauling," and on page 14 of the New York *Herald Tribune* the same dispatch appeared under the headline, "U.S. Cavalrymen Track Down Elusive Guerillas, Kill 159, Many Wounded on Both Sides."

The newsman is accustomed to this confrontation of opposing viewpoints in the interpretation of events. It is therefore quite logical for him to assume that a similar clash of opposing viewpoints on the part of different "polls" also represents merely a difference of interpretation.

In the fall of 1965, the American Association for Public Opinion Research formally objected to the use of street-corner interviewing by a newspaper which devoted enormous attention to a preelection survey, giving percentage figures on a district-by-district basis. The editors defended themselves by pointing out that this was not a scientific public opinion survey but merely a "straw poll"—as though the ordinary reader knows the distinction.

It is symptomatic of the low esteem in which media people hold the research fraternity that when the AAPOR Executive Council issued a statement condemning street-corner election polls it received no attention by any newspaper or news magazine. Obviously, editors see the whole matter as technical and academic, even though there are obviously important political news implications to a candidate's position in public favor, or to the state of public opinion on any important issue.

The solution—if there is one—to the problems I have raised

will not be found by arranging a better press room at meetings of
the American Sociological Association, or by adding a course in
sociology to the journalism school curriculum.

The need to apply social science knowledge and insights has
never been greater. We face crises today in race relations, in urban-
ism, in the creation of international order, in the planning of social
and economic development for the impoverished areas of the
world. On all of these subjects, which are the basis of the news each
day, there is a challenge to social scientists who claim expert jurisdiction over them.

The mass media, like any other conservative established institution, will not change their ways voluntarily. They must be goaded,
pressured, educated, and convinced. This does not happen by itself,
or as a result of isolated individual gestures. It will not happen, in
my opinion, until social scientists become much more concerned
than they are today about the action consequences of their studies,
about the uses of their knowledge.

---

1. Percy H. Tannenbaum, "Communication of Science Information," *Science*, Vol. 140 (May 19, 1963), pp. 579–583.

2. One need not look very far back into history to find examples of this.
On October 17, 1966, the *New York Times*, in a two-inch item at the bottom of
page 34, reported the death of 2,000 Brazilians in a malaria epidemic.

3. *The Airtight Cage*, New York: Harper and Row, 1966.

4. I am not extending this to include the field of economics. Professional
economists employed on the editorial side of newspapers are primarily involved
in finance or business economics rather than in pure economic research. A
great deal of economic news reporting both by the wire services and by newspapers is actually based on press releases from government agencies and business associations.

5. Kurt and Gladys Lang, "The Unique Perspective of Television," *American Sociological Review*, Vol. 18, No. 1 (February 1953), pp. 3–12.

6. A. William Bluem, *Documentary in American Television*, New York:
Hastings House, 1965.

7. John G. Schneider, *The Golden Kazoo*, New York: Rinehart & Company, 1956, p. 78.

8. Needless to say, I have been able to pick this and other horrible examples from newspapers only because newspapers carry vastly more information
than other media and vastly more information of social science interest. And
it is possible to pick on the *Times* only because it publishes more news and because our expectations of it are so high.

10
**Barriers to Communication:
The Problem of Jargon**

Ernest Havemann
WRITER

One of the dictionary meanings of *jargon* is perfectly straightforward and respectable; the word is defined simply as the technical vocabulary of a science or profession. The word is seldom used this way; it is almost always used pejoratively, and I am sure that the sponsors of this conference used it pejoratively when they asked us to address ourselves to its role in the behavioral sciences. However, I think we can profit from putting aside our semantic habits for a moment and talking about jargon merely as technical vocabulary, and not necessarily as gobbledygook or gibberish.

How much jargon—as technical vocabulary—do we really find in the writings of the behavioral scientists? I have a psychology textbook here on my desk, one that is recognized as more complete and difficult than most. I look through the table of contents and find such chapter headings as "Growth and Development," "Motivation," "Emotion," "Perception," "Learning," "Remembering and Forgetting," "Heredity and Environment," "Thinking," "Personality," "Conflict," "Adjustment." I open one of the classic textbooks on the family used by advanced and graduate students in sociology and find that it is divided into sections called "Nature and Origins of the Family," "Social Changes and the Family," "Life Cycle and Family Experience," "Crises and Family Organization." None of these words is exactly unfamiliar or esoteric. They are all good, common, everyday words at which no journalist, no matter how dedicated to keeping his prose simple enough for the man in the street, should boggle.

Now of course the behavioral scientists do use jargon. If they did not, we would have to worry about them. The growth of science and indeed of civilization must of necessity involve an increasingly rich jargon. We add new words to the English language every year; when we stop adding them, we will have stopped adding to our knowledge. Some of the most interesting recent findings of the behavioral scientists, as a matter of fact, concern the importance of language as the essential tool in human thinking. When we have a word for something—a good, sharp, precise word—we can perceive that something better. It has been found that we recognize it and remember it more easily. Thus societies coin words for the things that are important to them.. The Eskimos, to whom snow is important, have three words for snow. One of the Philippine tribes has 92 different words for rice. On the other hand, there is an African tribe that has only two words for all the colors of the rainbow, one describing everything at the blue-green end of the spectrum, the other lumping together all the colors at the red-orange end. We can imagine what would happen if an American cosmetics manufacturer tried to open a factory there and operate it with native labor.

So of course the behavioral scientists use jargon. But let us also examine the products of journalism for signs of jargon, still using the word without prejudice. On the front page of almost every newspaper almost every day, we find words like *reconnaissance, logistics, interdict, infiltration.* Up to the time of World War II, these were all unfamiliar words. They would have stumped the man in the street. Journalists, if they knew them, avoided their use. Now they are a standard part of the journalistic vocabulary. On the financial pages, we find words like *preferred, common, yield, discount rate, prime rate, debenture,* and *convertible debenture,* not to mention *subordinated debenture.* All highly technical words, unfamiliar to most Americans until the recent bull market (another technical term) got under way.

Or take a look at the sports page. Many phrases known to every American schoolboy and taken for granted by the least pretentious of sports writers are jargon in the sense that we are now using the word *jargon;* among them are *strike, ball, home run, double play.* But on top of these old and familiar jargon terms has been piled an increasingly complicated new vocabulary invented quite recently—in football, *red dog, blitz, cornerback, draw play, line-*

backer, flat; and in basketball, *post, turnover, one and one.* This new jargon has developed, at least in part, out of necessity. Football and basketball are much more scientific sports today than they were when most of us were watching our college teams, and they cannot be discussed without an enriched and more technical vocabulary. Moreover, sports writers seem to like to throw a little jargon around to prove that they are just as erudite as the more highbrow correspondents. I was listening recently to a television sports commentator discuss that lowbrow pastime called prizefighting—and heard him say "ancillary revenue," leading me to fear for a moment that I had tuned to "Wall Street Final" by mistake.

Many other examples could be cited, in many other fields such as the reporting of the law, medicine, and even women's fashions. The point is that modern journalism, without blinking an eye, without feeling the least bit self-conscious or worrying in the slightest about alienating its readers, uses tremendous amounts of jargon. The modern man in the street is not offended by this jargon; quite on the contrary, he apparently understands it perfectly and indeed relishes it.

Let us now abandon this exploration of jargon as technical vocabulary and return to the everyday or pejorative meaning. I think we can fairly define the word as follows: *Jargon (in the sense of gobbledygook and gibberish) is any terminology that we have not bothered to learn.* When a journalist accuses the behavioral scientists of an addiction to jargon, he is really saying only that they use words whose meaning he has not yet tried to understand. When an editor says that he avoids running stories on the behavioral sciences because his readers resent the jargon, he is really saying only that he has not educated his readers in the meaning of behavioral terminology to the same extent that he has educated them in the meaning of *interdict, debenture,* and *red dog.* In fact I have a feeling that editors might be surprised to discover how much of the jargon of the behavioral sciences is already more familiar to their readers, particularly younger readers, than it is to them and to their writers. In a nation where there are more than five million college students, most of whom take at least some kind of course in behavioral science, the terminology cannot be completely arcane.

At any rate, the discussion of jargon leads us to a rather strange

conclusion. For some reason, journalism condemns as jargon a vocabulary of the behavioral sciences that is surely not very much
more specialized and complex, if at all, than other vocabularies
that journalism has enthusiastically adopted and helped to popu-
larize. Why should this be?

The answer is not easy to find. But we can certainly say with
confidence that one thing is *not* the answer; we know beyond doubt
that journalism does not dislike the subject matter of the behavioral
sciences. What does journalism report on? With what does it fill
the columns of its newspapers and the pages of its magazines? The
answer is human behavior. Does journalism confine itself merely to
reporting the bare facts about specific items of behavior? No, it
does not. A substantial part of its effort is devoted to interpreting
behavior and making recommendations. In one morning paper I found advice on how to avoid heart attacks, how to protect
my children from allergies, how to behave when introduced to the
friend of a friend, how to patch up a quarrel with my wife, how to
save money on my income tax, how to make sure I will receive
Medicare, and what kind of perfume to buy my wife for Valentine's
Day, as well as several editorials that told me what to think about
the New York State lottery and Section 14-B, plus a horoscope
that warned me, as a Taurus, not to put too much faith in promises
until the stroke of midnight. My wife read advice on how to
choose her spring suit, build a new room in the unlikely event
that we should be confronted with a small child, do her shopping,
plan her week's menu, cook tonight's dinner, and crochet an orna-
ment for the dining-room table, as well as the warning that she, as
an astrological Leo, should beware of any interference by influential friends into her domestic arrangements, whatever that might
mean.

Thumbing through the contents pages of the magazines at the
local library—just the top magazines, not the cheap ones—I find
these titles: "What Famous Men Find Sexy in Women," "When Is a
Man Remarriageable?" "How to Get Over a Love Affair," "Why
Men Don't Listen or Talk to their Wives," "Breathe Right and Stay
Well," "How to Live with a Woman," "Why Good Parents Have

Problem Children," "Leisure and the Split Man," and "How Good is Your Mental Health?" The only thing unusual about the list is that by accident it does not cover that perennially popular magazine subject represented by past titles like "The Drinking Man's Diet" and "How to Lose Twenty Pounds Without Feeling Hungry."

Perhaps it is important to note that the newspaper stories I have mentioned, and the magazine articles as well, were not written by behavioral scientists. They were written by professional journalists, often without any advice or counsel at all from a behavioral scientist or a scientist's book. Journalism has its own experts on behavior. On psychology and sociology it has Helen Gurley Brown and Betty Friedan. On marriage and the family it has Dear Abby and Ann Landers. On mental health it has had a long succession of experts going all the way back to Walter Pitkin of *Life Begins at Forty,* in my earliest memory, and doubtless to others before that.

Here, I think, we come to the crux of the disagreements and misunderstandings that block communications between journalists and behavioral scientists. To the scientists, articles with titles like those I have mentioned, and the opinions of a Dear Abby or a Walter Pitkin, are totally ridiculous—unfounded in fact, misleading, and, because they present an overly simplified and rosy view of the solutions to human problems, downright dangerous. To many editors, the findings of the behavioral scientists are dull, inconclusive, pessimistic, and therefore unsalable. The copy in the horoscopes and in Betty Friedan is more glamorous; it has more sex appeal; it swings; it is what the readers want.

In this quarrel, I tend to sympathize with both sides. Let me speak as a journalist first, then as a friend of the behavioral sciences.

Journalism, unfortunately, is not blessed with the kind of independence and autonomy that the behavioral sciences enjoy. The scientist can perform his life's work without any concessions at all to public opinion; he can stay in business even if no one is listening to him but the captive audience in his classrooms and a few colleagues who read the books he publishes with the help of a subsidized university press. But the journalist ceases to be a journalist if he cannot find an editor to print his product, and the editor soon ceases to be an editor unless the product finds an audience that is willing to pay for it.

The history of journalism in America is littered with the wreckage of newspapers and magazines that were admired by professional journalists—and often by scientists and other intellectuals as well —yet did not sell enough copies to stay out of bankruptcy. In many commendable ways journalism serves as the leading edge of public education. Most editors sincerely want to improve their product and advance the level of public taste. Many of them have taken substantial risks in this direction. But we cannot ask them to go too far; we cannot expect them to commit professional suicide. Like politicians, they have to keep a finger in the wind—and we should encourage them in this, for the bankrupt magazine is of no more service to society than is the high-minded but badly defeated candidate.

The dependency of journalism on public acceptance sometimes has such unfortunate results that many people refuse to believe it; so let me emphasize it with an example. Many intellectuals living in the smaller cities of the nation complain bitterly that the local newspaper is not a *New York Times*. The reason is that even out of the 15 million people in the New York City area there are only about 700,000 a day willing to pay ten cents for the *Times*. In a metropolitan area of one million, like Cincinnati or Dallas, a paper like the *Times* presumably would have a circulation under 50,000 and go broke the first week. The *Times*'s own West Coast edition, you will remember, was a financial failure and had to be abandoned. Though we tend to forget it, newspapers and magazines face the same sort of dilemma that is so much more dramatically apparent in the case of television, which cannot simultaneously please Jack Gould and the millions of people who like to watch "Peyton Place" or "Green Acres."

The journalist has to go along with his public—or at least cannot get so far ahead of the public as to vanish out of sight. Thus it is very easy for an editor to prefer the opinions on sex of Helen Gurley Brown to those of Dr. Paul Gebhard, and the opinions on marriage of Dear Abby to those of Dr. Clifford Kirkpatrick. Mrs. Brown and Dear Abby offer quick and easy solutions. They promise

results. They and the other nonscientific "experts" can offer Ten
Easy Rules to be glamorous, find happiness, succeed at marriage,
stop worrying, win friends, live longer, and if necessary lose weight.
The behavioral scientists cannot offer the Ten Easy Rules, because
the Ten Easy Rules do not exist in fact and have to be made up. All
that Dr. Gebhard can offer, in the final analysis, is the rather melan-
choly observation that sex has been a considerable problem for most
people; and all that Dr. Kirkpatrick can offer is the suggestion that
if you work hard enough, and have chosen wisely to begin with,
you may be able to make your marriage go fairly smoothly a fairly
large part of the time. According to a long-standing journalistic
theory—backed, I presume, by some market research—this is hardly
what the public wants to hear.

All of us, even the behavioral scientists, would like to find solutions to our problems—and the faster and less laborious the solutions the better. If you were a young housewife who discovered in
the springtime that you could no longer fit into last year's bathing
suit (a happenstance which is in fact the inspiration for most diet-
ing), would you rather read about a new diet guaranteed to take off
ten pounds in ten days—or about the well-documented discovery of
the psychiatrically oriented physicians who have specialized in
weight problems that out of a hundred people who try to lose weight
only two of them have any real and lasting success? Perhaps many
of us here at this conference would find the physicians' article rather
comforting. It is the opinion of most editors that the average young
housewife would not.

The behavioral scientists, on the other hand, certainly have every right to complain that journalism still continues to foster super-
stition about human affairs in an age when every well-educated
and responsible person should know better. In a sense, journalism's
attitude is what the scientists would call a culture lag. It is a tradition that goes back to the days before there were any behavioral
scientists—when the journalist's opinions on human behavior were
as good as anybody's, and when the opinions of superjournalists
like Dostoevski and Will Rogers were better than anybody else's.
There has always been a Helen Gurley Brown. If an editor did not
have one, he created one. He had to, because, in bygone days, there

was no one else to satisfy the public demand for discussion of human behavior—a demand that goes back to the Delphic oracle and before that to even more primitive soothsayers and witch doctors.

From any kind of logical view, the day of the old-fashioned personal journalist should now be over. The behavioral scientists now have the facts—not all the facts, of course, but at least an impressive start on the collection—and one of their clearest and firmest findings is that most of the notions about human behavior held by the layman are largely incorrect. The personal journalist, with nothing to offer but opinions based on his own limited experiences, frequently distorted by the neuroticism that seems endemic among us writing people, should have disappeared.

Certainly some of the personal journalism is clearly dangerous. Mrs. Brown's magazine recently recommended flatly that every young woman should treat herself to the excitement and glamor of an affair before settling down to the humdrum of marriage. If Mrs. Brown wants to argue that there is nothing immoral about the premarital affair, that is her business. If she wants to argue that marriage is a drab kind of existence compared to the thrill of unmarried sex, that is still perhaps her business, though it does tend to undermine one of the pillars of our society. But I do not believe there is any way that we fellow journalists can defend Mrs. Brown against one accusation that behavioral science can level at her. Mrs. Brown ignores all individual differences in upbringing, moral teachings, and the learned standards of behavior which have such profound influences on our lives. Any impressionable young woman who took Mrs. Brown's advice—in contradiction to her own inner standards and rules—might very well find herself filled with anxiety and depression for the rest of her life.

Dear Abby, I suppose, is less dangerous. She is a fine professional humorist, and I myself read her every day without fail, for the laughs. I have known sociologists who feel, indeed, that Dear Abby renders a sort of service—as a channel for disseminating some of the prevailing ideas of our society relating to social behavior and conduct in marriage and toward children—that outweighs any harm she might do if somebody took her advice too seriously. But even Dear Abby is bad for human progress because there is a variation on the theme of Gresham's law at work here. Dear Abby takes up the space and dulls the appetite that might otherwise be reserved for a more solid kind of discussion. Just as the bad money drives out the good, the pseudoscience drives out the real behavioral science.

I believe there is a lot to be said on both sides. This is not an easy quarrel to resolve. But I do think things are getting better. It was not very long ago that journalism ignored the behavioral scientists almost completely, and printed nothing but the pseudoscience. *Collier's Magazine*, for example, though it had a good reputation in its day, was full of slipshod articles on social and political problems, highly opinionated and skimpy on fact, and tended to embrace every dubious medical expert who came along with a new surefire cure for a complicated ailment like headache or backache. Today we still have the Mrs. Browns and the Dear Abbys and the Betty Friedans; but we also have an increasing number of journalists who go to the behavioral scientists, report their findings and opinions with a fair amount of accuracy, and still get their stories published. Also an increasing number of editors expect this kind of reporting—at least from the working "stiffs" if not from the columnists and the personalities.

My own feeling is that journalism is discovering that the findings of the behavioral sciences are not unsalable at all. This may only represent my own background and continued interest in the behavioral sciences, of course; but I think not. I believe that most readers of a newspaper or magazine—in this day of cultural explosion and of those five million college students—are bound to be fascinated by such things as the Hebb and Lilly experiments on what happens to people deprived of sensory stimulation, all the recent work on the effect of electrical stimulation and various drugs upon the human brain, the Harlow findings about the monkeys raised by surrogate mothers, the fascinating and amusing experiment in which scientists at Walter Reed Hospital learned how to turn a monkey into an executive and thus give him an ulcer. To me this is all a great deal more exciting than anything Mrs. Brown and Dear Abby can dream up at their desks, and it has the added advantage of being truth. I think that it is bound to prevail—and probably a good deal sooner than most journalists and behavioral scientists expect.

11
**Barriers to Communication:
Another Journalist's View**

Emmett Dedmon
CHICAGO SUN-TIMES

It goes against the grain for a communicator to address himself
solely to the "barriers" to the achievement of his professional goal.
Yet this dour piece of research is my assignment, so I shall do my
best to accentuate the negative.

The first barrier to communications between behaviorial scientists and journalists arises, it seems to me, from the dual role that
both play in dealing with subject matter which is of mutual concern.

Professionally, both are cast in the role of observer-recorder
or—if you prefer quantitative social science—in the role of evalu-
ator. At the same time both are also cast in the role of participant in
the social process which is their natural subject matter.

When the behavioral scientist reads his morning paper, for
example, he reacts to it intellectually, emotionally, and, I suspect,
viscerally in terms of his own personal philosophy and politics. At
the same time he is judging it professionally as an instrument of
communication and social change, with a specialist's awareness of
where it has succeeded and where it has failed.

The editor, in turn, when he reads a social critique of the communications media is apt to react first with that great intellectual
disinterest which any of us show when we are criticized. "Don't
those social scientists realize," he will explode—editors traditionally
explode when criticized—"that we are dealing with a human equa-
tion and that imperfection is the essence of human nature?" In
short, it is a basic assumption of the editor's craft that his product

will be imperfect and transitory; but as a student of that craft, he does not like his academic observers to document those imperfections and codify them as social science.

For the second barrier to communications, I am somewhat indebted to Daniel Boorstin, who assisted me by sharing some of the technical vocabulary with me. The behaviorial scientist and the journalist have "alien models," Dan suggested; and, like a good teacher, translated this phrase for me in mundane journalistic terms.

The model which the social scientist has for the communicator is one in which the communications media are seen as having the capacity to cause social change and social improvement. Therefore, the social scientist, who most often starts from the premise that he is measuring social amelioration, tends to measure the effectiveness of the media in terms of how effective they have been in promoting or effecting such change.

The journalist acknowledges the capacity of his media to cause change but does not regard as the "model" by which he is judged (to borrow computer language) his effectiveness in promoting such change. His purpose is to provide communication; though the social scientist may see this as a means, the journalist tends to regard it as sufficient end. Ameliorative change is a satisfying by-product of such communication, but it is not its primary purpose in the eyes of the journalist.

Dan and I have argued, for example, over one of his theses in *The Image: Or What Happened to the American Dream* to the effect that press conferences and press questioning created, in his words, "pseudo-events." It was my view that, far from being "pseudo-events," press questioning merely brought to the surface for examination events which were already occurring.

Thus it was—and you are going to get my side of the discussion and not Dan's—that I laid claim to Socrates as an early journalist. He did not introduce new issues—or "pseudo-issues"—to Greek society. His questioning merely laid bare the issues which were already present and were having a bearing on the structure and development of his society.

Perhaps it would not be too bold to suggest that Socrates was both inquiring journalist and behaviorial scientist in one person.

(At this point it also might be prudent to recall the reward he earned for himself by his efforts.)

A third barrier to our communication is the difference in our scales of judgments. Not all our judgments are different, but one critical difference is that the behaviorial scientist can measure achievement by an intellectual scale (or hopes that he can), while the journalist operating in a free (and free enterprise) society must bear the judgment of the marketplace; in other words, he must be judged on a monetary scale.

Many people often fail to realize that the way to keep a press free is to keep it free of government support. In this respect, it is important to remember that the constitutional provisions for a free press prohibit support for the press as sternly as it prohibits interference with it.

Thus, both in law and in practice, the press must survive to be free. It is not an idealized mode of communications, but a series of media—reading, listening, and viewing—which are able to fulfill what the sociologist calls the role of the stranger. We must be able to communicate, not with a community of people whom we know, but with audiences measured in terms of hundreds of thousands or tens of millions whom we do not know.

If we do not communicate, we are out of business. What we communicate is not what these vast audiences *ought* to know, as our academic colleagues would sometimes have us do, but what these audiences are willing to accept as worth knowing.

If we are professionals, then like good lawyers we should be leading our clients along paths in their own self-interest. But like even the best lawyers, communicators cannot overcome the resistance of an obdurate client, either singly or in a mass audience.

The behaviorial scientist is not inclined to give us much sympathy on this point. He is trained and he is experienced. He knows what the criteria of good communications are and he expects us to live up to them.

Who is right I will leave to your judgment. But I believe it is clear that we have identified another barrier to communication between us.

Here it is probably worth taking time to view the American

communications media as we see ourselves. And to make the further distinction that communications media vary from country to country just as languages and vocabularies may be expected to be different.

I am indebted to the publisher of the *Manchester Guardian* for the suggestion—in fact, hypothesis—that American communications media divide the socioeconomic pyramid differently from the media in England.

In America, with its presupposition that "all men are created equal" (and continue that way), the newspapers, radio, and TV cut vertically through the pyramid. It is an article of our political faith that the man at the bottom of the pyramid must have access to the same quality of information as the man at the top.

The English are not so sanguine. From BBC to the *Guardian,* the English cut across the pyramid. The *Times* and the *Guardian* for the folk at the top of the pyramid; the *Express* for those in the middle; and the *News of the World* to titillate the vulgar sensibilities of those whom England's educational system has deprived of the potential from which curbstone statesmen are made.

Diagrammed, it would look like this:

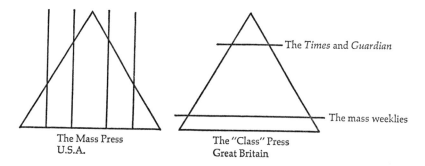

The Mass Press
U.S.A.

The "Class" Press
Great Britain

The *Times* and *Guardian*

The mass weeklies

You can see that whether we call it audience, market, or public, the press reflects the social structure in which it must exist. We hope, therefore, that when the press or other media are criticized for failing to live up to proper standards, our academic friends will realize those standards may not be accurate for that particular social structure in which these communications media exist.

I was also asked to speak briefly about the barriers of "jargon" between us. Happily, I think I can say that jargon is less of a problem in our relationships than in almost any other field of specialization. It is our prejudices that stand between us, not our jargon.

Finally, if I may be permitted to end on a positive note, let us look at how a better information flow may be initiated over these barriers.

One suggestion would be that we might institute a system of "reverse fellows" by which behaviorial scientists could participate in our continuum of communications just as an increasing number of individuals are returning to the campuses for further educational skills. The change in emphasis of newspapers, for example, from a combination of entertainment and information to primarily informational media, has already accelerated the amount of communications between social scientists and communicators. The raw stuff of the modern newspaper—and news shows on radio and TV—is no longer the sensational event, but the political, economic, and social questions of the day.

To deal with such issues as civil rights, poverty, urban renewal, demographic planning, and the rest, the communicator must be in constant contact with the scientist who is evaluating an ever-changing pattern of social data. This flow must be continued and expanded.

The differences, then, may be summarized as differences in standards of judgments rather than values. The reason for breaking down such barriers and communicating better will arise from a commonalty of interest and the need for the modern communicator to draw on the skills and research resources of the behavioral scientists.

12

**Barriers to Communication:
As Seen
by a Social Psychologist**

Ronald Lippitt
UNIVERSITY OF MICHIGAN

I accept the assumption implicit in the topic of behavioral scientists and communications professionals, and I would like to use the word *professionals* instead of *craftsmen* because my contacts with journalists have convinced me that it is a profession rather than a craft or a business.

I accept the fact that the behavioral scientists and the communications professionals do have joint interests in the communication of science-based knowledge to various publics and that we do encounter a variety of problems of collaboration and communication with each other in trying to carry out this common mission. Although there are a number of special cases in which the scientist attempts to go directly to various publics and to bypass the professionals, I think the modal situation, and certainly the one we are talking about here, is the situation in which the communications professional is in the role of linkage agent between the scientist and the lay public. I am not assuming that this type of linking role is the only type of information creating and processing role played by most communications professionals. One of their valued activities is also that of inquirer and producer of knowledge, initiating original inquiry into events selected by criteria of newsworthiness other than scientific resource. I think this value of creative inquiry in generating newsworthy communications is often incompatible with the function of being an effective linking agent between science and potential science consumers.

There are, of course, a great many linking agent roles between scientific resources and potential users. The county agent, for example, has a defined role of linking new agricultural research and technology to the population called farmers. So do the more vested-interest salesmen who are pushing farm implements and new fertilizers, for example. Eli Ginzberg mentioned the record of productivity in the agricultural segment. As far as I have been able to see from some of our inquiries, one of the reasons for this productivity is the tremendous apparatus of linkage between research and innovation and practice. The time gap is remarkably closed as compared to other segments. The medical education extension agent has a relatively undeveloped role in linkage to doctors. Much more developed in this field is the vested interest of the detail man in linking the drug company to the doctor.

Now one of the points of inquiry I would like to initiate is an exploration of just what type of possible linkage role the journalist has in regard to behavioral scientists. What values, commitments, and expectations guide his decisions and his behavior as a linkage agent? I would like to do this by identifying a few typical problem issues in my experience and those of my colleagues, giving the scientist's viewpoint, and then make an attempt to infer some of the reactions of the journalist colleagues as I have experienced them. Next, I would like to make a quick effort to identify some of the causes of the difficulties, and to suggest a few directions for improvement of collaboration.

Here is a brief set of typical confrontation events. Here is one, almost a quote. "He wrote it up [this happens to be a particular innovation in educational practice] and assumed he was expert enough to get it straight without checking back. The assumption he made was that he had it all straight, and there were two major errors in the communication." Here we see the competing role of interpreter that in many of our experiences has so often had such results when there was no dialogue, but a one-way flow in the communication. Another one: "He made universal generalizations from what I tried to communicate to him, and he did not qualify the sample. I talked to him about a gang of delinquents who were older teenagers, who were from central cities, and were Negro. He talked about discoveries concerning delinquency in general." Another one;

it's from a recent series of notes: "He seemed to lack sensitivity to the potential side effects or unforeseen consequences." This happened to be a situation in which the communication was about the new math and in a small community paper; the parents became very agitated because the material was written up in order to demand immediate action, and there were no resources to give immediate training for the teachers; the effort that followed as a consequence was a disaster for the kids, the teachers, and the parents because of the lack of facilities for training and for internalization of the innovation in the local situation. Another one: "The news he seemed to enjoy was that scientists disagree, and their disagreement became the news story rather than the effects of punishment on children. There did not seem to be any attempt to integrate the conflicting views of the scientists or to help the reader become in any way a problem solver." Another quote: "He seemed to want to give the answers, not help the reader acquire knowledge to help solve problems. He left out all multicausation in his interpretation." Another: "He did not seem to listen to the whole story; he tried to cream off a couple of interest stories to use and then ran away." Another: "He acted as though he knew as much about conflict resolution as I did from the research we tried to do. He knew the answers really before he interviewed me, and he was just using me as a source for a story."

Now some of the confrontations, of course, are very therapeutic. Some of these confrontations may create barriers to interaction between the journalist and the scientist, but on the other hand, may greatly reduce the barriers to communication to the laymen in the results that come out. For example, there are great correctives, certainly in my own experience, in challenges to vagueness and inconsistency of interpretation, to gaps in logic, to unnecessary use of technical terms, and to overgeneralization. A whole variety of things emerge frequently at creative confrontation in the effort to work through the linkage problem with a communications professional.

What seem to be some of the themes and the bases of these problems of communication from the point of view of the behavioral scientist?

First, it is not clear just how much to trust the objectivity and competence of the communications professional as a thinker in the realm of social science. What are his values and what is his training? We don't know. What kind of effort will he make to control his own projections in interpreting the behavior of middle-class parents of delinquent sons? Or the reasons fourteen-year-old girls get pregnant? Or the causes of resocialization of gang leaders? Or the effect of a testing program on the behavior of teachers and students?

Second, in addition to this problem of trust in regard to objectivity and competence, it is unclear what interpretation the journalist is making of his responsibility in the interchange with the behavioral scientist. Does he regard it as a joint effort to get an accurate and appropriate communication developed, or is it a one-way process with no chance for testing and reacting? What kind of role definition does he have about the interaction?

Third, it is often unclear what the values are of our responsibility to the client or consumer of the information. What values go into the judgment of "newsworthy"? Does it include, in any way, concern for the consequences of the news impact, or is there primarily a value of what will attract readers, which is, I suppose, one of the values in any decision to put energy into a mass media communication effort.

Fourth, often through lack of time for minor considerations, journalists neglect to deal with some of the unique aspects of social science communications in light of what we know about the reader consumption process.

And finally, I find myself frequently questioning the validity of the assumptions being made about the readiness of readers to consume more confronting messages. Let me just report briefly a few observations from our work on the utilization of research by practitioners and laymen, observations that I feel are important in the collaboration between behavioral scientists and professional communicators—newspapers, TV, radio, tape libraries. I want to make just two generalizations and a couple of subobservations on each.

First of all, there are a number of critical differences between, on the one hand, communication and use of social scientific resources that my colleagues and I want to practice as behavioral scientists and, on the other, the communication situation of my colleagues in the natural and biological sciences. First, in dealing with behavioral science communications, the reader must become involved if he is to read and in any sense understand. He must become involved in confrontation of personal values and attitudes and very often current personal behavior patterns, such as smoking, for example, or child-rearing, or attitudes toward teen-agers. So the message can and must support the legitimacy and the relevance of making such an effort on the part of the reader.

Second, it is less required by society or less obvious to the reader that many units of relevant information require direct use of technical help. For example, the message about the significance of getting teen-agers involved in responsibility in order to reduce alienation is a pretty meaningless piece of information to try to act on without recognizing and seeking some help in the kind of involvement technology and training required. Otherwise, there is almost a guarantee of doom to failure for the party trying to act on the information. So the question of referral information and qualification are important in the message—this is the whole issue of quality of understanding and action. To use the new knowledge about deviant behavior, or social action, or conflict-resolution, or whatever it may be requires understanding of concepts and ideas, about causation and consequences. It is not a matter typically of thinking or doing as someone else has done, using a new drug or fertilizer, for example. It is a process of adapting innovated ideas, procedures, or behaviors to one's unique self and situation. It is an *adaptation issue* as we talk about it rather than an *adoption issue* that is involved in making any use of the message. We found this recently in work with a rather wide population of teachers where we were communicating three kinds of messages to them on material for classroom use. One message involved new concepts with which to think about the kids in their classrooms. The second was a set of new tools, actually instruments, for diagnosing what is going on in their classrooms. And the third was a set of new practices, developed by others, that they might want to adopt. At the end of six months, the teachers reported that the most practical material given them in the communication process was the new concepts because the theory they had acquired was of more help continuously in seeing their situations differently and guiding decisions about them. I think Dr. Bressler's point about using new bits of knowledge means that there is much more than cognitive information involved if the information is to lead to any kind of decision-making or sense of commitment to action or effort.

The second generalization is that we tend greatly to underestimate the ability and readiness of children and adults to cope with more complex and challenging ideas and problems than we typically provide them. If the meaning of becoming active is felt to be relevant to the self or it helps make the here-and-now world more understandable, therefore usable, there is, in our experience and our observations, a much higher level of readiness than is typically assumed. I would like to pass on some examples from my observations of nine-, ten-, and eleven-year-olds involved in an experimental behavioral science curriculum that was begun two years ago. This curriculum was set up to train these young consumers in the activities and meanings of social science and social science inquiry. I observed one fourth-grade class outlining their first trip to the planet Earth after having grown up on Mars. Only part of the class was going to Earth; those who remained charged them with learning all they could learn in a day to understand how the people on Earth lived and why they acted as they did. They went over all the questions they were going to ask and who they were going to seek out for the answers. Following this, the class was shown a short filmstrip on people who study other people and the distinctions between natural scientists and social scientists. I visited another class, a third grade, where the pupils were arguing vigorously over the reliability of their observations and the adequacy of their sample in a study they had just completed on how time was being spent in their classroom. I visited an all-Negro fourth-grade class in Central City. The seats held 43 kids with a reading level of 2.9. They were arguing with their teacher over whether their decision to have the lightest child in the room play the role of the angel in the cast was a value judgment or inference from data. They had a significant and very basic dialogue under way.

It is these kinds of experiences, and I could give you many, many more, that have convinced me there is great consumer readiness and consumer eagerness when the material is meaningful, when it relates in some relevant way to the here and now of life.

I close with just four observations. First, it seems to me that we need to collaborate with experimentation on the presentation of behavioral science materials to readers or viewers or listeners stretching beyond the limits of our present assumptions. Second, we need to experiment with several reporters on behavioral science beats. Third, we need some collaborative teaching in journalism and behavioral science in both the professional school and the college department, or preferably in joint courses. Fourth, we need to do serious joint work on the question of what ways of communicating can integrate the values of freedom of the press and professional responsibility in regard to being sophisticated about the issues of side effects, of half-truths, of providing information without use-potential. I think we should give emphasis, not to the kinds of limitations or restrictions there should be on what is communicated, but to the ways issues can be communicated so that they will have a significant and meaningful impact on the various publics we are concerned about.

13

Barriers to Communication: As Seen by a Sociologist

Edgar F. Borgatta
UNIVERSITY OF WISCONSIN

As a social scientist, I should like to note that the title of this paper implies a particular model of communication. There are obviously two groups, journalists and behavioral scientists, and the model implies that, except for certain barriers, communication would be greater or better. This is a model that is practical and appealing, but from the point of view of social science it is a naive one.

Of course, in the social sciences such models occur, as in the work of Kurt Lewin. That doesn't make the models productive, no matter how appealing. In fact, using another popular approach known as the "sociology of knowledge" and assuming the "functionalist" paradigm of analysis, one could assert that by distracting social scientists from other approaches, such appealing but naive models may be "dysfunctional" for the science. That bit of jargon is a mouthful. Obviously, we could add to the jargon. But a number of questions have already been raised to which we can give attention. Let us look at a few of these.

Let us note that the statement that the title assigned for this paper implies a particular model, one that is relatively simple to understand and grasp, points to an important problem in communication between journalists and behavioral scientists. Let me phrase the situation as follows. If journalists are not social scientists, then they may respond to the model which *appeals to them*, or which may be commonplace in society already. There are many such common expectations, and they may or may not correspond to the empirically based theories in the social sciences. Thus, there may be some propensity for whoever chose the titles of this program to make an error. If a journalist, possibly the author of the program titles imposed on them his particular model of the process that is involved. Or possibly a social scientist was the author of the titles, and he tried to formulate a model that the journalist could "understand." Or possibly the social scientist tried to formulate a model that most social scientists could "understand."

But what is all the fuss about? What is a better model from the point of view of the social scientist? Well, says the social scientist, we could have a title such as: "The Interaction of Journalists and Social Scientists and Social Science Reporting." But it may be objected that this is not as specific a title. Our interest is in the fact that there seem to be some barriers between the two groups and in learning what can be done to remove them. Well, yes, but before we can speak in those terms, wouldn't it be necessary for us to know a little bit more about the process of communication between the journalists and the social scientists as it currently exists? There may be the impression that there *are* barriers, but this is an evaluation of a particular condition in a particular way. What exactly *is* the evaluation? Is it that there is insufficient coverage in the newspapers of advances in the social sciences? Is it that the advances in the social sciences that are reported are not the ones that should be reported? And if the latter question is appropriate, from whose point of view —that of the journalist, the social scientist, or the public? Or is it that social science research is not being reported accurately?

The Relevance of the Status of the Science

There is some value in turning attention to the status of social science in order to examine whether or not, say, there is inaccuracy in social science reporting. In assessing sociology, for example, it is necessary to compare it to other sciences and indeed to emphasize whether one is speaking of sociology as art or as science. If we may assume the latter, then by almost any criterion, sociology must be viewed as a most rudimentary science. Its most marked characteristic in contrast to our higher biological and physical sciences is the fact that it does not accumulate knowledge in the sense of empirically based, well-interrelated theories. Rather, it is characterized by the existence of many loose theories based on equally loosely generated facts. Surely *experience* accumulates over time, but this is quite different from accumulating knowledge in the sense of empirically based scientific theory. If the caricature is correct, then, what is it that social scientists have to communicate in which journalists should be interested? This is a good question.

When journalists are viewed as no different from social scientists who are concerned with finding out what new facts are being developed in social science, they may not be greatly aided in their task of reporting. It may be that they would just find very little to report, since professional readers of sociological journals frequently suggest that they find little in the journals that either interests them or is essentially an increase in the store of accumulated knowledge.

Of further interest, we may reflect on the fact that there is a continuing debate between segments of the sociological profession as to what the character of the professional journals should be. In particular, a segment of the profession has constantly complained that much of the journal content has been overly technical, and the complaint has even been phrased in the form: "I can't even read what they publish any more." The distinction between "soft" sociology and "hard" sociology tends to follow this alignment of a tradition of humanistic interests as contrasted to the formulation of a rigorous science. Editors of journals sometimes editorialize on how they are going to emphasize articles of theoretical importance as well as those that emphasize empirical research findings. By this they often mean that they want more discursive articles that have "insights" and "new ideas" in them. But some of the more cynical of the social scientists point out that nothing ruins "insights" and "new ideas" quite so well as empirical research.

What these comments have led to may now be phrased more directly as an assertion that much of what passes for sociology certainly is not social *science* at all, where the emphasis is on the word *science*. There is a definition that goes, "Sociology is what sociologists do." Thus, if sociologists have interest in action programs, that is sociology. By the same logic, of course, being a family member and going to the theater are sociology. The importance of this distinction is certainly not trivial, as it has great bearing on what it is in the social science that may be reportable from the point of view of journalists.

One can readily maintain that very few products of social science are reportable. Further, one can draw the analogy that very few products of physical science are reportable. For example, experimentation with nuclear energy never really was big news. The *application* to the development of the atom bomb, however, was important as news. Thus, there is a large distinction between the pure science, if you will, and the practical or applied science. The engineering or practical applications are those that become newsworthy, not the developments of the more basic science on which these are based.

The analogy to physical sciences has relevance, and it may be remarked that there has been a tremendous proliferation of scientific journals in the biological and physical sciences. There has also been some increment in the reporting of science news, but little of it gets into the major segments of the newspapers, and most is reported either in the occasional science pages that exist in a few of the newspapers in the country or as incidental information in business pages when it may have relevance for product development. Much of the science information that is received particularly descriptive charting of characteristics of chemicals, for example, is of little interest as news. On a per capita basis, surely basic scientists in the physical sciences are no more the subject matter of news stories than is the case for the social sciences.

Returning to sociology, we may phrase the problem relatively simply. There are very few advances in the basic science to which we turn. In fact, the development, as I have intimated earlier, is more of experience than it is of an accumulation of systematic empirically based theory. And much of that experience tells us that some of our assertions or assumptions may be wrong. It does not tell us necessarily what is correct. It means that we may often be prevented from making the error of predicting, but it does not necessarily mean that we can improve our predictions.

Journalists as More Sophisticated Through Access to Social Sciences

It may be that much of the experience that is accumulated in social science is communicable, and if so, certainly journalists should have access to it. During the last two or three decades we have had some improvement in data-gathering procedures, and also in analytic procedures in the social sciences. Some of these have been of particular importance for news reporting, since news reporting tends in some ways to be quite similar to some descriptive aspects of social science. For example, there have been substantial advances in the area of sampling procedures. Notions of appropriate samples in order to make generalizations about the population from which the samples are drawn are reasonably current. But such a notion is not necessarily new to persons who are news reporters. If they are concerned with reporting the opinions of the population, the pulse of the community, or the nation, certainly they must have some confidence that they are indeed representing these opinions appropriately.

A parallel between public opinion polling and news reporting is easy to make. If public opinion polling (or survey research) is viewed as an aspect of social science, then the further analyses that are based on breakdowns by particular variables to "explain" particular variations or positions in the public opinion area constitute part of the descriptive science. Similarly, the news reporter may be interested in reporting the opinions of salient segments of the population. Thus, at the descriptive level, sophisticated reporting may differ little from the social science approaches, at least in principle. At this stage of the game, however, we expect very few errors from survey researchers, if they are defined as social scientists, but that does not mean that journalists will make few errors in their presentations.

I might illustrate the latter by a particular example in Madison, Wisconsin, where the major segment of the University of Wisconsin is located—some 30,000 students. The *Capital Times* recently ran a story, presented to indicate that they believed it, to the effect that there are from 3,000 to 5,000 persons who have used narcotics or illegal drugs at the Madison campus. The immediate question raised was how this estimate was obtained. Were students interviewed in some representative way? The supporting facts for the assertions were quite meager, and as practical evidence for the 3,000 or 5,000 users, two students had been arrested in 1966 for possessing "pot." From a point of view of sophistication of the analysis, there is considerable peculiarity to the story. Possibly what is supposed to make it newsworthy is what makes it so implausible. Like the stories of nude parties, of sex on the rampage, or any of the other mass violations of morality that on occasion are reported, someone has in the process forgotten that these youngsters are drawn from the core of the middle class that seems to personify that conserve of morality. Even a reasonable attempt to get facts in a way remotely related to social science standards might negate the impression that newspaper created.

As an aside, when I arrived on the Madison UW campus, I heard that the place was "great," and stories of nude parties were the big thing. With the normal curiosity in what the youth are doing, I started to interview students on a reasonably broad scale on the question, simply using the "Oh, by the way," technique. I suppose that they could have been systematically lying to me, but I could not find a single person who knew a person who had been to a nude party, although the vast majority of persons to whom I talked knew they were "going on all the time."

Translating Social Science Findings for Public Consumption

The problem of translating scientific findings for public consumption is one that is constantly raised in the social sciences. A skeptic may raise the question, however, as I did earlier: "What social science facts would you like to have translated for public consumption?" I am not sure that a reasonable answer can be given by the social scientist. To the contrary, I would suspect that much of the social scientist's response, when it calls for greater attention to his work, is instead a feeling that social scientists should be more consulted in social planning. Further, possibly, social scientists may feel that they are for some reason also more qualified to select social goals, as well as to advise on how to implement them.

14

Perceptions of a Mass Audience

John Mack Carter
LADIES' HOME JOURNAL

Let us pull aside the veil: How does an editor of a mass magazine perceive his audience? What kinds of research does he use?

1. Audience research to determine the size. This is equivalent to the marks on the kitchen door recording the growth of the children.
2. Market research. How much money the subscriber makes and how he spends it. Enormous sums of money are spent in this research because the rewards are immediate and great.
3. Editorial research on what he reads and how he responds to it. I have been most interested in this kind of research, of course, with a view toward planning future editorial content. With what success?

Well, in trying to predict reader interest, the old-fashioned demographic approach has failed because it lacks sophistication. (This approach, however, still has a good deal of validity in predicting customers' buying patterns—apparently a much less sophisticated activity than reading.)

One exception to the general failure of the demographic approach is that sex does differentiate reading interests in mass magazines most sharply with reading of the lowest social class and increasingly less sharply as you rise in the social class structure.

Also, some differences can be made on the basis of age of reader, the differences between reading interests of teen-agers, say, and those over forty. But even this seems to be fading, and I suppose it isn't hard to explain. Go down and look at the baby-doll dresses in Saks—for grandmothers—or watch the wrinkled knees popping out of the latest young fashions. Or go down to Shepheard's and see who is dancing the monkey.

So how does all this research help determine what I put in my magazine? Very little. It leads inevitably to an editor's idealized perception of his audience, to a gap between perception and reality, to the recognition that the proper editorial goal is to condition appetites as well as feed them.

At this point I must interrupt to retitle my paper—not "Perceptions of a Mass Audience," but "Mysteries of a Mass Audience."

The mass audience in this country is free somehow from the tyranny of mass communication. The reader is too sophisticated, too well-to-do, too distracted even. And I'm rather glad, because it leads to the triumph of the individual. Last December, for instance, I ran a Christmas appeal called "The Children Santa Forgot" and asked readers to make a miracle come true for 17 about-to-be-forgotten children being cared for by local welfare agencies: for Rickie, eight, the only child of normal intelligence in a family of mental defectives, who wanted an encyclopedia. And for Ellen, eight, whose dream of a trip to Disneyland might recast her shadowy world. How could I perceive—in a mass audience—the little girl who sent half her allowance (five cents) to Rickie, or the two children who put on a Christmas play and raised $3.10 toward Ellen's trip?

Or the surprisingly light volume of "hate" mail from readers when the *Journal* ran the autobiography of Sammy Davis, Jr., with his detailed description of his romance and marriage to Mai Britt. Only to be stung six months later with vicious response to a cover photograph of a deeply tanned Sophia Loren.

It reminds me sometimes of the three-legged race at the old community picnics. First we are pulling, then we are being pushed. With confidence in reader agreement, I use the editorial columns to support marriage, sobriety, the church, and occasionally, when the climate seems especially favorable, even chastity. Even in these positions I find myself being dragged along, struggling, behind the audience.

It is possible to lead the audience, all right, if it is where it wants to go. The famous early *Ladies' Home Journal* editor, Edward Bok, was credited with success in his crusade to do away with the common drinking cup. But he spent more space and greater effort in his fight against women's suffrage.

Even the patently simple business of predicting best sellers among books defies formula. An almost unreadable novel by James Gould Cozzens, *By Love Possessed*, becomes one of the all-time top sellers. As, indeed, does *The World of Mathematics*. And, currently, Dr. Berne's *Games People Play*, not even written for the public, is a coffee-table fixture. Perhaps it's the law of the hula hoop at work. And the Superball. And Batman. (Is it possible for a television program with no killing, no bloodshed, and absolutely no sex, to succeed? Obviously not, but Batman does.)

In line with the charge that mass magazine editors have broad commercial responsibilities that tend to restrict them, it is my feeling that the audience has been willing to move up faster than editors will allow. Our magazines are lagging further behind the times today than ever in the past, and editors don't believe it. I think there needs to be a wider appreciation of a new application of Gresham's law of money. Bad editorial material drives out good. And slavish use of research leads to a downward spiral of taste. The public hasn't nearly so set a notion as to what it wants to read. It is waiting for the editor to say. So the editor who pauses, panders, and prostitutes will fail.

What is my perception of a mass audience? The audience of any mass magazine is composed of an aggregate of minorities. There are the bridge players, the knitters, the mothers of three-year-olds in need of toilet training, the new house buyers, the Frank Sinatra fans, even those concerned enough to read about Vietnam.

Which brings me to the behavioral sciences. Why haven't we done a better job of reporting your work? Why haven't you done a more creative job of making use of our media? Perhaps because we haven't gathered often enough for this kind of Arden House Conference. You have to keep after us. One of your number Edward Glaser of Los Angeles, who has put together a group of consulting psychologists under the banner of Edward Glaser and Associates, has been trying for years to shame me into doing a better job in my magazine. As a result we are trying a small-scale experiment which at least indicates a measure of good faith on our part. Dr. Glaser and his group are attempting to provide a monthly screening of current social science research and demonstration projects that might be of significant interest and appeal to the readers of *Ladies' Home Journal*. This includes government agencies and foundations as well as relevant journals and abstracts. It's an impossible job, of course, but neither of us is willing as yet to admit this to the other. And certainly it is worth the effort. I remember while serving last year on the President's Commission on Heart Disease, Cancer and Stroke, I was startled by the scientists' statement that 17 per cent of the cancer deaths each year are unnecessary. We could prevent these deaths simply by diligent application of the scientific knowledge we already possess. This is the role communication can play. Perhaps it can do the same in enabling us to take better advantage of the knowledge you have acquired. The audiences are massed and ready.

15
A Review of Session Three

Joseph T. Klapper
COLUMBIA BROADCASTING
COMPANY, INC.

I am struck first by a willingness, a reluctant willingness, if you like, on the part of both journalists and social scientists to achieve some sort of rapport. Each group agreed that they were both in the same game, that they should understand each other, and that obviously they do not. Secondly, I perceived what at first seemed to me a rather appalling lack of knowledge on the part of both journalists and social scientists regarding the goals, activities, values, and problems of the other. On second thought, it occurred to me that this was a rather positive thing, because I found, curiously, that in several instances the roles seem to have been reversed. I was somewhat startled, for example, by the following statement by a journalist: "The model which the social scientist has for the communicator is one in which the communications media are seen as having the capacity to cause social change and social improvement. Therefore, the social scientist, who most often starts from the premise that he is measuring social amelioration, tends to measure the effectiveness of the media in terms of how effective they have been in promoting or effecting such change." I did not know that was the model of the social scientist. I had been under the impression for the last twenty-five years that the mass media very rarely effect mass social change and social amelioration except under the most unusual conditions. So I was rather surprised to find that the social scientist's role was being taken by the journalist.

What is the problem to which we are addressing ourselves here? Are we talking about whether journalists ignore all the great gifts the social scientists have provided them? Are we talking about the fact that we should in some unspecified way be helping each other? Are we talking about the possibility that social scientists should be contributing to policy decisions among the media? Clearly all of these are legitimate problems, and each has different answers. I am not so precocious as to attempt to answer all of these nor even to formulate them. But I do suggest, however, that a clear delineation of the problems is the first step to their solution.

Let me address myself to the topic of "barriers." I would like to suggest one reason for their existence and a possible way to make a start in overcoming them. Some years ago several behavioral scientists—Ithiel de Sola Pool, Raymond Bauer, and Claire Zimmerman—demonstrated in soft-nosed research that newsmen tended to write not exclusively or, in some cases, not even primarily to communicate information to readers. Rather, they wrote to satisfy those criteria by which they thought they would be judged by their fellow newsmen. I am not referring in this case to an editor; I am referring to the competent, regular, workaday journalist, not the editor of the *Milwaukee Journal* or the *Chicago Sun-Times*. Pool, Bauer, and Zimmerman did this, as I recall, simply by setting journalists to writing a story and asking them, while they were doing it and afterwards, how they came to certain decisions, why they decided to say certain things in certain ways, and whom they were thinking about at the time. And they discovered, as I said, that to a great extent, newsmen were writing for other newsmen.

Now for whom are behavioral scientists writing? Obviously it depends on the behavioral scientist, but I submit that many of them are writing largely for other behavioral scientists. Their aim is not primarily or even importantly to write for the public who read newspapers but for other behavioral scientists. And I would go somewhat further and say that I am personally firmly convinced that a certain portion of younger social scientists whose work appears in the more technical journals may not be writing to communicate anything to anyone except the fact that they are writing something, which as you know is an important achievement for academic advancement. I am not being wholly sarcastic; I am exaggerating slightly, but I think it is something to be considered.

I do seriously submit then, that the two parties, the journalists and the behavioral scientists, tend to write for different reference groups—using that loosely. I think that from this stems a certain amount of trouble, part of which is due to what has been called jargon. I take some slight issue with the statement that jargon is a specialized language which we have not learned to understand. This it may be in some instances, but I think that in other instances, it is an esoteric language which is not absolutely necessary for purposes of communication although it may be convenient. I was exiled to the West Coast for a year or two—it is now Paradise, but in those days it was exile—and I was bewildered by the material from New York which kept referring to a technique called "secondary analysis," and I wondered what this was. When I returned to New York—I decided to ask somebody, and I found that every graduate student was talking about secondary analysis, and I was rather ashamed to inquire. I finally took my courage in hand and asked. For those of you who do not know, it refers to the procedure of analyzing data which has already been analyzed before for some other purpose. The term "secondary analysis" is convenient, but it is not essential. Another example: suppose a social scientist wishes to report that he has observed differences between two groups of people—an experimental and a control group, let us say—and that these differences are almost certainly due to the fact that one group was exposed to a communication and the other was not, or that one group was one thing and the other was not. Whatever the cause of the experiment was, if the social scientist wishes to say that these differences are almost certainly due to this factor, not to some chance variation, he will, in writing for behavioral scientists, not say so in these words, but will say that the differences are significant beyond the .01 level. Now here again, I think that one is talking about a kind of jargon which, although not wild and although convenient within the specialized group, could well be dropped in more public communication.

Enough of the jargon. I use it merely as an indication of the kind of thing that I think stems from the different reference groups, the different writing groups. My major point is that behavioral scientists and journalists have different audiences and are writing for different reference groups. Now, assuming that we are agreed on

the desirability of behavioral scientists and journalists coming to
understand each other, how can this be done? This seems to me
nothing in any way very mysterious. I agree entirely that there must
be a dialogue. I would think that each of the parties concerned
ought to begin talking in his own area of expertise and advance to
meet the other, but I do not think it is very realistic to expect either one to go the whole way. There are a dozen ways in which this
might be done. Ronald Lippitt and John Riley have both in one or
another way suggested some sort of teamwork. Lippitt has reported,
from my point of view, all too briefly on some rather interesting
case histories. Whatever way it is done, I do not think that the social scientist has any responsibility to provide newsworthy findings,
but I think that perhaps social science, if not the social scientists
themselves, has a responsibility for rendering findings comprehensible. Many social scientists will not be able to do this. They are not
trained to do it. On the other side, I do not believe the journalists
can reasonably be expected to become social scientists. I do not believe that they need to become experts in methodology. I think it is
unreasonable to assume that they are going to be able to criticize a
study with methodological flaws. But I do believe that they have the
responsibility of becoming familiar with the basic concepts of behavioral science methodology and, perhaps more importantly, with
the ethos of behavioral science—the concept of objective information as opposed to personal opinion, hearsay, and the like. I believe
that the meeting point will vary, depending on the individual social
scientist and the individual journalist, and an intermediary may
often be necessary. Surely not all social scientists and not all journalists will be able to have the fortune to be involved in teamwork.
This intermediary can be a specially trained individual; it can also
be that the intermediary may be a journal. I call your attention, for
example, to a journal, with which I have no personal connections,
so that I can speak freely, called *Trans-Action*, which has attempted,
in my opinion very well, to render social science findings and social
science activities comprehensible to educated persons who are not
themselves social scientists.

There is one point I would like to add; behavioral sciences,
and the sociological sciences in particular, seem to me to be largely
unknown to the bulk of newspaper readers. The high school grad-

uate is not ready, obviously, to become a nuclear physicist nor to become an engineer of mission control at Cape Kennedy, but he has some vague idea of what physics is about. He is not ready to go to Dupont as a researcher, but he has a general concept of what chemistry is about. To some slight extent, if he still hates his mother, he has some vague idea of what Freudian psychology is about, erroneous as the idea may be. But sociology, it seems to me, has no such area of contact among persons who have not gone to college or who have gone to college and not taken sociology. Its findings have not been translated so as to impinge upon the average man—with a very few exceptions. Automation impinges upon the average man. In rather incidental ways, some of the lesser accomplishments of social science have come to impinge on journalists and editors. I venture to say that there is not an editor or journalist who would have any difficulty whatever understanding the phrase "readership study with aided recall." Now that is jargon. Lippitt made the point that when new ideas impinge actively on people, they will exert the effort to learn the language, and I would suspect that they will often exert it without even being aware that they are doing so. I would suggest that when the findings of social science impinge on the average man or can be translated by journalists so that they impinge on the average man, they will become newsworthy and the jargon will be understood.

Herbert H. Hyman
COLUMBIA UNIVERSITY

Let me start with the paper by Edgar Borgatta. I think he showed admirable honesty and modesty throughout the session in remarking that we don't have a substantial number of definitives, final truth on pressing social problems. That's so. But it seems to me that this shouldn't stop journalism from using what might be provisional knowledge, if that provisional knowledge were better than no knowledge at all or better than opinion. I think it is self-evident that there isn't any science whose knowledge is final. The physical sciences and medicine change too, in five years or two years or six months. It's all provisional. But there is a quantum of something in it which gives one some sense of confidence. So I don't think that this should be construed as a barrier—the lack of, so to speak, pure and final truth. By the same token, I don't think the smallness of the archive of knowledge on pressing social problems is really the central issue. I assume that the media present many things that simply give people some understanding of something they're curious about. Not every bit of knowledge is useful in solving a problem. It's interesting. And I think the media publish items all the time that are interesting, if not necessarily helpful in solving a critical problem. So while I grant that Borgatta is correct in one of the prime assertions he makes, it seems to me that it should not deter us from using more of what is available.

I note in the Borgatta paper another correct point. He remarks, and we know from a good deal of work in a fascinating field, psycholinguistics, that a word or a label or a title implicitly guides and narrows thought and therefore makes it hard to see some element of a problem. He remarks that the title "Barriers to Communication" pushes you to see our topic in one way and that perhaps you should see it more broadly. I think that's well taken, but I somehow feel that in his paper he, too, is victimized, as we all are, by the very words we choose to label our propositions. I believe the paper focuses to some extent too exclusively on barriers to the coverage and accurate treatment of social science knowledge in one particular medium—the newspaper. Granted that that's an important class of problems in a most important medium, the problems there may be somewhat peculiar to the capacity of that particular medium to incorporate social science in optimal, not utopian or ideal, but simply optimal fashion. The capacity of journalists working in other media, magazines, perhaps radio and television, to absorb certain kinds of extended reports of social science research or extended treatments of a complex problem to which social scientists have addressed themselves may be greater. I take as one illustration the fact that the newspapers now certainly use in great measure public opinion polls. We may describe polls as a kind of superficial skimming of a much deeper type of social science research that I might call survey research, which might be the depth dimension of the poll. Perhaps it's easy to carry the top of the survey, namely the poll, in the paper, but you could only treat it in depth in some other way, in a feature, in a magazine, perhaps in some other fashion. For example, I compare the way the *Scientific American* in the United States or the *Listener Magazine* in England can report a deep and complex survey or other social science research to the way that a daily newspaper, not deliberately but because of its limitations, could report the same thing. I grant that I may not be on firm ground in arguing the potential of all magazines to cover surveys or other social science reports adequately.

I think that Borgatta stresses the reporting by media of advances in social sciences. I take that to mean recent social sciences, so to speak, new facts that were uncovered yesterday or last week. But it's obvious that some of the old established facts, the things on which we haven't advanced in thirty or fifty years or maybe more, are probably just some of those facts in which there is a very high quantity of truth and definitiveness and which might be new to the readers of media and worthy of reporting in some kinds of media even if they're not new in the sense of being recent. On this score, I lean on the authority of Ernest Havemann, who, at the end of his paper, I was delighted to see, cited Donald Hebb's work on sensory deprivation as highly exciting to readers, albeit not new or recent. I might pursue that a bit, if I may, without intending to be esoteric; Hebb's work in that area is certainly exciting. Despite the fact that his great work dates back to 1949, it is as exciting to read today. And that work leaned heavily on a classic work published in Germany in 1932, which I'm sure is as exciting for American readers today as the day it hit the German bookstores in 1932. (It wasn't translated until 1960, so it certainly is new.) That book from 1932 dealt with an exotic problem, and I'm sure Havemann could write a fabulous piece on it. The book written by Von Senden summarized all the cases that had ever been reported in all the literatures of the world of adults who had never seen the world before in their lives because they had been blinded from birth, and who then described that world when they were miraculously restored to sight following surgical operations as adults. Hebb went

beyond Von Senden, and I'll tell you that Von Senden went as far
back as a chronicle by an Arab surgeon in the year 1020. Apropos
of Havemann's reference to the excitement that inheres in some scientific chronicles, old or new, I shall quote a passage on one of the
Von Senden cases from its original source in the great journal of its
day, *The Tattler*, for the week of August 13, 1709. It's as good a
tearjerker today as it was then. In this particular case, the human
interest that attracted the correspondent of *The Tattler* was the fact
that when the blind man was about to be restored to sight, the
young girl whom he loved became worried that he might not love
her anymore when he saw her, because, as the correspondent notes,
she wasn't very pretty. She therefore asks him to make a declaration before she removes the bandages from his eyes. And he answers her in these words: "Dear Lydia. If I am to lose by sight the
soft pantings which I have always felt when I heard your voice, if I
am no more to distinguish the step of her I love when she approaches me, but to change that sweet and frequent pleasure for
such an amazement as I knew the little time I lately saw, if I am to
have anything besides which may take from me the sense I have of
what appeared most pleasing to me at that time—which apparition
it seems was you—pull out these eyes before they lead me to be un-
grateful to you or undo myself. I wish for them but to see you.
Pull them out if they are to make me forget you." I think that's better than a soap opera, and it's science! The correspondent of *The
Tattler* prefaced the story with a heading that makes the point. On
that particular day in 1709 a great battle between Sweden and other
European powers was in the news. But he starts, "While others are
busied in relations which concern the interests of princes, nations,
and revolutions, I think though these are very large prospects, my
subject of discourse is sometimes to be of matters of a yet higher
consideration."

The literature is full of such pieces if you simply do not confine
yourself to the recent and present. And if, instead of just covering
scientific speeches or conventions or interviewing scholars, you covered the literature, the choice is vast. I found John Mack Carter's
remarks most interesting, and I sympathize with his requirement to
get what he needs for his readers. But there's so much there, you can

find something to suit any reader. I'm not telling you how to pick, but there's enough to pick from.

Let me turn for just a few minutes to the other papers. I've already implied that I am very much in agreement with the Havemann paper. I take exception to nothing. It's written with clarity and sophistication and punch, and I wish we social scientists could write that way. I think it has just about the right combination of sympathy toward both parties and toughness toward each.

The Dedmon paper seems to me a most thoughtful analysis of the relations between the social scientist and the journalist and the differing perspectives they have because of their roles. I think the paper couched matters correctly and I especially liked the broad, comparative vista—putting the problem in the context of societies other than the United States in order to understand it better. Obviously the mix of social science with journalism varies not only by types of media, for example magazines or papers or TV, but that mix and the tolerance for a certain mixture of social science may vary by country, as Dedmon conveys by his description of the class media versus the mass media in England and the United States. Now certainly we also have some class media in the United States. And I believe these media can certainly do the biggest and the best job in the use of social science. But I might elaborate one point of difference from the inference Dedmon draws about the mass media in the United States. To be sure, you can argue that media catering to different social classes are worlds apart and that heavy doses of social science are only appropriate to what one might call the elite media or the class media. But I wonder if it's right to conceive of the media and the corresponding classes as being that much isolated from each other. I recall a fine Ph.D. dissertation done in our department by a man named Warren Breed, who started out in life as a newspaperman, working, I think, on a paper in York, Pennsylvania. From his observations of newsrooms of smallish papers, he talked of the dendritic process of smallish papers, a very nice metaphor. He meant that the little paper, perhaps the lower-class paper, stretches out its dendrites, its antennae, trying to feel the way the big, classy paper handles itself. It then, so to speak, models itself and thereby elevates itself. Now, even if that is not true of papers, certainly it's true of the masses to some extent, as the sociologists of many societies, particularly America, stress. People are mobile, trying to rise on the ladder. Perhaps they want their mass media to help them in achieving that, if you wish, vulgar goal or American dream. I don't care what you call it. But certainly if that be true and if you wish to exploit that motive, the mass media can, as it were, introduce more social science into the mix without losing the audience. If anything, the audience will like it because the audience thereby learns in that school the manners and repertoire and, if you will, air of knowledge that they haven't had opportunity to learn in the more conventional schools of life.

I'll make one more remark about the general topic of barriers (and perhaps here I'm on Borgatta's side). I wonder if the problem in some instances is not that of too many or too few barriers, but rather of the shaping, the quality of the barriers. For example, I have the sense, perhaps because of my vulnerable position in New York at Columbia University, that the barriers between the journalists and the social scientists are let down impulsively and temporarily when each week writers on Madison Avenue from every kind of medium you can think of call Columbia University, and each writer, depending on the question, is shuffled to anthropology, medicine, biology, archaeology, or, part of the time, to me. Then he asks a terribly difficult question, and when I reply that I have to think about it, he says, "I gotta write the piece in ten minutes." He wants an off-the-cuff judgment. The barrier there ought to be raised, not lowered, or at least the shape of it ought to be changed. Consider another quality of the barrier. It seems to me the barrier is down and the channel is a kind of narrow rut. I perhaps misunderstand to some extent the term "beat." But I have a sense that a beat involves a habitual contact. There's a fellow on the beat who's the easy one from whom you get the poop. Thus the barrier is down and forms a kind of rut. There's a rut worn between you people and a particular coterie of social scientists, and because that rut is so smooth and so obvious, you run back and forth in it and the social science you get is the accident of a long-established friendship with a self-appointed social scientist in contrast with the knowledge you would get from, let us say, a better representative of the discipline who has not made himself prominent for you or available to you as a result of that beating process.

I would end by saying it's perhaps less the height of the barriers or the lowness of them than the shaping of them, and perhaps that is worthy of discussion.

Session Four:

PROSPECTS: TRAINING OF JOURNALISTS IN THE
BEHAVIORAL SCIENCES

16
The Russell Sage-Columbia Program in Journalism and the Behavioral Sciences

W. Phillips Davison
COLUMBIA UNIVERSITY

Having successfully avoided academic administration for twenty-five years, I suddenly find myself a vest-pocket-sized academic administrator. After examining this unfamiliar role from the viewpoint of a new incumbent, I have concluded that it somewhat resembles the role of the mother-in-law as described by Max Scheler. Like the mother-in-law, the academic administrator is necessary to a vital process, but is not part of it. He is doomed to remain on the outside, making attempts to influence a primary relationship in which he is not directly involved, often resented as a troublesome busybody by the two principals, and suffering, himself, from the pangs of *ressentiment*—a combination of jealousy and frustration.

At the same time, both roles have certain compensating advantages and rewards. As is the case with the maternal in-law, the academic administrator is privileged to comment on a very broad range of subjects, to concern himself with the highest values and most ambitious goals, to speak in generalities. If his comments fail to come to grips with certain realities of the day-to-day educational process he is usually forgiven, since such mundane matters are the province of those engaged in actual teaching and research.

Nevertheless, I shall not be able to take full advantage of this license to speak in generalities, since in making a generous grant that provides fellowships for mid-career journalists who wish to spend a year at Columbia familiarizing themselves with the behavioral sciences, the Russell Sage Foundation has also posed two very immediate questions: First, how can news reporting of developments in the behavioral sciences be improved? Second, can journalistic writing about current social issues be deepened and enriched if journalists are acquainted with the behavioral sciences? As coordinator of this fellowship program, it is my responsibility, if not to answer these questions, at least to suggest ways in which answers might be obtained.

It is therefore necessary to ask: What should the emphasis of the program be? Of what elements should the program consist? What results can one realistically expect?

The problem of what the emphasis of the program should be is a more difficult one than may be evident at first, because the two questions imply rather different educational approaches. The first question involves writing *about* the behavioral sciences. To answer this, one would have to look at what behavioral scientists were doing and then determine how to communicate their findings to a wider audience. The second question involves *using* the behavioral sciences. It implies that one's primary interest is in current social issues, and that behavioral science can be used as a tool that will enable one to obtain a better understanding of these issues and to interpret them more meaningfully.

My tendency is to place the emphasis of the program on the second question without, of course, ignoring the first. One reason for this preference is a selfish one—curiosity. I have been influenced by the fact that this is not the first such program that has been initiated by the Russell Sage Foundation. A somewhat similar undertaking was started at the University of Wisconsin in 1964, and is continuing. The aim of the Wisconsin program, while closely related to this one, is not identical. It has dealt primarily with the problem of improving public understanding of the social sciences—including economics and political science—while at Columbia we have been urged to give primary attention to the behavioral sciences: social psychology, sociology, and anthropology. The point in which I am most interested, however, is that the Wisconsin program has thus far been devoted largely to the problem of improving writing *about* the social sciences, and I understand that it has achieved good results. Since considerable progress has already been made in this area, it would seem more interesting to give primary attention to the question that has been less thoroughly explored: namely, will the journalist who is writing about social issues be able to do a better job if he takes a look at them through the spectacles of the behavioral scientist as well as viewing them from his own professional perspective?

A second reason for preferring this approach has to do with the subject matter of the behavioral sciences. While the natural scientist is usually sovereign in his own field, the behavioral scientist studies many phenomena that are also properly within the purview of the politician, economist, lawyer, theologian, physician, or educator; indeed, he treads on almost everybody's toes. He concerns himself not only with subjects that are rarely analyzed by other specialists, such as motivation, attitudes, social mobility, and group behavior, but also with such subjects as crime, poverty, mental health, and marriage. He is thus a source of information both about developments in behavioral science and about certain aspects of social phenomena that are also in the domain of other specialists, or even in the domain of the general public. The behavioral sciences can therefore contribute to the understanding and interpretation of certain classes of news events, even though the individual events may not have been studied by sociologists, psychologists, or anthropologists.

Whether or not a year's exposure to the behavioral sciences will actually make possible better news analysis and interpretation in certain cases remains to be seen, but I think it will. Let me give a very minor example. During the New York power failure last November, many of the news media reported that, in the face of the shared calamity, New Yorkers became more friendly, more neighborly. A survey conducted by the Columbia Bureau of Applied Social Research during the blackout found that such a reaction was indeed characteristic of those belonging to the higher educational and income groups. Poorer, and more ignorant people, on the other hand, tended to feel more isolated and to show more signs of apprehension. The research thus suggests that journalists assigned to cover popular reactions during similar emergencies might be well advised to seek out representatives of different social classes when making interviews. Indeed, awareness of class structure and of the different reaction patterns of different population strata is probably relevant to a great many news stories in addition to those about elections, where it is already taken into account as a matter of course. For instance, I suspect that stories about the population explosion and birth control would benefit if class structure were given greater consideration.

One might also look at the top news stories of recent years and ask whether the behavioral sciences could have had anything significant to contribute to the way these stories were reported, analyzed, and interpreted. Here are some of the top stories from AP and UPI polls, as listed by *Editor and Publisher*.

1963—Civil rights crisis, Profumo scandal in Great Britain, Buddhist suicides in Viet Nam, Pope Paul reconvenes the Ecumenical Council, Supreme Court declares required Bible reading in schools unconstitutional.

1964—Johnson landslide, Civil Rights Act becomes law, Negro rioting in northern cities, U.S. Surgeon General finds cigarettes a health hazard.

1965—War in Viet Nam, Watts riot in Los Angeles, Northeast power failure, Selma civil rights march, India-Pakistan fighting.

My suspicion is that, in writing on quite a few of these subjects, journalists might have been able to draw considerably more from the behavioral sciences than was in fact done, and I believe that this would have contributed to better public understanding of the issues involved. Certainly, Gunnar Myrdal's *American Dilemma* could be considered relevant background for reporting on race relations; *The American Voter* by Angus Campbell and his associates provides basic information about voting patterns that could contribute to a wide variety of news stories; and Gardner Murphy's *In the Minds of Men*—a study of social tensions in India—might very well provide a new slant on stories from the Indian subcontinent.

If journalists are able to *use* the behavioral sciences in this way, namely, as an added resource that can be tapped when reporting and analyzing social issues, they should also be able to write *about* new developments in sociology, psychology, and anthropology. In other words, by focusing on the second question that was posed by the Russell Sage Foundation, we may be able to answer the first at the same time. This is, at least, a convenient rationalization for the approach I would like to follow.

The problem then becomes: How can the journalist tap this resource? There are at least three possible answers. The most obvious is that he can improve his ability to squeeze relevant information out of individual behavioral scientists. To do this, he has to be able to locate those who are most likely to have the necessary knowledge, to communicate easily with them, and to evaluate what they have to say.

A second answer—possibly less congenial to the always overloaded newsman—is that he can draw on the body of behavioral science literature. If he is going to take this avenue, he will have to know where to find the literature, how to discriminate good research from bad research, and how to relate the information thus laboriously acquired to the facts of the story he is writing.

The third answer—and here we tread on shaky ground—is that the journalist can himself apply some of the concepts and methods of behavioral science in pursuing his own investigations, in deciding what sources to explore, in determining which questions to ask, and in interpreting the information he has obtained. I refer to this as shaky ground since all specialists tend to be skeptical about recommending a do-it-yourself approach to laymen. This is especially true of the medical profession, but lawyers are scarcely less tolerant of those who attempt to do their own legal work, and when the writer suggested a program of do-it-yourself social research to foreign service officers a number of years ago he found that he had inadvertently stirred up a swarm of bees among his own colleagues. Nevertheless, we all do resort to self-medication on occasion, and we take care of our own traffic tickets. It is to be expected that journalists will employ any concepts and methods of the behavioral sciences with which they are familiar whenever they feel that these will be useful in their work.

How is the journalist to become qualified to use any one—or all three—of these approaches most fruitfully? This is the heart of the question facing the Columbia-Russell Sage program. An immediate and obvious answer is a negative one. It is neither possible nor desirable to turn journalists into behavioral scientists in a single year. At the most, one could transform good newsmen into bad researchers—a poor bargain however one looks at it.

When we look for more constructive answers to the question, it is clear that a primary objective of the program should be to create conditions for improved communication between the two groups: communication on a personal level, and communication through the medium of publication. The journalist should have a road map that will help him find his way to the major stockpiles of behavioral science information, both human and published. A second objective should be to develop critical ability: how to distinguish between a good researcher and a bad researcher, a good book and a bad book. A third objective might be—to resort again to a medical analogy—to develop a program of first aid for those interested in reporting social issues: to familiarize them with concepts and techniques that they can use themselves, and to sensitize them as to when it would be advisable to call the doctor.

All these objectives involve solving the problem of language. It is probable that half of the persons at this conference don't know what "B copy" is, while the other half would be baffled by a reference to cognitive dissonance. Some acquaintance with the language of the behavioral sciences will certainly be necessary for the journalist who wishes to exploit either human or published sources of behavioral science information.

A fourth objective of the program should be to enable the journalist to become familiar in somewhat greater depth with at least one subject that is of interest to both behavioral scientists and newsmen, and to do some writing in this field. This would test out the hypothesis that knowledge of the behavioral sciences can be used to provide greater enlightenment to the public without making a managing editor or TV news director any unhappier than he was before.

Now we come to the nuts and bolts phase of planning. If these objectives are accepted as reasonable, how should Russell Sage Fellows spend their time in order to achieve them? Perhaps most important is that they have adequate leisure for independent reading and writing. In addition, I envisage four types of more specific ac-

tivities: first, participation in a seminar to discuss important research studies under the guidance of academic specialists; second,
visits to leading research centers and professional gatherings;
third, election of two to three courses in subject areas of interest to
journalists; fourth, preparation of one or more papers involving the
application of behavioral science knowledge to journalism.

The seminar is the heart of the program. It will include some
thirty sessions of approximately three hours each. All sessions will
be built around one or more books, but will not be limited to them.
The principal book will be an empirical study of a social problem or
issue; others may be works that helped develop one or more of the
conceptual tools used in the empirical study. The discussion will be
led by an expert in the subject area, occasionally assisted by one
or two other behavioral scientists who will serve as interlocutors and
discussants. The role of the Fellows will be to represent the journalistic interest, to ferret out applications, to demand clarity, and to
raise embarrassing questions.

Out of these seminar discussions I hope that there will grow
not only an appreciation of the books themselves, but also a specification of the theories and concepts that are used in them, an appraisal of the methodology and techniques of investigation, a picture
of current work that is going on in the same area, and an inventory
of possible applications in journalism. The basic strategy of the seminar is thus to start with an empirical study, and to work back from
there to a discussion of theory, method, other research, and current
applications. As examples of the subject areas with which we expect to be dealing, I might mention aging, crime, population, race
relations, education, industrial relations, communication, mental
health, psychological testing, and poverty. Undoubtedly many other
areas will be added.

In discussing these empirical studies, I should hope that we
would encounter theories and concepts dealing with social organization and disorganization, socialization, motivation, personality,
learning, attitudes, cognition, group behavior, mass phenomena, social change, and cultural innovation and diffusion.

As to methodological tools, it is probable that we would encounter sampling, tests of significant difference, content analysis,

simulation and gaming, projective methods, interviewing, and questionnaire construction, as well as—more generally—experimental design and the scientific method.

Let me take one book, by way of example, and attempt to follow through the probable course of discussion. Suppose we selected Floyd Hunter's *Community Power Structure*. We would first of all be interested in Hunter's conclusions regarding the distribution of power in Regional City and the way decisions were made. Then we might look at some of his assumptions about social classes, formal and informal organization, the relationships between power and status, and the role of informal groups. It might be worthwhile to ask the seminar participants to read also Gaetano Mosca's *The Ruling Class,* Harold Lasswell's *Politics, Who Gets What, When, and How,* or Charles Merriam's *Political Power.* I expect that in discussing *Community Power Structure,* we would spend some time examining the way Hunter chose his respondents, his methods of interviewing, possible sources of bias, and the adequacy of his pre-test. I would also hope that the discussion leaders would be able to acquaint us with more recent studies of community power structure, criticisms that have been made of the reputational method of identifying community leaders, and some of the other methods that have been used. Finally, we would inquire whether the studies of local power structures made by behavioral scientists have any relevance for reporters covering city halls, or writing on other aspects of urban affairs. We might also ask how social scientists interested in this area could be of value as news sources, or as commentators on local political developments.

So much for the central seminar. I think the purpose of the elective courses, and visits to research institutions and professional meetings, are sufficiently obvious. The elective courses will provide an opportunity to explore one or two subject areas in greater depth, while visits to research institutions and professional meetings will enable Fellows to investigate the problems and possibilities of reporting current behavioral science activities.

The writing assignments will have two major purposes. One type of assignment, as has been mentioned already, will test the assumption that the behavioral sciences have something to contrib-

ute to news stories or other types of coverage that are aimed at the
general public. A second kind of assignment will have a somewhat
more devious purpose. Our assumption here is that the Russell Sage
Fellows will be able to describe for the benefit of other journalists
how behavioral science can be useful in reporting on one or more
subjects—for instance, race relations, mental health, or poverty.
These papers would thus have for their primary audience other
journalists, and they would be submitted for possible publication in
periodicals aimed at the journalistic profession. In this way, we
would try to achieve a multiplier effect for the program. A man who
had discovered ways of utilizing research on population or military
sociology in the reporting of current events would be asked to describe this for the benefit and critical appraisal of his professional
colleagues in journalism, who could then make use of his insights if
they cared to do so.

It is our hope that in connection with these papers some of the
Fellows will also define and pursue research projects of their own.
For example, one may wish to make a systematic examination of
the way different styles of reporting race relations have affected
race relations in a given area. Another might become interested in
examining the unstated assumptions about human behavior that are
made in the writings of one or more leading journalists and then
comparing these assumptions with such empirical social science
findings as are available. We do not, however, plan to assign research topics; these should be self-generated.

This is a brief outline of our proposed program. What kinds of
results can we expect from it? The most obvious result will be feedback that will influence the shape of the program itself. It can hardly
be right the first time; if I were presenting this description to you
a year from now instead of today, it would certainly differ in a
number of important respects.

In the longer range, we expect that the program will contribute to the development of a better-informed public by encouraging
more meaningful journalistic coverage of social issues that are already in the news, and by stimulating reports about some subjects
that have not yet been recognized as deserving extensive public attention. In the latter category, among subjects that have hitherto

been reported only cursorily, are some developments in the behavioral sciences themselves.

A third probable result will be an unintended one. The program aims to have an effect on journalism, and thus on the level of public information. It is likely also to have some effect on the behavioral sciences. If an intelligent mid-career journalist diligently explores the work done by sociologists, psychologists, or anthropologists in one or more subject areas, he is likely to be of considerable help in pointing out problems that have not yet been sufficiently explored and in suggesting new subjects and new priorities for research. At the least he will be able to pinpoint cases where expression has been fuzzy and the communication of results imperfect. One can hope, therefore, that the program will have a beneficial effect on both behavioral science and journalism.

Finally, there is an anticipated effect about which I can speak with considerable confidence. This is that the program will have a pronounced educational influence on its coordinator. Indeed, this process has already become evident. If this is the only result of the program, then it will achieve a certain distinction as being the most expensive educational undertaking in history. If, however, our assumption holds that new insights about social issues on the part of a few journalists can be communicated to many journalists, and from them to the attentive public, then the educational cost per human unit will be remarkably low, and the program will establish a new benchmark for economy in public education.

17
Techniques for Improving Access to Social Science Data and Resources

Wayne A. Danielson
UNIVERSITY OF NORTH CAROLINA

Others have had a chance to deal with barriers to communication; my job is to suggest some ways of overcoming these barriers.

My first suggestion is that the social sciences in general must do more than they have in the past to disseminate their own findings. Wilbur Schramm has written of the fraction of selection which determines whether a person will attend to a particular communication. In the numerator of this term is the *Expectation of Reward*. In the denominator is the *Effort Required to Obtain the Information*.

Realistically appraising the mass media as potential users of social science data and resources, we must reluctantly conclude that their expectation of reward is not very high. That is putting it mildly, perhaps. Newspapers have gradually come to the conclusion that it takes a man who knows something about natural science to cover a natural science story; in my opinion, they have not yet reached a similar conclusion with regard to the social science story. To many an editor, unfortunately, social science is a vast elaboration of something he thinks of as "just human nature." As a consequence, he is likely to believe that the social science story can be successfully covered by the meanest intelligence in the newsroom.

With a small value in the numerator of our fraction, therefore, it is unlikely that the news medium will cover a social science story unless that story is very easy to get. Practically speaking, this means that the story must come to the news medium, the news medium will not go after the story.

How are social scientists to be convinced that *they* must pre-pare versions of their scientific findings suitable for dissemination to the public? There is little reward for such dissemination for the average young sociologist, for example. He gets no points toward promotion in his institution for a newspaper story or a magazine article or a television show about his work. As a matter of fact he may have points subtracted for popular as opposed to academic publication.

What can be done? Perhaps the best and the easiest answer is to convince social scientists that publicity is the shortest way to the public purse.

I believe that a good case can be made for this proposition by studying the campaigns of voluntary health organizations, the gov-ernment programs in health and natural science, and the activities of some of the private foundations. All of these groups, to a greater or lesser extent, seem to favor popular research projects—that is, projects which appeal to voters.

Social science projects may not have the natural appeal of heart research, for example, or the fight to cure cancer. Nevertheless, they are not hopelessly plain. The great lesson of Hollywood must be remembered: If you don't have IT naturally, hire a press agent who can convince people that you do!

I have not expressed the point in a very dignified fashion. I be-lieve that it is basically true, nevertheless. The social sciences will not attract the funds they deserve until they deliberately devote some attention to their public image. Conditions being what they are, the social sciences cannot expect that the information media will come to them; they must go to the media.

A logical place to begin, in my opinion, is in the university news bureaus. A great deal of coverage of the social sciences orig-inates here—and much of it is poorly done. I would recommend that the Russell Sage Foundation and other organizations interested in changing the present situation devote some time and money to (1) promoting the idea that university news bureaus need men ca-pable of covering the social sciences, and (2) helping to see that the men selected for these jobs have the education they need in the social sciences. Certainly the professional associations in the various social science disciplines should also be encouraged to set up news bureaus and staff them with well-trained men and women.

Now, the mass media will use these social science handouts we have been discussing, but they will not like them. They distrust almost all public relations efforts—they depend upon them, but they distrust them. They want their own avenues of access to the social sciences on those occasions when a story comes along that interests them.

How can they find someone to talk to who will speak in the common tongue—who will give them the story in words they can understand?

I have two suggestions: The first is that the mass media concentrate on the Grand Old Men, the acknowledged "names" in the social sciences. These men are usually willing to talk to the press. They have made their reputations. They have their professorships. They spend much of their time consulting. They are used to dealing with men of commerce and industry. They are not afraid to paraphrase results for newsmen. They do not mind slight inaccuracies in quotations. They are too big to be hurt by popularization. They are excellent news sources.

Of course, they may not really understand what the younger men are up to, but they have a vague idea, and they *can* often put a new finding in the long-range perspective of the discipline better than the younger men.

A second suggestion is that the mass media improve their reference libraries generally and in the social sciences in particular. Social scientists can almost never understand the need of the mass media for information *now*. "I'd be happy to look that up for you," the old political scientist says, "why don't you come by for a chat after commencement next June?"

The best solution to this problem is for the mass media to have an adequate, internally controlled information retrieval system —in other words, a good, fast, usable *library*. The mass media have libraries now, of course, but as special research libraries go, those in the mass media (with a few shining exceptions) are pretty poor. In newspapers, for example, the libraries are often still called "morgues," and the term aptly describes their cheerful decor, their friendly, helpful personnel, and the vitality of the information they contain.

There have been marvelous advances in automation recently that make excellent, fast-access libraries possible. In addition, the schools of library science are increasingly turning out young people who are well equipped to perform the translation function the mass media need.

As a primitive indication of what can be done, I would like to cite a special-purpose bibliography commissioned by the Magazine Publishers Association and currently being compiled at the School of Journalism of the University of North Carolina.[1]

This bibliography is to cover postwar research in the social sciences of interest to magazine editors. The bibliography is entirely automated. That is, once items go into the computer—on punched paper tape—they are never keyboarded again, unless mistakes have to be corrected. The items are stored on magnetic tape and may be searched for and found at electronic speeds. The annotations are being made (we hope) in terms the editors can understand and use.

The final result of this project will be a printed bibliography indexed and sorted in a variety of ways. If the magazine publishers were interested, however, the final result could be a dynamic, always improving, automated reference service associated with a central computer somewhere.

Good libraries and good librarians, in my opinion, could aid substantially in the matter of improving access to social science data and resources. I would suggest that the mass media, together with the computer companies, the schools of library science, and some foundations interested in the problem, investigate the matter further.

My final suggestion for improving access to social science data and resources is made both to the social sciences and to the mass media. It is simply this: The social sciences should be more helpful to the mass media, or, putting it the other way, the mass media should make greater use of the social sciences in solving some of their own problems.

An outstanding recent example in this regard is the improved television coverage of elections made possible by social science research. I refer, of course, to the various computer-assisted vote-prediction programs written for election night, and to the general-purpose, background-information programs also provided for the use of newscasters and analysts. The voters have a better image of social science research as a result of these cooperative efforts. And so do the mass media. They have seen—in a practical and useful way—how social science research can improve the product they offer the public.

Therefore, my final plea is that social researchers suggest some projects which will benefit the mass media, and that the mass media support some of the projects. Out of such cooperative efforts will come, not only an improved product, but improved understanding between the mass media and the social sciences. On such an understanding our long-range hopes for improving access to social science data and resources must depend.

------

1. Wayne A. Danielson and G. C. Wilhoit, *A Computerized Bibliography of Mass Communication Research, 1944–1964,* New York: Magazine Publishers Association, 1967.

18

Should There Be a Behavioral Science Beat?

Earl Ubell
SCIENCE EDITOR
WCBS-TV, NEW YORK
NEW YORK HERALD TRIBUNE

Let me say at the outset that I do not believe that a newspaper should have a behavioral science beat. That goes for all other mass news organizations as well. Now, in any decent argument one must give one's reasons. To be sure, I did not think of reasons until I had been asked to examine the problem. I doubt that I will convince anybody either way. In the long run irrational factors over which few individuals have control determine many fundamental aspects of the organization of newspapers, newsmagazines, and broadcasting companies.

My major reason for opposing a behavioral science beat on a newspaper or in any other news organization has to do with the behavioral sciences themselves rather than with the coverage of the news. I supposed that in the course of this program many attempts would have been made to define the behavioral sciences.

Behavioral sciences are the soft sciences, as opposed to the hard sciences, which, I guess, are so named because from the point of view of news reporting they are hard to understand and hard to explain. For newspapermen, behavioral science reporting is a soft job—it deals mainly with people, and anxiety is easier to explain than the atom; it is dramatic, concerned with interesting problems. However, as has perhaps been made clear many times, the difference between the sciences is more fundamental than that which concerns newspapermen.

When one lists behavioral sciences in one column and the so-called hard sciences in another, some striking differences emerge.

The soft sciences include, to name the most prominent, psychology, psychiatry, anthropology, sociology, and to a large extent economics. Medicine is sometimes included in the behavioral sciences, but I feel it falls between the two schools. And then there are chemistry, physics, astronomy, oceanography, biology, and mathematics, among many others. Column A in this menu of science deals with man, although psychology has in the past dealt hugely with rats, while Column B concerns subjects considered outside of man (although there is a biology of man). That difference is superficial; there is something in the quality of the evidence in the various fields that really differentiates the two columns.

I need not labor the point. It is a matter of constant controversy on many college and university campuses. In behavioral sciences there is a sticky subjectivity in the observations. In the hard sciences the observer has nearly refined himself out of existence. In this respect, I would like to quote a paragraph from James Joyce's *Portrait of the Artist as a Young Man* in which the rather pompous Stephen Dedalus discusses art. I made a slight alteration in the quotation, substituting the words "science" and "scientist" for "art" and "artist" in the correct places. Making the substitutions, you will see that what Joyce is talking about in literature is what the men in the hard sciences are up to.

The personality of the *Scientist*, at first a cry or a cadence or a mood and then a fluid lambent *synthesis*, finally refines itself out of existence, impersonalises itself, so to speak. The *realistic* image in *scientific* form is life *and reality* purified in and reprojected from the human imagination. The mystery of *symbolic representation* like that of material creation is accomplished. The *scientist*, like the God of the creation, remains within or behind or beyond or above his handiwork, invisible, refined out of existtence, indifferent, paring his fingernails.

In my opinion, and I underline the word *opinion*, real progress in the behavioral sciences will be made when the observer refines himself out of existence. Real progress will be made in understanding man's behavioral characteristics both as an individual and in society when the evidence is reproducible in the large and in the small, when the experiments performed (and there will be many experiments) have the same qualities of control that one finds more and more in biology, and in physics always, and when there is a theoretical framework into which those observations fit.

I think it is a good idea to quote Ubell's law, which differentiates the hard sciences from the soft sciences. It is the law of hypotheses—the number of hypotheses in a field is inversely proportional to the amount of data.

I am not saying that all of the behavioral sciences are pervaded by softness, i.e., by subjectivity. That would be fatuous in the extreme. I am saying that there is more softness than I for one find myself comfortable with. Indeed, in sociology we have a distinct cleavage between good data-gatherers who are trying to understand the societal dynamics of our complex world and those who are merely essayists. In anthropology, essayists rather outweigh the data-gatherers, or at least this is my impression.

It is interesting that when Ralph Linton attempted to make a cross-cultural survey for an estimate of the worldwide incidence of psychosis he came across the incredible situation in which anthropologists in many instances simply forgot to count the number of people in the tribes they were studying. I need not tell this group that variability of incidence from society to society could tell us a great deal about the etiology of mental illness. However, it was not to be.

With respect to experimentation, an amusing situation exists in psychotherapy. I will only state the conclusion. Despite the pervasion of psychotherapeutic ideas in schools, prisons, and social agencies, only ten experiments exist which test the efficacy of this particular treatment. Four or five have adequate numbers and controls. I would venture to say that if a manufacturer of drugs put forth the amount of evidence for the efficacy of any particular medicine that is now put forth for the effectiveness of psychotherapy, that drug would not be approved under the current drug laws.

One final comment about the behavioral sciences in order to avoid being completely misunderstood (some behavioral scientists tell me that no matter what I do, I will be). When I speak of subjectivity in the sciences, I am not speaking about the art of discovery or the art of knowing what sorts of things are important. I am speaking rather about evidence. A scientist's ability to conceptualize, to have insights, and to be intuitive about what he is doing are parts of the unexplored art of being a scientist. The gathering of data and demonstration of hypotheses brought forth by the art are part of the scientist's craft, and it is in craft that the soft sciences are weak.

Now with that as a background for my ideas, I wish to state categorically that despite what some of you may have heard I do not believe that the behavioral sciences are "junk," although there is a great deal of "junk" in them. In fact, although we are now seeing an explosion in the biological sciences through the application of just the hard kind of craft I have been talking about, that particular explosion with its monstrous implications for genetics and medicine which is said by some to make the atom bomb pale by comparison, will in itself be picayune when compared to the explosion of knowledge that will come when the craft of the behavioral sciences achieves a state of rigor which chemistry, physics, and biology now have.

I do not say that the behavioral sciences should adopt the concepts of physics. I am amused by those who put forth the argument that what I am suggesting would make the behavioral sciences subservient to physics and chemistry. They are just those who fail to recognize that Freud and the early sociologists did not hesitate to take over crude physical principles into their fields.

At bottom what I am saying is that the standards of evidence should be the same. Observation should be less subjective, more quantitative, controlled, repeatable, crucial, i.e., it should test important hypotheses. Perhaps I am overstepping my ground with this large production, but it is central to the thesis I am going to state about a behavioral science beat in the news media.

To establish such a beat apart from the regular science beat in a newspaper is to put the behavioral sciences apart from the other sciences. That would reinforce in the public's view the ideas of different standards for behavioral sciences as opposed to the others. We, at the *Herald Tribune,* who have a "large" science staff with three science reporters, hold to the idea that each of us should be prepared to cover the news of science in all the fields. That is not to say that we are experts. We recognize, or should have enough sense to ask someone to help us to recognize, those developments in the various fields which are important or at least interesting. I must hasten to add that this is not so on many other newspapers, where the physical science beat is separated from the medical science beat.

The *New York Times* does have what one might call a behavioral reporter who covers psychiatry, sociology, social work, and what has been generally classed by crude rewrite men as "nuts and screws." I remember that about six or eight years ago one could meet at conventions of the American Psychiatric Association, reporters whose newspapers had assigned them specifically to cover psychiatry, not medicine. In recent years those specialists have declined in number. I believe that is all to the good.

The science reporter who covers all sciences comes in contact with many different scientists, gets to know the mode of thought and the standards of evidence in each field. As a result there are very few science reporters today who will report on the efficacy of a drug that is not backed up by a controlled experiment in which double blinds are employed. Dr. Beecher of Harvard has demonstrated repeatedly that placebo effects are real and that they enter into the evaluation of every drug. And science reporters know that all too well.

Such science reporters who cover science broadly will be applying a standard to the behavioral sciences that would present to the public those advances which are thoroughly backed up by good evidence, by hard scientific methods. They will shun the essayists and the opinionizers.

On the other hand, while a behavioral science reporter specializing in that field may have the advantage of more knowledge and background in a specific area and more acquaintanceship with scientists in this area, he may fall prey to many of the same sort of standards which prevail in the field. In this respect I have an amusing experience to relate. The Council for the Advancement of Science Writing has organized a number of seminars for science reporters on biostatistics and epidemiology. The last one concerned biostatistics and epidemiology in relation to psychiatry.

Dr. Joseph Zubin of the Psychiatric Institute organized the program, devoted to an explication of the standards and methods of good objective experiment and observational work in psychiatry. It was a brilliant program. All those who attended found it exciting and revealing. The next week the American Psychiatric Association met in New York, and many of the reporters who attended the seminar also covered the meeting for their papers. Along about the second day I bumped into one of the seminar members and asked him if he found anything at the APA Meeting interesting. He said, "I have nothing to write. You guys have ruined me. Every paper I look at seems full of flaws and completely void of any strong evidence." He actually used a slightly vulgar word. That is the kind of feeling which one would like to produce in a general science reporter facing the problem of reporting behavioral science.

We turn to another problem of a behavioral science beat. The average newspaper has finally become aware of the necessity to have medical reporters. But there are relatively few daily newspapers which have them full time. I should point out that none of the television networks have such reporters. ABC and NBC have science reporters who devote themselves largely to space and the hard sciences.

The Council for the Advancement of Science Writing is now engaged in a process to increase the number of science reporters on relatively small newspapers throughout the country. We have 135 fellows now in training. We have given them materials related to the behavioral sciences. To have a reporter who covers the behavioral sciences alone would add another burden to many newspapers which can ill afford it.

The largest science reporting staff in the country consists of about eight people. The next largest has about four, and following that there are a number which have two, and after that most have only one and he may be only part time. Nevertheless, I have some answers to the problems of increasing the coverage of behavioral sciences, since I do really believe that the behavioral sciences ought to be better covered. I think at least three things might be done to increase the quantity and quality of reporting behavioral science to the public. First, rather than establish a behavioral science beat, it would be easier to add to the existing science staff additional science reporters, to encourage editors to do so. Needless to say, this approach would work only for the very large newspapers. Next, one would encourage the existing science reporters to broaden their backgrounds to include behavioral sciences. Many have done so in the past out of necessity.

But good materials are hard to come by. Seminars are few. The Council for the Advancement of Science Writing stands ready to help in any such venture. We have done so in the past and will do more in the future.

A third approach would be to make editors aware of the news in the behavioral science field, as they have been made aware of the news in the hard science field by the atom bomb and in the medical sciences by antibiotics and heart surgery. That, again, might be done by seminars with appropriate attention by the scientific societies involved to the distribution of news releases to more than just a few of the technical journals.

With respect to the last, it should be noted that the American Chemical Society, the Federation of American Societies for Experimental Biology, the American Physical Society, and many of the medical and other hard scientific societies employ full- or part-time public information people whose duty it is to distribute the news of the particular science to the various news channels. Except for the American Psychological Association and the American Psychiatric Association, most of the other behavioral science societies do not have such individuals.

Accordingly, their meetings are not fully covered. Their journals do not get into the mainstream of the reading of the average science reporter, and one only hears about the findings when a university public information officer puts out a news release about a particular professor or when it becomes the subject of a governmental action. For the smaller behavioral science societies much could be done toward establishing a central news office to make sure, at the very least, that résumés of the journals are sent out and that notices and programs of their meetings get into the hands of editors and science reporters.

One should also mention the activity of the American Physical Society, the American Chemical Society, and the American Institute of Biological Sciences in sending out science stories to weekly newspapers across the country as part of their effort in informing the public of what is going on in their fields.

As each of the various methods begins to take effect, we shall see an increasing number of behavioral science stories in newspapers, magazines, and, hopefully, in the broadcast media. That in turn would create a pressure among editors and among science writers themselves to produce more of the same material. (Lord knows that is usually much more exciting than writing about atoms.) That in turn would lead to increases in the number of science-writing hours devoted to the behavioral sciences and to the pressure for increasing the science-writing staffs in various newspapers. I recall that I said I was against the behavioral science beats as such. It may be that such a program in the long run will provoke editors who believe in such subspecialties to establish behavioral science beats. For particular newspapers in particular situations that might be all to the good. Having come full circle, I now end my peroration.

19
A Review of Session Four

Robert L. Jones
UNIVERSITY OF MINNESOTA

It is perhaps interesting to note that the number of journalists with behavioral science backgrounds is quite small, and that we are working with a deficit that has been accumulating for some time. The problem is not just what the perennial needs may be, but one of coping with an accumulation of deficit. We can start with a general assumption: There is a desirability of more and better social science coverage. Even if attention is devoted to making some progress in solving the problem of manpower, agreed that the need is there for the area to be covered, we also need to consider making life simpler for the manpower that we have. So under these general headings, I will continue with some additional remarks.

First of all, I would like to talk about the Columbia and Wisconsin programs. These are early career special efforts, which have some aspects of a crash program to reduce the severe deficiency that we sense. They are characterized by high cost per unit of persons trained, and they require, at least at the start, rather generous external subsidies. The number which can be accommodated per annum is small. These programs are diversified, imaginative, generously staffed, and flexible, and they do anticipate adjustments and modifications in their initial structures as feedback from trainees comes in. All of this is fine. Perhaps we could think for a moment, under the heading of behavioral science training for journalists, of two ways of bracketing the excellent programs at Columbia and Wisconsin. (1) What are some of the trends and patterns in the undergraduate study of journalism prior to a possible Russell Sage Fellowship, and (2) what are some of the things that might happen beyond these fellowships for even more experienced and senior science graduates?

First of all, I would like to speak about the traditional journalism school efforts and some of the happy trends that one can see in the programs of those schools. I had the good fortune to attend recently the annual meeting of the journalism school accreditation committee; there we can see from year to year trends in the curricula of the national group of accredited schools. There is a distinct swing—not massive but distinct—toward behavioral science areas as supporting programs for the undergraduate major in journalism. This year, two institutions in the Southwest which previously had insisted upon English minors for their journalism majors have now swung away from this requirement. Such a move does not necessarily mean any de-emphasis on humanities or lessening of regard and appreciation for fine writing, but it does suggest that the ability of students to elect greater concentrations, minors, or supporting programs in the behavioral sciences as undergraduates has increased substantially—particularly at these two units and in a general trend across the country. I think this is encouraging, for it means that the students with initial interest in this area have a better chance, and are taking that chance, to strengthen their backgrounds in the behavioral sciences.

Secondly, there is a marked swing toward the undergraduate journalism major taking a second full major. Increasingly, this is in the behavioral sciences. So the solution of the problem of range and depth in the liberal arts area as an accompaniment to journalism education is moving with noticeable steps toward the provision of a second major field, and, increasingly, this second major field is one of the behavioral sciences. Then there is an increasing swing toward five-year programs as necessary and proper preparation for journalism. Universities taking this direction are among the most distinguished in the land. More and better behavioral science work is available in five-year programs.

New programs are getting under way in science communications. These are not specifically programs in the behavioral science aspects but in science communications more generally. One of these

is at Boston University. A second is at Minnesota, where we are beginning a brief program with just a pair of courses, and are concen-
trating on a few students per year. There has been a great deal of
additional work in the journalism curriculum *per se* on the application of behavioral science techniques and research methods to problems in journalism; and these courses no longer are entirely confined
to the graduate curriculum. Again a national trend is discernible in
the undergraduate research methods course on the processes and
effects of the mass media. These kinds of courses, even though intended somewhat more for consumers of research than doers of research, nevertheless do acquaint the undergraduate student, far
more than formerly, with the procedures and key findings of the
behavioral sciences as they relate to mass communications. This
clearly is an additional steering ingredient for students who may
eventually become reporters or specialists in behavioral science
journalism.

There is new recruit effort which I think is interesting. Many
schools are now examining, as a football coach would, where their
prospects are coming from and the backgrounds they have. If you
take the journalism prospects that come to the gate, say in a large
state university, you find that fate is bringing you an increasing
number of women students. This represents a certain demographic
shift. You will find that taking what comes to the gate will bring
you many literary, poetic, and humanistic students with an interest
in writing for writing's sake or because of an expressive urge. What
you will find, I am sure, is that very few students naturally gravitate
toward a school or a department of journalism because of a strong
high school or early college background in the natural or behavioral
sciences. Yet we are finding that if even a moderate amount of attention is paid to seeking out a certain kind of talent for one's journalism school, it is possible to balance the group of humanitic students with a selection of students who are interested in the sciences,
both natural and behavioral. What we discovered at Minnesota,
and what is being found at other schools around the country, is that
the extent to which one may successfully bring into journalism at
an early date a number of fine prospects for science communication
and the reporting of the behavioral sciences is greatly increased by

even a moderately aggressive, outgoing effort to find the kinds of students who do not just naturally appear at the gate.

So much for comments about feeding in talent—younger than that which appears in the Russell Sage program, but which would be excellent material for such programs ultimately. It has occurred to a group of us that there is a need for a kind of sabbatical year, not for early mid-career science writers but for late mid-career science communicators. I came from a conference recently with a distinguished middle western science writer. This journalist was very much interested, after a long and distinguished career in reporting medicine and the hard sciences, in backgrounding himself more deeply in the behavioral sciences and in the philosophy of science —in the area we have been discussing. What he wanted was to take a sabbatical year, which would require some very special arrangements. He represents, then, Example A of the kind of thing that needs doing beyond the Russell Sage program as presently defined. I was pleased to learn that the National Association of Science Writers has itself been working on this idea and has been looking toward some realization of it in the near future. The National Conference of Science Writers has also been actively engaged in seeking to help younger members of the society, not through formal academic work but through a program of materials, encouragement, and counseling by senior members. This development, too, is helping with the training of journalists in the behavioral sciences.

I want to echo briefly something that has been said three or four times in the conference—by Danielson, by Ubell, by Wald, and by others—that universities do a pretty wretched job of reporting upon themselves and that the news bureau of an average university is harassed and undermanned. I think this is indeed true. In many states, the major universities are the centers, the fountainheads, of behavioral science research and activity. And there is a great deal of slippage in the reporting of what is going on and the interpretation of it. I think that an inquiry into and an effort to upgrade and improve the news bureaus in universities would be a marvelous thing, and I could not be happier to hear some of our speakers ask that this be considered and that support be sought to make it possible.

I want to echo also the notion of better access to social science facilities. And I repeat that you have got to make life easier for the behavioral science writers. I learned from Mr. Dedmon's paper of some of the progress being made by the *Chicago Sun-Times* in an effort to move along on this matter of better newspaper libraries and better information retrieval systems. Mr. Dedmon told me that his librarian is consulting with a special library division of the American Library Association, and that they are working hard on the problems of categories and on getting the basic systems ready to make some rather striking advances in this area of librarianship and retrieval of material for newsmen of major newspapers.

Let me close by making two or three remarks of a more general nature. One idea that struck me is that the newspapers increasingly have research men on their staffs. They may be fully implemented, as is the *Des Moines Register-Tribune* or the *Milwaukee Journal*, with a research department. Increasingly there are personnel on the staffs of newspapers who are charged with doing research or contracting for research in the interests of the marketing and audience curiosities of the management. These persons are in effect the behavioral scientists in the organization, frequently with a rather considerable degree of skill, working operationally on problems. And it seems rather clear to me that to use these men as bridges and links to the area of behavioral science outside the research shop itself might be a way to capitalize upon the existing talent that the papers already have aboard.

Another comment, the general run of syndicated material in the behavioral sciences does seem to be rather dismal. We have "Let's Explore Your Mind," a chapter from Dr. Zilch, and so on. Something should be done about the general run of such material. I am aware that Mr. Ubell and others are syndicated rather widely —that is not the kind of syndication I mean, as I hope I have made clear. But the kind of fly-by-night, believe-it-or-not, isn't-this-a-funny-thing-we-see-here kind of syndicated material could be jettisoned with little loss and could indeed be replaced with great gain by sound material.

Session Five:

SUMMARY AND CONCLUSIONS

20
Summary and Conclusions

Daniel Lerner
MASSACHUSETTS INSTITUTE OF
TECHNOLOGY

I have been asked to present the summary and conclusions of this
conference, and will begin with Session One. Marvin Bressler and
Richard C. Wald were quite right in the strategy they followed.
They had to get us social scientists and journalists divorced right
at the start so we could later make up and really enjoy a honeymoon. They set up the "two cultures" situation, which is always
a wonderful way to divide and drool. When C. P. Snow came to
the M.I.T. Centennial and gave his "two cultures" speech, one of
my cynical colleagues, an engineer, said, "If ever we build a bridge
between the two cultures, it's going to be strong enough to resist a
Snow job." Now, I was a bit struck by the amiable hostility at these
meetings, because I know a lot of people here and have known them
for a very long time; it's obvious that many know each other even
better and have for a long time. So, I came thinking we were going
to have a "coffee klatsch" kind of conference; instead we have had
fireworks with some sparkle and much noise.

As the first session developed, Wald and Bressler stated their
cases so bluntly and made so many points which really hurt, that
everybody rushed in to bind the wounds. The discussants took particular note of the need for moderation. Ben H. Bagdikian warned
us against what he called egocentricity. Our two sects, which seem
to be in the same chapel, nevertheless exaggerate the ritual devia-
tion that they burn their candles at different lengths. He indicated
very aptly, I think, that journalists are now mainly college graduates—which means they are literate, and I just don't believe that

they can't understand much of what's written by social scientists.

One might conclude that Bressler and Wald differ on more than their contrary notions as to who is God and as to what constitutes a divine tone of voice. But I think many of the differences stem from their very determined, and probably quite deliberate, overstatements of their basically reasonable points of view. I think Wald overstated the moral responsibility of research for relieving his concern that the times are out of joint; he also overstated the vacuousness of current contributions from research. Bressler, by contrast, overstated the moral *irresponsibility* of research. He talked in an excessively light way of research which considers people as "residuals." He especially exaggerated the position which hard-nosed behavioral research holds in the total flow of social science around the country today. I'm rather in agreement with one participant's comment that there is a good deal of important, interesting, relevant work that doesn't correspond to this Bressler image of behavioral research, and I say this as an occasionally hard-nosed behaviorist. Much of the interesting material in my book *The Passing of Traditional Society*, which was mentioned several times in this context, is no more hard-nosed, despite its apparatus of concepts and techniques, than good journalistic reporting.

Behaviorism today is descended from, but really is quite transmuted from (and I think improved on), the behaviorism that was taught forty years ago by that grand man William Cornell Casey and by J. B. Watson. If one wants to put it in a sentence, the central theorem on which behaviorists operate today is that—owing largely to statistical and computer techniques that have been made available during the past forty years—we can draw aggregated conclusions about whole processes and whole groups from data on individuals. The inferences can be drawn from, and only from, individuals. In this sense, while a presumptuous graduate student may dismiss individuals as "residuals," in fact, individuals are the base of behavioral research. We just can't do without them. If we didn't have them, we'd have nothing over the older social science.

I think it's important, not for honeymoon purposes but to set the historical record a bit straighter, to recognize that the relations between research and journalism in this country have been very intimate. American sociology, with all respect to Lester Ward and the book writers of the last century, really grew out of the womb of journalism. The only competing source for American sociology, besides journalism, was social work as done by Jane Addams and Jacob Riis and others. As this work—notably through the historical auspices of the Russell Sage Foundation—merged with sociology, we began to get our impetus to research, to find out facts about how social things work, particularly about things that weren't working right.

It was precisely the muckrakers—Steffens and Baker and Tarbell and Upton Sinclair—who really motivated young students to go into sociology rather than some other field. Possibly the greatest chairman of a sociology department this country has ever known—Robert E. Park—was himself a professional journalist during a good part of his life. His "Chicago School," which all through the 1920's represented the most interesting and probably the best of American sociology, was essentially journalistic. The topics it dealt with were the topics which are still the staples of journalism today—street corner society, white collar crime, the ghetto, the gang, and so on. It seems to me important that these joint traditions have a long, long history. They grew out of each other and nurtured each other.

The joint tradition still lives in this conference. Irving Dilliard, W. Phillips Davison, and I—we learned to work together at SHAEF. Edward Barrett and others were part of the OWI group. Robin Williams and others were in the Army Information and Education group. Most of us, in these World War II groups, learned that researchers and journalists can cope with some kinds of communication problems better if they do it together than if they try to do it separately. This seems to me the sort of comment one should add to the first session.

Moreover, this joint growth of social research and journalism is not just American. It's also true of the great tradition of European sociology. I would date all research sociology, as we understand it today, from a Frenchman named Frederick Le Play. In the 1840's he went out and counted up the household budgets of urban industrial workers in Europe. He did it first in France, wasn't sure he had adequate controls, and so he went on to Germany. Finally he covered much of Europe and Asia, doing empirical, quantitative, comparative studies of the major new social phenomenon in nineteenth-century Europe. Le Play's study of the industrial worker—the urban industrial worker—how much money he got, and how he spent it, is still one of the great classics of sociology. I would say that, with all of our new techniques today, many of us would do well indeed if we did as well as that.

Note that Le Play's work was carefully and closely drawn from the real social problems of his day. Further, he tried in every way he could to influence social policy to correct ills and to shape thinking about social betterment. He went at it in a way very different from what was then current in Europe, and this way is perhaps the most distinctive thing in the historical origins of social science, particularly sociology. He didn't operate the way Marx, for example, did. He didn't construct a magnificent architecture of ideology to explain why the new urban industrial class existed, why it had to exist, why it had to dominate society in the future. He tried, by a more careful, reportorial, journalistic technique to find out how the new social thing really was. This makes him the father of the kind of work we today call empirical social research.

This European tradition continued right through to the present generation of leading social researchers in America. Paul Lazarsfeld, back in his Vienna days, had his young people go out and study what really happened to the unemployed of Marienbad. When he came to this country, his first piece of work, with Samuel Stouffer at Harvard, was to study what really happened to families in the Depression. Always the basic techniques were essentially journalistic—interviewing people and recording what they said. To which one adds only those elements of systematic control and comparison that distinguish social research when it's good from journalism when it's good. Journalism simply doesn't use that apparatus of control technique; that's perhaps the critical difference.

But what I want to emphasize is that the great tradition which we come from, which we all come from, is the tradition of working on real problems—problems that arise not from last month's professional journal, but from the life of human society. This is why I would chide Bressler for having stressed, I think deliberately, what interests him the most (and what often interests me the most)—the kind of work on instruments, concepts, tools, techniques, which is really the in-house business of behavioral sciences. We really oughtn't to bother other people about this stuff at all. In the measure that they want to take the time and make the effort to inform themselves about these games that we play, they will make better critics, better evaluators of our work when they have to deal with it. Aside from that, I know no reason why a journalist who has a certain job of work to do would want to spend a lot of his time going through all of the massive literature on scaling. I haven't gone through it myself, and I teach courses in it. So that, I think, is the sum of Session One.

I think that Session Two was really the high point of this conference. It demonstrated the continuing vitality of the great historical tradition of working on real problems, the tradition in which researchers and journalists have most fruitfully engaged each other. However much they may disagree about vocabulary and fight about interpretations, clearly this is their common ground. The problems that Session Two reported on—race, poverty, crime, mental disorder, technological change—these are problems in our society that interest journalists just as much as they do researchers. As a social scientist, I am particularly pleased that my colleagues were able to give such a remarkable, I think really superb, demonstration of just what good, careful, well-thought-out, well-executed social research can do to clear up all kinds of misunderstandings, errors, and inadequacies which may not be cleared up quite so efficiently by journalistic techniques. I have the impression that this was the session that hit the journalists where they live. I had the impression that the journalists were more moved by these reports than they were by much of the discussion preceding and following. In fact, there were several points at which individuals who presented these papers were asked about the possibility of utilizing their research results for journalistic purposes.

Having said that, something which casts the social scientist a bit in the role of a reporter working with somewhat specialized techniques that are superior for some purposes—particularly finding out whether a thing is true or not, a kind of reporting which is easy, interesting, and useful to the journalist—I would be unfair to my colleagues if I didn't point out that their work also rests on an important conceptual apparatus. There is an apparatus of ideas here, and a tradition of working on these problems, that becomes the matrix out of which their own work grows. Robin Williams was appropriately modest in pointing out that this very important insight he had on the development of intergroup tensions came to him out of the literature which he had studied as a student and worked with as a scholar. That he carried it forward is to his great credit. But it is also to his credit that he is cognizant of the importance of his own sociological tradition in this case.

Now, just for purposes of illustration rather than argumentation, let me simply mention that concepts are important. It has been said that there is nothing in social science which gives you a conceptual framework. I disagree. We can profit by taking somewhat more seriously the important conceptual apparatus of the social sciences. Let me mention the kinds of concepts which went into the writing of these papers in the second session. The most important of these, and the most often referred to, was reference group theory—the concept that a person can belong, by some psychological process, to a group of which he is not physically a member. From the body of reference group theory, or within it, can be integrated such concepts as the levels of aspiration of people, their expectations of mobility, as in Mr. Kahn's paper, their levels of frustration and relative deprivation, as Mr. Williams points out. This is the Williams concept that is so important I quote it: "Militant protest is most likely to occur, not under stable conditions of maximum poverty and social oppression, but under conditions of rapid change and relative deprivation." Which means, if you're way down at the bottom of the heap, you're not as likely to engage in protest movements as when you've got somewhere in sight of (or identify yourself with) the possibility of a better life than the one you've got. This means you've got to get up off the bottom before you get active about going higher.

Stanton Wheeler dealt with this and so did Eli Ginzberg. I'm not going to quote all these papers. Let me, because Mr. Ginzberg's written paper was so terse, just remind you of one point that he made. At the very end, he said he had calculated that the United States needs a growth rate of approximately 4 per cent in order to maintain its level of employment. Now what this suggests to me, in terms of the conceptual apparatus in the other papers, the concepts I've just named without explaining, is this: if you take his figure seriously, if it's confirmed by other economists who work in different ways, whenever we get a falling off below 4 per cent in the growth rate, we should begin to look for all of the symptomatology of relative deprivation. Researchers and journalists alike should then expect sharp rises in militant protest, in race conflict, in violence and crime, and even in serious mental disorder. Melvin Kohn was a model of care and modesty in the way he presented his own explorations and his own conclusions, but he would likely accept this inference from available research.

Putting the "conceptual apparatus" together in a framework of this kind alerts us as social scientists to the signs of the times. Now perhaps we don't read them well or we don't read them well enough; perhaps we don't adequately plan our work ahead in terms of the signs of the times. I have the impression that college-educated journalists might even do better than social scientists can in relating the kinds of work we do to the signs of the times in which we live. That's the main inference I draw from the discussion in Session Two.

Session Three brought out many interesting points. It continued the sense of the meeting established in Session Two. Ronald Lippitt gave us a fascinating set of examples illustrating what he calls "confrontation events" and particularly the "linkage problem." Ernest Havemann, still in the mood of Session Two, stated that every one of the papers in that session could be put into a good, printable magazine article—and I haven't the slightest doubt that he could do it if he wanted to take the time and make the effort. Mr. Havemann said another thing which belongs in a résumé, however hasty, of the third session. He said that the facts don't matter all that much—it's more important to get your attitude right on some of these social problems. I agree.

The question of facts came up for discussion. Edgar Borgatta, again in the hard-nosed role, taking off from the observation that there is no accuracy of perception in the social sciences, concluded that there are margins of error. I think he drew the inference that given the margin of error that is bound to exist—somehow with our present instruments of observation we don't get things quite right —it would be at least premature to demand of behavioral scientists that they produce copy for the journalists. Don't ask us to report to you the things about which we have a considerable amount of indeterminacy ourselves.

Herbert Hyman attempted to answer this by saying that all knowledge is provisional; physicists, chemists, and so on revise their theories, their concepts, their findings every ten, five, or two years—or even every six months. We do the same. There's no particular reason why our errors should be considered as of a different order of magnitude than theirs. In any case, ours are more likely to be less erroneous than what one gets by unaided observation without controls.

Emmett Dedmon made two points that seem to me worth bearing in mind. I'm not sure what to make of the first: it's a forecast that the technological advance in newspapers over the next ten years is likely to release people now involved in technical jobs, which will then presumably be done by machines, in such a way that newspapers will have (and use) a greater quantity of professional and editorial skills. I only hope he's right; this would enormously improve the quality of our press, and certainly it would improve the social science component of the press. Mr. Dedmon said another thing on which, again, I only hope he's right. He said that today names no longer make news; issues make news. If he is correct, that's a very good sign for anybody involved in the social sciences as a mode of getting and spreading relevant information about the world we live in.

Joseph Klapper, in his humorous way, reminded us of a point which had been bugging us right from the start—that newsmen tend to write for their own reference group, other newsmen. They're mainly concerned, when they write a story, about what other newsmen whom they respect will think of it. And so, in fact, are the social scientists. It matters more to me, when I write something, that my colleagues should think it good than that a journalist should.

I'd like to return to the issues raised by Bressler and Wald and perhaps pose them in a somewhat different form. They did us a great service; getting us divorced was a fine stimulus to the search for common ground. I think Bressler does speak for the ego ideal— if I may call it that rather than egocentrism as Ben Bagdikian did —of a considerable portion of behavioral scientists, particularly the younger ones. He retreated, and considerably reduced and consolidated his position, after the pincher action by Wald. With some rephrasing, the consolidated position could probably stand as an acceptable testament that speaks for very many people in the social sciences.

So, I think, does the consolidated Wald—though I'm on less certain grounds here. I think that there are many journalists who may be hard-nosed but who are also genuinely high-minded in their concern for their profession and its responsibilities in the world. I think this is what Wald had in mind. He made clear that when he said, "Talk English," he didn't mean just get your commas in the right places. He's concerned with the apparent decay and deterioration of many aspects of American life, of which the abuse of the English language is only one instance. I have pulled out some of the rather poetic sequences in Wald's paper, not to make fun of them (it's sometimes embarrassing when somebody reads out loud a poetic formulation that was written to be read silently) but because I think they raise deep questions that do concern us and should concern us.

In repeating these questions I want to remind us all of the great Talmudic wisdom which says that the existence of a question does not always imply the existence of an answer. But with that caution, here is a fine sentence: "This country is the disease of the world's future and possibly, in its antibodies, the hope of its salvation." That's poetic. Later he says, "We're in a wild dislocation of sensibility." That may be less poetic. And then he says, speaking of TV, and I think these three quotes are related: "The thrust of the medium becomes a way of life even as its literal message becomes a rule. Clearly, its emphasis is on numbers. There is nothing immoral in that. To reach the numbers, the programs must seek the lowest common denominator. That denominator is what is within a man that is most like the things that are in every other man." He goes on from this to draw conclusions that are not unfamiliar. He expresses them more gracefully, and in some places more modestly, than the Cassandras who have been screaming the doom of American society, complete degeneracy, and so on—because we no longer do things like we used to do them, like write good English. But all the same, Wald fits himself into a rather gloomy view of the future based largely on its departures from the past and present. I wonder whether he really would not profit, marginally, from considering what the social sciences have to contribute to this prophecy.

There is, I think, a humane response that comes out of the social sciences which deals with these somber images, these apocalyptic views of the future. It was expressed very humanely by a social scientist who said that the wisdom of social science, if there is any, begins with the recognition that in each man there is something like *all* other men, something like *some* other men, something like *no* other man. This is a premise on which behavioral science and virtually all of social science are built. I wonder if that isn't a somewhat more qualified, somewhat more usable, even somewhat more poetic formulation of Wald's worries about the future: like *all* other men; like *some* other men; like *no* other man. Could one more aptly conjoin our sense of human individuality with our common humanity?

I close with a comment on the value of these large speculations for all of us. The value of poetry is taken for granted. But on this level the social sciences, despite all their hard-nosed technology and in some ways even because of it, also have something valuable to say.

We journalists and social scientists are jointly engaged in the process of demystifying the human mind in some sense—reducing ignorance and prejudice, increasing rationality and enlightenment. With all of Earl Ubell's cautions in mind about the number of Americans who don't know this, that, or the other thing, we are still the most educated country in the world, the greatest media-consuming country in the world. The journalists *have* to be involved in this process of demystification. So do the humanists, or those who regard themselves as humanists. We social scientists, in our professional role, also have things to say that are useful for shaping and sharing the values, as well as the facts, in our images of the future.

For example, there was a period after World War II when humanists, journalists, and others were talking about the "age of anxiety." Tension was said to be mounting everywhere; it was more and more difficult to live in an urban and industrial civilization. The real trouble with all that rather self-indulgent prophecy of doom was shown by two social scientists, who conducted a study of the incidence of mental disease over the past century. They discovered that the actual rate of increase, as far as they could determine objectively—this was the study by Marshall and Goldhamer, just the kind of careful study that Mr. Kohn has reported to us at this meeting—brings into question these gloomy prophecies about the future.

We make, all of us, very sweeping statements about television and what it's doing to children. But the best *studies* of television —such as Himmelweit's in England—make it perfectly clear that what television actually does to any child is largely a function of its family background: the role of parents in helping select and counsel; the reintegration of television stimuli with other stimuli from reading, family discussion, and school. Any sweeping generalization is just wrong. So, we in the social sciences do have a common stake in investigating these important social problems with you.

You have a stake in paying attention to us, not just when we're grubbing out little pieces of fact and information, but also when we're using the big conceptual apparatus that all of us are beholden to. And even in our speculations about the future, journalists and humanists (and many social scientists) would do well to think about the kinds of ideas represented by Merton's "theories of the middle range," by Parsons' ideas of systems-analysis, by Harold Lasswell's idea of policy sciences generating information that can serve the public policy. All prophecy can be disciplined by Lasswell's idea of "developmental constructs" projecting a future based on evidence that one can collect now, next week, next month, next year. All of these seem to me levels of thinking on which, now that the honeymoon is over, we can usefully seek our common concerns for public enlightenment and public welfare—concerns for which we might even stay married from time to time and from place to place.

Index

Communications technology, 53

Community Action Program, 106, 107, 108–112, 115

Community Mental Health Amendments of 1965, 114

Community Power Structure (Hunter), 226

Computers, impact of, 124–130; in medicine, 149

Conservatism, of the press, 48

Consumer-oriented crime statistics, 148–149

Council for the Advancement of Science Writing, 238, 239, 240

Council of Economic Advisers, 95, 113

Cozzens, James Gould, 204

Crime: and administration of justice, 144–147; age, rates by, 134; characteristics of in United States, 131–135; cities, rates in, 134; and history of lawlessness, 139–141; and mass media, 147–150; minority groups, rates among, 134–135; organized, 132; prevention of, and social policy, 141–144; against property, 132; reporting of, 148–149; and response to failure, 139; sex, rates by, 133; socioeconomic groups, rates by, 133–134; and struggle for success, 139; and violence, 131–150; white collar, 133; by youth-gangs, 133

"Crime and Violence" (Wheeler), 131–150

Criminology, 7

Cultural goals, and crime, 139

Culture of poverty, 99–102

Custody arrangements, 145

Danielson, Wayne A., 245; paper by, 229–233

Davison, W. Phillips, 251; paper by, 219–228

Day, Juliana, 92

Dear Abby, 179, 180, 182–183

Dedmon, Emmett, 214, 246, 256; paper by, 184–188

Defense, Department of, 120

Delinquency and Opportunity (Cloward and Ohlin), 143

Demography, 18–19

Des Moines Register-Tribune, 246

Dexter, Lewis Anthony, 76

Differential opportunity, and crime, 139

Dilliard, Irving, 251

Discrimination, 63, 66; Negro reaction to, 66–67; as overt behavior, 65

Disparity consequences, in action research, 13

Documentaries, 167

Dohrenwend, Barbara Snell, 91

Dohrenwend, Bruce P., 91

Dorn, Harold F., 19, 27

Drift hypothesis, and schizophrenia, 80, 84

Dropouts, 32–35

Drug Abuse Control Amendments of 1965, 114

Duncan, Otis Dudley, 27

Dunham, Barrows, 10, 27

Dunham, H. Warren, 78, 79, 81, 90

Durkheim, Emile, 139

Easton, David, 5

Economic Opportunity Act of 1964, 102, 104, 106–112, 114, 115, 118

Economic Opportunity Council, 108

Electronic data processing, 129

Elementary and Secondary Education Act of 1964, 114

Elites, as audience of behavioral sciences, 20

Elizabethan Poor Law, 102, 103

Employment: of Negroes, 130; and technology, 124

Employment Act of 1946, 103

Employment and Investment Incentive Loans, 107

Equality of educational opportunity, action research steps in, 12–13

Essen-Möller, Erik, 79, 81, 82, 90, 91

Ethnic composition, and mental disorder, 83